The Macroeconomy of Central America

The Macroeconomy of Central America

Edited by

Robert Rennhack

and

Erik Offerdal
International Monetary Fund

palgrave
macmillan

First published 2004 by
PALGRAVE MACMILLAN
Houndmills, Basingstoke, Hampshire RG21 6XS and
175 Fifth Avenue, New York, N.Y. 10010
Companies and representatives throughout the world

PALGRAVE MACMILLAN is the global academic imprint of the Palgrave Macmillan division of St. Martin's Press, LLC and of Palgrave Macmillan Ltd. Macmillan® is a registered trademark in the United States, United Kingdom and other countries. Palgrave is a registered trademark in the European Union and other countries.

ISBN 1–4039–3652–8

This book is printed on paper suitable for recycling and made from fully managed and sustained forest sources.

A catalogue record for this book is available from the British Library.

Library of Congress Cataloging-in-Publication Data
The macroeconomy of Central America / edited by Robert Rennhack and Erik Offerdal.
p. cm.
1–4039–3652–8 (cloth)
Papers from a conference held by the Central American Monetary Council and the Western Hemisphere Department of the IMF from July 25–26, 2002, in Antigua, Guatemala.
ISBN 1–4039–3652–8 (cloth)
1. Central America – Economic policy – Congresses. 2. Fiscal policy – Central America – Congresses. 3. Taxation – Central America Congresses. 4. Central America – Appropriations and expenditures – Congresses. 5. Central America – Commercial policy – Congresses. 6. Monetary policy – Central America – Congresses. I. Rennhack, Robert. II. Offerdal, Erik. III. Consejo Monetario Centroamericano. IV. International Monetary Fund. Western Hemisphere Dept.

HC141.M25 2004
339.5'09728—dc22 2004045623

10 9 8 7 6 5 4 3 2 1
13 12 11 10 09 08 07 06 05 04

Printed and bound in Great Britain by
Antony Rowe Ltd, Chippenham and Eastbourne

Contents

List of Tables, Figures, and Boxes

Tables

Figures

Boxes

Foreword

The countries of Central America have a long tradition of regional cooperation, with the oldest system of regional integration in Latin America. These ties have been growing closer each year, as trade among the countries expands and banks engage in more cross-border lending within the region. A free trade agreement between the United States and Central America would most likely integrate the region further.

Against this background, the Central American Monetary Council and the Western Hemisphere Department of the IMF sponsored a conference on 25–26 July 2002 in Antigua Guatemala to strengthen the regional dialogue on the key macroeconomic policy issues facing the region. Participants included the ministers of finance, presidents of central banks and bank superintendents from most countries in the region, as well as staff from the IMF, the World Bank and the Inter-American Development Bank. This occasional paper presents most of the papers that were prepared to provide background for the policy discussions among the participants in the conference.

The conference opened by discussing how to set fiscal policy to keep public debt on a sustainable path, while allowing for effective programs to improve education and health and social safety nets. Chapter 1 sets the stage for this discussion by assessing the outlook for public debt in the region, highlighting the risks arising from several factors including external shocks and natural disasters. This chapter also reviews the debate on the usefulness of fiscal policy rules. Chapter 2 analyzes the trends in public expenditure in the region. In particular this chapter notes that public education on spending in Central America remains well below the average for Latin America. The level of spending on health appears adequate, but steps could be taken to improve the efficiency of this spending. Also the region would benefit from better targeting of social safety nets. Chapter 3 compares tax policy in Central America to other developing countries and confirms that tax revenues in the region are low by Latin American standards. It stresses that tax policy reform in the region should continue to emphasize the importance of strengthening domestic tax systems by relying on a wide range of taxes and taking steps to broaden the tax bases.

The conference then, focused on how to strengthen the competitiveness of exports through further trade liberalization and the proper choice of the exchange rate regime. Chapter 4 points out that the region reduced import tariffs considerably between the mid-1980s and the late 1990s, and identifies several issues to be considered in the negotiations on a free trade agreement with the United States and in the Doha round of trade negotiations. It also suggests that monetary integration with the United States might be the next step once the region enters into a free trade agreement with the United States. Chapter 5 analyzes the variety of exchange rate regimes in the region, which ranges from full dollarization to managed floats, and concludes that the countries' choice of regime is consistent with the choices made by developing countries in other parts of the world.

The conference also covered the issue of financial supervision. Chapter 6 analyzes the trend of growing dollarization in the financial systems in many countries of the region and proposes steps to adapt prudential regulations to guard against the risks of partial dollarization.

The main conclusions of the conference were:

- Many countries in the region would benefit from stronger fiscal policies to keep public debt on a sustainable path, although there was no agreement on the value of fiscal rules.
- Countries should seek to strengthen public investment in basic infrastructure and primary health care and education, which would most likely require raising tax revenues through better enforcement, simpler taxes and broader tax bases.
- Implementing effective consolidated financial supervision is crucial, because a number of banking conglomerates in Central America are expanding their cross-border operations.
- Partial dollarization – if it is present – creates a need for higher bank liquidity requirements and general provisioning requirements, as well as for strong macroeconomic policies.
- Most countries seem to have adopted exchange regimes that make sense based on the structure of their economies.
- It is important to provide thorough and clear explanations of policy proposals to legislatures and to the public to help build broad support for sound economic policies.

Finally, the editors would like to thank all the participants in the conference for their time and energy and Mr Miguel Chorro of the Central American Council for his invaluable help in organizing the conference. We would like to give special thanks to Ms Lita Ali and Ms Hilda Scioville for their untiring dedication to organize all aspects of the conference, which made it a success.

Robert Rennhack
Division Chief
International Monetary Fund

Notes on Contributors

Ana Corbacho Ana Corbacho is an economist in the Fiscal Affairs Department of the International Monetary Fund, and has work experience in Latin America, Eastern Europe, and Asia. Previously, she was a researcher for the Central Bank of Argentina, and for the Harvard Institute for International Development. She holds a BA in economics (*summa cum laude*) from Universidad de San Andrés in Buenos Aires, and a PhD in economics from Columbia University in the city of New York. Her dissertation on 'Education, Income Distribution and Growth' was awarded a distinction from Columbia University. She was a fellow of the Bradley Foundation, the Organization of American States, and the Public Policy Consortium at Columbia University.

Hamid R. Davoodi Hamid R. Davoodi is currently a senior economist in the Middle East and Central Asia Department of the International Monetary Fund. He joined the IMF in 1997 and has worked previously at the World Bank, Federal Reserve Bank of San Francisco and taught at Georgetown University in Washington DC. He has published papers in economic journals the areas of governance, poverty, economic growth, and fiscal policy.

Alain Ize Alain Ize is currently an advisor in the Monetary and Financial Systems Department (MFD) of the IMF. Prior to joining MFD, he worked in the Fiscal Affairs Department, also of the IMF. Prior to joining the IMF, he was a professor at El Colegio de Mexico and an economist at Banco de Mexico.

Daniel Lederman Daniel Lederman is Senior Economist in the World Bank's Office of the Chief Economist (LCRCE) of the Latin America and Caribbean region. Before joining the Bank, Mr Lederman was an economist with the United Nations' Economic Commission for Latin America and the Caribbean (ECLAC). Mr Lederman received a BA degree from Yale University (1989), where he studied economics and political science. Mr Lederman then went on to receive his MA (1991) and PhD (2001) degree in international economics and politics from the Johns Hopkins University, School of Advanced International Studies (SAIS). Mr Lederman has written extensively on issues related to financial crises in emerging markets, violent crime, the political economy of economic reforms, institutional reforms, economic growth, and international trade.

Valerie Mercer-Blackman She is an economist at the Western Hemisphere Department, International Monetary Fund (IMF). Since 1996 she has worked on fiscal and macroeconomic issues of Central American and Transition economies. Prior to that she was at the Council of Economic Advisors during the Clinton Administration. She holds a PhD in Economics from the University of Pennsylvania and a BA from Yale University.

Erik Offerdal Erik Offerdal, a Norwegian national, has a masters degree in economics from the University of Oslo, Norway. His early career, while working for the Norwegian government and as a Visiting Scholar at Harvard University, focused on general equilibrium modeling, the macroeconomic impact of petroleum revenues, and tax policy analysis. He joined the International Monetary Fund in 1990, and has since been engaged in macroeconomic surveillance and policy formulation in Eastern Europe, Asia, and Latin America. He was the Fund's resident representative in Vietnam 1997–99 and is currently the resident representative in Guatemala.

Guillermo Perry Guillermo Perry has been Chief Economist of the Latin America and Caribbean Region at the World Bank since 1996, where he is responsible for leading the Bank's position on economic policy issues in the dialogue with regional authorities and for designing, together with the Vice President, the Bank's strategy for lending and advisory services in Latin America. Prior to joining the World Bank, Mr Perry served in several senior policy-making positions in his native country, Colombia, including that of Minister of Finance and Public Credit, Minister of Mining and Energy; and Director of the General Directorate of National Taxes. He was also Director of two of Colombia's leading economic think-tanks, and has served as a member of the Constitutional Assembly and of the Senate of the Republic. Mr Perry undertook doctoral studies in Economics and Operational Research at the Massachusetts Institute of Technology between 1968 and 1970. He has published several books (including, most recently, Closing the Gap in Education and Technology (2002), co-authored with David de Ferranti *et al.*) and numerous articles on a range of subjects covering macroeconomics, fiscal policy, financial policy, international finance, and energy policy issues.

Robert Rennhack Robert Rennhack is currently Division Chief for Colombia, Ecuador and Belize in the Western Hemisphere Department of the Fund. At the time of the regional conference on Central America, he was chief of the Central American Division. He has worked extensively on macroeconomic issues in Latin America for the past 20 years, and has written papers on capital mobility, monetary policy, and energy demand. He holds an undergraduate degree from the University of Michigan and a graduate degree in economics from Yale University.

Janet Stotsky This was written while she was a deputy division chief in the Tax Policy Division of the Fiscal Affairs Department of the International Monetary Fund. She has also been in the Western Hemisphere Department. Prior to joining the Fund, she was an assistant professor of economics at Rutgers University and a financial economist with the Office of Tax Policy in the United States Department of the Treasury. She has a BA degree with high honors from Princeton University and a PhD from Stanford University in economics and has published in the areas of public finance and tax policy, and was a contributor to the IMF's Tax Policy Handbook.

Rodrigo De J. Suescún Melo Rodrigo Suescún is Senior Economist in the World Bank's Office of the Chief Economist (LCRCE) of the Latin America and the Caribbean region. Before joining the Bank he worked at the Center for Studies on Economic Development (CEDE) of the University of the Andes, where he was also Professor of macroeconomics in the graduate school. He was Director of the Financial and Monetary Affairs Department at the Banco de la República, Colombia's central bank, and Senior Economist in its research department. Mr Suescún received a BA degree from Universidad de los Andes, Bogotá, where he studied economics. He holds MA and PhD degrees in economics from the University of Pennsylvania.

Asegedech WoldeMariam Asegedech WoldeMariam is a Senior Research Officer in the Tax Policy Division of the Fiscal Affairs

Department of the International Monetary Fund (IMF). She has also worked in the IMF's African Department. She previously worked as a Consultant for a non-profit consulting firm in Washington DC – PPF International. She has a BA Degree in Business (International Finance) and an MA in Economics from Syracuse University. She has co-authored and published working papers on tax policy and public finance issues and was a contributor to the IMF's Tax Policy Handbook.

1
Fiscal Sustainability

Erik Offerdal

Introduction

The overall theme of this chapter is: How concerned should policy-makers in Central America be about current levels of public sector debt?[1] The general answer is that there is reason to be quite concerned, not only because debt levels are high in some of the countries, but equally important because: (i) all Central American countries remain highly vulnerable to adverse shocks; and (ii) they are constrained in their ability to formulate effective policy responses to such shocks. Thus, the basic policy recommendation of this chapter is similar to that suggested by Fischer (2001): 'Countries that are vulnerable because they operate in emerging markets need to make themselves less vulnerable by having smaller debts.'

The assessment of public sector debt in the Central American region focuses on five questions:

- What are the most important factors behind recent developments in public debt?
- Is there an 'appropriate' level of public debt for the Central American countries?
- What are the main sources of long-term vulnerability to public debt in the region?
- How would adverse shocks, given these vulnerabilities, impact on the long-term debt position and the need for fiscal adjustment?
- Would fiscal rules, similar to those in use in other countries, be helpful in addressing these vulnerabilities?

Several factors suggest the critical importance of these five questions for policy makers. One such factor is that the *current ratios of debt to Gross Domestic Product (GDP)* – while generally lower than in South America, are increasing rapidly in some Central American countries, and are large enough that interest obligations place a significant burden on the public finances (Interest obligations have averaged 3 to 7 per cent of GDP in Costa Rica, Honduras, Nicaragua, and Panamá in recent years). Related to this is the *'emerging market' status* of Costa Rica, the Dominican Republic, El Salvador, Guatemala, and Panamá, all of which have raised substantial amounts in international markets in recent years, generally at quite favorable terms.[2] This increased exposure to private capital markets also means that these countries are becoming more exposed to sudden *shifts in market sentiment*, and thus to 'contagion' from financial crises – contagion that may be entirely unrelated to the fundamentals of their economies. These economies are also *small and highly sensitive* to terms of trade changes (e.g. higher oil and lower coffee prices) and natural disasters such as hurricanes and earthquakes. These shocks can put a substantial strain on the public finances, partly through their adverse impact on economic activity and fiscal revenues, and partly through the need for additional capital expenditures to repair damaged infrastructure. The limited size of these economies therefore makes such shocks more difficult to absorb by the domestic economy.

The next section raises some accounting issues pertinent to an analysis of public debt, and the subsequent five sections address each of the questions above.

A basic accounting framework

The accounting framework used in this chapter is 'conventional' in that it focuses on gross debt, generated through the public sector borrowing requirement. Although widely used, and chosen here primarily for reasons of comparability across countries, this framework has some important limitations.

Ideally, an assessment of public debt sustainability should be based on an analysis of the balance sheet of the public sector, defined as comprehensively as possible. Such an approach would explicitly recognize that, for the purpose of long-term sustainability, the focus should be on current and expected future changes in public sector net worth rather than gross debt. The public sector frequently holds significant assets (buildings, infrastructure, mineral deposits, and various forms of liquid reserves), and changes in net worth could potentially be very different from changes in gross debt. Moreover, by looking at future changes in net worth one would incorporate factors such as an increase in the liabilities of public pension schemes caused by demographic changes. A balance sheet approach would also allow for a symmetrical treatment of public investment expenditures (which increases net worth) and privatization receipts (which, assuming they are converted into another asset or held as cash, do not increase net worth).[3] Moreover, a comprehensive definition of the public sector should incorporate all public sector entities. This is important in an analysis of public sector debt since the central government, as the majority shareholder in public enterprises and public financial institutions, has a direct fiduciary responsibility for the operating losses and for debt contracted by these entities.

In practice, however, a complete balance sheet approach – while analytically more appropriate – is fraught with data difficulties, in particular in establishing reliable estimates of the assets of the public sector. The valuations of these assets is frequently made difficult, either because they have no market price (e.g. roads and bridges) or because the market price is uncertain and subject to large fluctuations (oil prices in the case of unexplored petroleum deposits).[4] Moreover, the focus of this paper is on the macroeconomic vulnerabilities emanating from public debt; many public assets, such as infrastructure, cannot be easily liquidated to retire debt. The discussion that follows is therefore based on a 'conventional' approach in that it is focused primarily on gross debt, generated through the public sector borrowing requirement. The coverage is the nonfinancial public sector, that is, excluding operations of the central bank and public financial institutions, mainly to ensure comparability across countries.

The accounting of public sector debt dynamics simply states that the overall fiscal balance – the primary balance plus interest cost on domestic and foreign debt – is financed by increasing the stock of debt, either domestic or foreign.[5]

$$D + i \cdot B + i^* \cdot B^* \cdot E = \dot{B} + \dot{B}^* \cdot E \qquad (1)$$

where D is the primary fiscal balance, i (i^*) is the nominal interest rate on domestic (foreign) debt, B (B^*) is the stock of domestic (foreign) debt, E is the nominal exchange rate, and a 'dot' over a variable indicates its (absolute) change over time. Through some straightforward transformations, detailed in the appendix, this identity can be expressed in terms of ratios to GDP:

$$d + b(r - g) + b^*(r^* - g + \hat{e}) = \dot{b} + \dot{b}^* \qquad (2)$$

where lower-case letters for b, b^*, d, indicate the ratios to GDP of the upper-case equivalent in (1), g is the growth rate of real GDP, r and r^* are the domestic and foreign **real** interest rates, and ê is the rate of change in the real exchange rate (vis-à-vis the US dollar). This basic accounting framework directly identifies two key factors behind changes in the overall ratio of public debt to GDP:[6]

- *the primary fiscal balance*, where a higher primary deficit (positive d) would increase the growth of debt (*cet. par.*), and a higher primary surplus (negative d) would lower it;
- *the interest service* on domestic and foreign debt, where an increase in the real interest rates r and r^* or a lower GDP growth g would increase the net borrowing requirement and thus the debt stock relative to GDP. In particular, if $g > r$, domestic interest service will contribute negatively to the borrowing requirement as a ratio to GDP, that is, the growth in nominal GDP outpaces the interest service on domestic debt. A similar point applies to interest service on external debt: a higher real interest rate, lower growth, or real depreciation (i.e. negative $\hat{e}$) would increase the net borrowing requirement.

However, equation (2) captures only changes in the ratio of debt to GDP directly related to net borrowing requirements derived from above the line. Additional changes in the debt to GDP ratio may arise from a number of 'debt stock operations', the most common of which is the assumption of contingent liabilities (private sector loan guarantees, deposit insurance schemes, bank recapitalization operations, commodity price guarantee schemes etc.), which would tend to increase the debt ratio, privatization receipts, and debt reschedulings (either debt-stock reductions or debt-service reductions/deferrals if the latter is treated as below-the-line financing in the fiscal accounts), which would tend to reduce the debt-to-GDP ratio.[7]

What are the factors behind recent developments in debt in Central America?

In the last three to five years, Costa Rica, El Salvador, and Guatemala have all experienced fairly substantial increases in their debt ratios (Table 1.1). These increases have largely been driven by deficits financed by private market borrowing. By contrast, in the Dominican Republic, Honduras, and Nicaragua, debt ratios have declined, mainly reflecting declines in debt to multilateral and bilateral creditors.[8]

The most important contributions to these changes in debt since 1998 can be assessed using the decomposition of changes in total debt into contributions from the primary balance, interest service,[9] and a residual as suggested in the previous section. On a cumulative basis since 1998 (Table 1.2):

- the residual was, by far, the largest contributor to changes in debt in Costa Rica, El Salvador, and Honduras, and were also significant in Nicaragua and Panamá. Except in Honduras, this residual contributed to an increasing public debt ratio;
- the primary fiscal position was the most important contributor not only in Guatemala and Panamá, but was large also in Costa Rica. In the latter two countries, however, the primary surpluses only served to offset or partially offset the negative impact of stock operations;
- in the Dominican Republic and Nicaragua, the declines in the debt ratios to GDP were primarily the result of a negative contribution from interest service, which in turn can be traced back to buoyant GDP growth, fairly low interest rates, and substantial appreciation of the real exchange rate over the period (Table 1.3). These factors also played an important role in Honduras, but their importance was outweighed by this country's debt rescheduling in 2001;
- more generally, a weakening of GDP growth for all countries in 2000 and 2001, and a weakening fiscal position, especially in Honduras and Nicaragua, have contributed to increasing the debt-to-GDP ratios.

Table 1.1 Central America: level and composition of nonfinancial public sector debt (in per cent of GDP)

	1995	1996	1997	1998	1999	2000	2001
Costa Rica							
Total public debt	39.7	36.8	32.4	33.6	27.7	30.3	38.6
Held by domestic residents	22.7	22.2	19.6	20.2	14.1	15.7	20.1
Held by foreign residents	17.0	14.6	12.8	13.4	13.6	14.5	18.5
Multilateral/Bilateral	16.2	13.9	12.2	11.4	10.0	9.5	11.7
Private	0.8	0.8	0.6	2.0	3.6	5.1	6.8
Dominican Republic							
Total public debt			29.5	28.4	26.8	26.0	23.6
Held by domestic residents			5.9	6.3	5.8	7.3	4.3
Held by foreign residents			23.6	22.1	21.0	18.7	19.3
Multilateral/Bilateral			18.2	17.8	17.2	15.1	13.9
Private			5.3	4.3	3.8	3.5	5.4
El Salvador							
Total public debt	26.6	27.3	28.5	24.8	25.6	27.5	31.4
Held by domestic residents	3.0	3.0	1.9	1.9	2.3	4.3	6.8
Held by foreign residents	23.6	24.3	26.6	22.9	23.3	23.2	24.7
Multilateral/Bilateral	21.3	21.6	21.6	21.2	20.4	20.0	20.2
Private	2.3	2.7	5.0	1.7	2.8	3.3	4.4
Guatemala							
Total public debt	15.4	15.0	15.9	15.5	18.4	18.0	19.3
Held by domestic residents	4.4	4.6	4.3	3.7	3.6	3.4	4.2

Held by foreign residents	11.0	10.3	11.6	11.8	14.8	14.5	15.1
Multilateral/Bilateral	10.1	9.7	8.8	9.6	11.8	11.3	11.3
Private	0.9	0.7	2.8	2.2	3.0	3.2	3.8
Honduras							
Total public debt	108.5	99.0	82.5	76.1	78.6	72.4	66.6
Held by domestic residents	8.7	6.7	5.7	4.1	2.7	3.2	2.8
Held by foreign residents	99.8	92.3	76.8	72.1	75.9	69.3	63.7
Multilateral/Bilateral	96.6	89.9	75.7	71.7	75.6	69.0	63.5
Private	3.2	2.4	1.1	0.4	0.3	0.3	0.3
Nicaragua							
Total public debt			330.2	340.2	324.4	303.8	311.3
Held by domestic residents			25.4	36.2	28.4	29.9	45.5
Held by foreign residents			304.9	304.0	296.0	273.9	265.8
Multilateral/Bilateral			288.8	290.7	282.7	262.5	255.9
Private			16.1	13.3	13.3	11.3	9.8
Panamá							
Total public debt					82.6	81.2	84.2
Held by domestic residents					21.2	22.0	19.8
Held by foreign residents					61.4	59.3	64.4
Multilateral/Bilateral					20.3	18.2	16.9
Private					41.1	41.0	47.5

Sources: National authorities; and Fund staff estimates.

Table 1.2 Central America: contributions to changes in public debt (in per cent of GDP)

	1998	1999	2000	2001	Cumulative 1998–2001	Share of cumulative change
Costa Rica						
Change in debt (as per cent of GDP)	1.1	−5.8	2.6	8.3	6.2	100.0
Contribution from:						
Primary balance	−2.0	−1.4	−1.0	−1.8	−6.3	−101.7
Interest service (external and domestic)	−2.2	−0.2	0.1	0.2	−2.0	−32.9
Residual	5.4	−4.2	3.4	10.0	14.5	234.5
Dominican Republic						
Change in debt (as per cent of GDP)	−1.1	−1.6	−0.8	−2.4	−5.8	100.0
Contribution from:						
Primary balance	1.2	1.2	1.1	1.0	4.6	−77.8
Interest service (external and domestic)	−2.9	−4.4	−4.1	−1.1	−12.5	213.6
Residual	0.6	1.5	2.2	−2.3	2.1	−35.8
El Salvador						
Change in debt (as per cent of GDP)	−1.0	1.7	1.8	3.3	5.8	100.0
Contribution from:						
Primary balance	0.1	0.2	0.2	0.3	0.8	13.8
Interest service (external and domestic)	0.3	0.0	0.0	−0.1	0.2	4.0
Residual	−1.5	1.5	1.6	3.1	4.8	82.2

Guatemala						
Change in debt (as per cent of GDP)	−0.5	3.0	−0.5	1.4	3.4	100.0
Contribution from:						
Primary balance	0.3	1.4	0.7	0.8	3.2	94.9
Interest service (external and domestic)	0.0	0.2	−0.1	0.2	0.4	10.6
Residual	−0.8	1.3	−1.1	0.3	−0.2	−5.6
Honduras						
Change in debt (as per cent of GDP)	−6.4	2.4	−6.1	−5.9	−16.0	100.0
Contribution from:						
Primary balance	−5.6	−1.8	−0.2	4.1	−3.6	22.2
Interest service (external and domestic)	−0.8	2.8	−4.2	−1.2	−3.4	21.1
Residual	0.0	1.4	−1.8	−8.7	−9.1	56.7
Nicaragua						
Change in debt (as per cent of GDP)	0.8	−17.0	−19.1	12.5	−22.8	100.0
Contribution from:						
Primary balance	−4.8	0.5	2.1	4.7	2.5	−11.1
Interest service (external and domestic)	−18.6	−27.9	−23.2	−11.6	−81.3	357.0
Residual	24.2	10.5	2.0	19.3	56.0	−245.9
Panamá						
Change in debt (as per cent of GDP)			−1.4	2.9	1.6	100.0
Contribution from:						
Primary balance			−4.1	−3.0	−7.1	−443.8
Interest service (external and domestic)			0.2	2.1	2.3	143.5
Residual			2.5	3.8	6.4	400.4

Sources: National Authorities; and Fund staff estimates.

Table 1.3 Central America: key macroeconomic indicators

	1995	1996	1997	1998	1999	2000	2001
Costa Rica							
Real GDP growth (annual percentage change)	3.9	0.9	5.6	8.4	8.4	1.7	0.4
GDP deflator (annual percentage change)	22.2	15.8	14.9	12.3	14.1	7.1	8.1
Real exchange rate depreciation (vis-à-vis US$)	1.9	0.7	2.5	1.6	−1.3	3.2	4.7
Nominal effective interest rate, domestic debt	16.4	18.4	17.6	14.1	22.6	19.4	16.3
Nominal effective interest rate, external debt	3.5	3.7	2.8	2.6	3.5	3.7	4.1
Dominican Republic							
Real GDP growth (annual percentage change)	4.7	7.2	8.3	7.3	8.0	7.8	3.0
GDP deflator (annual percentage change)	12.7	5.4	8.2	5.0	6.4	7.9	8.8
Real exchange rate depreciation (vis-à-vis US$)	2.9	2.3	4.9	−0.6	−1.0	4.5	6.0
Nominal effective interest rate, domestic debt			2.0	2.7	2.5	3.3	5.9
Nominal effective interest rate, external debt			3.4	3.4	3.4	3.8	3.4
El Salvador							
Real GDP growth (annual percentage change)	6.4	1.8	4.3	3.2	3.4	2.0	2.0
GDP deflator (annual percentage change)	10.4	6.8	3.5	3.8	0.6	3.1	2.7
Real exchange rate depreciation (vis-à-vis US$)	4.4	7.9	4.9	2.9	0.9	2.6	3.4
Nominal effective interest rate, domestic debt	20.8	26.1	32.7	35.2	23.3	14.7	6.6
Nominal effective interest rate, external debt	4.5	4.3	3.9	3.7	3.8	4.1	4.3
Guatemala							
Real GDP growth (annual percentage change)	4.9	3.0	4.1	5.1	3.8	3.6	1.8
GDP deflator (annual percentage change)	8.7	8.9	8.5	9.4	5.4	6.0	7.6

Real exchange rate depreciation (vis-à-vis US$)	1.5	6.7	13.0	2.4	−9.0	1.6	5.5
Nominal effective interest rate, domestic debt	18.0	16.4	11.0	20.5	23.1	17.0	13.4
Nominal effective interest rate, external debt	5.4	5.4	3.3	3.4	3.6	4.5	5.6
Honduras							
Real GDP growth (annual percentage change)	4.1	3.6	5.1	2.9	−1.9	5.0	2.5
GDP deflator (annual percentage change)	31.7	22.4	24.0	9.4	6.4	16.2	7.1
Real exchange rate depreciation (vis-à-vis US$)	8.6	−0.7	11.9	11.8	5.2	7.4	6.0
Nominal effective interest rate, domestic debt	10.6	13.0	10.3	9.6	33.6	28.9	50.5
Nominal effective interest rate, external debt	4.7	4.5	4.1	3.9	2.9	2.1	2.0
Nicaragua							
Real GDP growth (annual percentage change)	4.2	4.7	5.1	4.1	7.4	4.3	3.0
GDP deflator (annual percentage change)	11.0	11.6	9.2	13.0	11.2	11.9	7.9
Real exchange rate depreciation (vis-à-vis US$)	−8.1	−1.7	2.5	2.8	0.8	8.4	3.0
Nominal effective interest rate, domestic debt			4.0	5.3	4.6	3.8	8.2
Nominal effective interest rate, external debt			1.7	1.1	1.2	1.2	1.5
Panamá							
Real GDP growth (annual percentage change)	1.8	2.4	4.4	4.0	4.1	2.3	2.0
GDP deflator (annual percentage change)	0.5	0.3	1.7	3.4	−0.1	1.4	1.2
Real exchange rate depreciation (vis-à-vis US$)	−4.1	0.5	1.0	0.5	1.7	1.4	−1.9
Nominal effective interest rate, domestic debt					2.1	5.5	5.1
Nominal effective interest rate, external debt					4.7	6.0	6.5

Sources: National authorities; and Fund staff estimates.

The residual – in effect the difference between the left- and right-hand side of equation (2) earlier – clearly captures the factors mentioned in note 8; the underestimation of the GDP data in Nicaragua is part of the reason why this country has a particularly large residual. There is, however, no question that this residual also reflects a 'real' phenomenon, namely 'stock operations'[10] such as the assumption of various forms of contingent liabilities and/or debt rescheduling (e.g. a bank resolution operation in Nicaragua in 2001).

The policy implications of these 'stock operations' will be explored later in the chapter, for now it suffices to conclude that (i) these stock operations have contributed significantly to recent changes in public debt ratios; and (ii) in most cases these operations seem to have a bias toward increasing, rather than reducing, the ratio of public debt to GDP.

What level of public debt?

The fact that ratios of public debt to GDP in Central America are either increasing or already 'high' raises a simple question with no straightforward answer: Is there a ratio of public debt to GDP for these countries that is broadly 'appropriate'?

From a Latin American perspective, the *external* debt ratios in our sample of countries are not particularly high (Table 1.4). In 2001, the average level of external debt to GDP in the non-Heavily Indebted Poor Countries (HIPC) Central American countries was only about half of that in the larger countries in South American and México. Debt service was also considerably lower, especially relative to exports of goods and services, but also relative to government revenues. Among the factors contributing to this is the greater openness of the Central American countries, and a larger share of debt being to multilateral and bilateral creditors, with longer maturities and less need for annual roll-overs.

Recent econometric evidence – discussed below – suggest that when *external* debt reaches a certain point, around 40 per cent of GDP, it may start to have an adverse impact on economic growth and/or represent a sharp increase in the likelihood of a debt crisis.

Patillo *et al.* (2002), using data for 93 countries, estimate that, on average, the impact of debt on per capita growth appears to become negative for debt levels around 35–40 per cent of GDP, while, on the

Table 1.4 Selected Latin American countries: public external debt and debt service

	1995	1996	1997	1998	1999	2000	2001
Costa Rica							
Public external debt[1]	22.7	22.2	19.6	20.2	14.1	15.7	20.1
Debt service							
In per cent of exports[2]	13.6	12.1	12.5	6.9	7.0	7.0	6.3
In per cent of government revenues[3]	41.3	37.1	40.2	25.7	29.7	30.8	27.9
Dominican Republic							
Public external debt[1]			23.6	22.1	21.0	18.7	19.3
Debt service							
In per cent of exports[2]	9.3	10.0	10.1	12.4	9.9	12.0	12.1
In per cent of government revenues[3]	26.7	35.2	27.1	31.0	24.9	33.4	31.3
El Salvador							
Public external debt[1]	23.6	24.3	24.1	21.7	22.5	22.9	24.1
Debt service							
In per cent of exports[2]	13.2	12.9	9.9	15.0	15.1	13.5	14.4
In per cent of government revenues[3]	18.2	17.5	17.0	24.9	23.4	19.7	20.6
Guatemala							
Public external debt[1]	11.0	10.3	11.6	11.8	14.8	14.5	15.1
Debt service							
In per cent of exports[2]	15.3	12.0	17.2	15.3	13.6	8.8	8.2
In per cent of government revenues[3]	24.2	16.3	24.6	22.0	21.3	14.2	14.0
Honduras							
Public external debt[1]		92.3	76.8	72.1	75.9	69.3	63.7

Table 1.4 Continued

	1995	1996	1997	1998	1999	2000	2001
Debt service							
In per cent of exports[2]	24.3	25.4	20.5	16.4	15.9	13.6	9.2
In per cent of government revenues[3]	46.9	56.4	43.4	28.5	24.0	19.7	14.9
Nicaragua							
Public external debt[1]			304.9	304.0	296.0	274.7	271.2
Debt service							
In per cent of exports[2]	133.2	38.1	30.6	27.6	19.9	18.9	17.5
In per cent of government revenues[3]	137.5	36.1	34.0	29.9	18.9	19.8	17.0
Panamá							
Public external debt[1]					61.4	59.3	64.4
Debt service							
In per cent of exports[2]	10.3	20.9	44.1	21.5	24.6	22.9	24.2
In per cent of government revenues[3]	13.0	29.0	60.8	25.6	27.9	24.9	31.3
Argentina							
Public external debt[1]	38.1	40.4	42.7	47.3	51.0	51.4	55.1
Debt service							
In per cent of exports[2]	57.1	62.9	70.2	77.5	102.3	107.9	118.1
In per cent of government revenues[3]	23.6	29.4	31.9	33.9	41.2	47.8	56.5
Bolivia							
Public external debt[1]	71.4	63.0	56.6	55.3	55.3	53.9	48.7
Debt service							
In per cent of exports[2]	42.2	25.5	25.2	28.8	19.1	18.3	16.4
In per cent of government revenues[3]	32.8	19.1	19.1	18.5	11.7	12.7	12.6
Brazil							
Public external debt[1]	22.6	23.2	24.8	30.7	45.6	39.8	42.1

Debt service							
In per cent of exports[2]	43.6	51.1	69.2	89.0	135.3	94.2	80.2
In per cent of government revenues[3]	9.4	12.1	17.7	21.6	41.8	29.7	32.1
Chile							
Public external debt[1]	30.2	30.3	32.3	40.0	46.8	49.2	56.9
Debt service							
In per cent of exports[2]	25.3	31.9	20.8	20.6	25.2	26.2	39.9
In per cent of government revenues[3]	31.3	36.7	24.1	23.4	32.9	35.7	54.2
Ecuador							
Public external debt[1]	77.7	76.6	76.9	82.2	120.3	136.7	101.4
Debt service							
In per cent of exports[2]	61.2	79.8	90.1	143.8	109.5	77.3	76.3
In per cent of government revenues[3]	78.6	108.2	124.8	175.8	178.7	118.1	91.2
México							
Public external debt[1]	59.0	49.7	38.5	39.4	36.9	28.4	26.6
Debt service							
In per cent of exports[2]	54.6	68.2	66.5	51.3	46.6	44.3	41.9
In per cent of government revenues[3]	52.7	71.6	64.2	52.6	46.5	42.9	36.4
Péru							
Public external debt[1]	62.1	60.4	48.3	51.6	55.5	53.6	53.6
Debt service							
In per cent of exports[2]	29.1	34.3	39.0	49.4	54.6	52.5	44.0
In per cent of government revenues[3]	20.2	23.7	29.1	34.1	46.4	47.5	44.8

[1] In per cent of GDP.
[2] Data refer to paid interest and amortization of public external debt in per cent of exports of goods and nonfactor services, including net maquila.
[3] In per cent of general government revenues and grants.

Source: World Economic Outlook.

margin, the impact on growth becomes negative at about half of these debt levels. While the transmission mechanism from levels of external debt to growth is not modeled explicitly, these authors suggest that an important part of the transmission has a fiscal component, either by 'crowding out' through the public sector borrowing or because high debt will generate expectations that future debt service will be financed with distortionary taxes and cuts in public investments.[11]

IMF (2002) uses data for all IMF member countries, except advanced industrialized countries, for the period 1979–2001, and estimates a 'threshold' level of external debt where the likelihood of a debt crisis or debt correction (i.e. a sudden decline in the debt-to-GDP ratio) increases significantly. They find that the conditional probability of a debt crisis or correction is typically 2–5 per cent for a debt ratio below 40 per cent of GDP; for a debt ratio above this threshold the conditional probability increases to 15–20 per cent.[12]

Although interesting in their own right, these empirical results do not provide much guidance to policymakers in the region as to whether current *public sector* debt ratios are broadly appropriate or potentially excessive. In particular, this does not provide much guidance on what debt ratio might be a potential 'trigger-point' for a crisis. This becomes quite evident when one looks at some summary fiscal indicators for countries that have experienced more or less severe capital account crises in recent years (Table 1.5).

These indicators suggest three general points:

- crises have afflicted countries with a wide range of recorded fiscal positions, including gross debt ratios well below 20 per cent of GDP (Czech Republic, Thailand, and Korea), and fiscal balances (surplus or deficit) within 1 per cent of GDP (México, Indonesia, and the Philippines).
- several countries (México, Argentina, and the Czech Republic) had significant unrecorded fiscal deficits, mainly in the form of quasi-fiscal activities in state-owned banks.
- gross public debt increased sharply as a result of the crises, partly reflecting the assumption of various contingent liabilities and partly reflecting large nominal devaluations associated with the crises, which increased the domestic currency value of foreign currency debt.

Table 1.5 Crisis countries: selected fiscal indicators of vulnerability[1] (in per cent of GDP, unless otherwise indicated)

Country/date of crisis	Capital account restrictions (Index)[2]	Pre-crisis overall fiscal balance		Gross public debt	
		Recorded	Other[3]	Pre-crisis	End-2000
Large recorded deficit (≥6% of GDP)					
Turkey (1994 Q1)	0.26	−13	—	36	68
Russia (1998 Q3)	0.56	−8	—	46	65
Brazil (1999 Q1)	0.47	−8	—	42	47
Ecuador (1999 Q1)	0.13	−6	—	83	123[5]
Significant (including unrecorded) deficit					
México (1994 Q4)	0.21	—	−4	41	55
Argentina (1995 Q1)	0.11	−2	−1	36	50
Czech Rep. (1997 Q2)	0.19	−2	−4	13	35[4]
Small deficit or surplus (≤2% of GDP)					
Thailand (1997 Q3)	0.40	−2	—	5	57
Indonesia (1997 Q3)	0.34	1	—	24	102
Philippines (1997 Q3)	0.32	−1	—	57	112[5]
Korea (1997 Q4)	0.40	−2	—	12	57[5]

Notes

[1] Pre-crisis indicators of general government (or consoliodated public sector) refer to period on, or prior to, the date of abandonment of the fixed or preannounced crawling peg, or (for Argentina, Philippines, and Turkey) of sudden and substantial private capital outflows – date of crisis shown in parentheses.

[2] Index value ranges from 0 (lowest) for absence of controls, to 1 (highest) for most restrictive exchange and capital controls.

[3] Estimates (official for México; Teijeiro (2001) for Argentina; World Bank for Czech Republic) of unrecorded balance encompassing mainly quasi-fiscal activities by state-owned banks.

[4] Includes World Bank estimated of unrecorded public sector liabilities mainly involving state-owned banks.

[5] Data for end-1999.

Source: Kopits (2002).

In general, all of these crises were triggered by *a combination of growing domestic weakness and external shocks*. As examples, in México, the domestic weakness was a rapidly growing external current account deficit; in Brazil a deteriorating fiscal position; and in Ecuador systemic banking sector problems, combined with a fiscal position excessively dependent on volatile oil prices. The external shocks were quite similar in México and Brazil – a fundamental shift in investor sentiment in México caused by a combination of higher interest rates in the United States and attractive investment opportunities in other emerging markets,[13] and in Brazil a drying up of financing to emerging market borrowers triggered by the Asian crisis. In Ecuador, the crisis was triggered in part by a sharp deterioration in fiscal revenues as oil prices plummeted in the wake of the Asian crisis.

The most important, and not very surprising, lesson to emerge from this discussion is that it is doubtful that one can establish any benchmarks or guidelines for an appropriate public debt ratio for the Central American countries. In particular, the experience of several countries suggests that *an external debt-to-GDP ratio well below the 40 per cent 'threshold' may be necessary, but is certainly not sufficient, to be out of the 'danger zone'*.[14,15] Moreover, the ability to respond to or counteract emerging domestic weaknesses and external vulnerabilities, especially with regard to debt management, is hampered by high debt and deteriorates as economic problems mount. Both México and Brazil sharply increased the share of domestic debt that were on variable interest rates or were dollar-indexed/dollar-denominated in the months leading up to the crisis. In both countries this calmed nervous financial markets for some months, but also sharply increased the vulnerability of the country to increases in public debt from exchange and interest rate increases.

Although none of the Central American countries are in a crisis, or in the 'run-up' to one, they are nonetheless vulnerable to shocks, both domestic and external. These vulnerabilities, and a policy flexibility sufficient to respond effectively to shocks are critical elements in deciding what is an appropriate ratio of public debt to GDP.

Potential fiscal vulnerabilities and policy flexibility

The vulnerabilities facing Central American countries can be broadly classified into three categories: *adverse shocks to growth, interest and exchange rates; contingent liabilities; and limited fiscal policy flexibility*.

Shocks with adverse implications for growth and interest rates

These shocks could arise from natural disasters such as earthquakes or hurricanes, or from external sources such as changes in terms of trade, decline in export demand, higher international interest rates, or shifts in investor sentiment (which would be reflected in country risk premiums). While this type of vulnerability is well known, it is still worth noting a few simple points:

- The 'price' for being a small, open economy is vulnerability to changes in terms of trade. In many of these countries (e.g. Costa Rica, the Dominican Republic, El Salvador, and Panamá), the simple correlation between such shocks and real GDP growth is about 0.65–0.95, either contemporaneous or lagged one year. This volatility reflects in part a limited diversification of the export base in Central America.
- Interest rates on domestic public debt have, over the past three to five years, been quite high in real effective terms in Costa Rica, El Salvador, Guatemala, and Honduras (Table 1.3).[16] Given the relatively thin domestic financial markets in the region, one would expect that domestic interest rates are significantly influenced by public sector borrowing requirements. Such high interest rates may well result in fiscal policy 'crowding out' private investment and undermining future growth.
- Market confidence in fiscal policy depends not only on the fiscal stance (e.g. the primary balance) alone but also on the gross financing requirement (i.e. the primary balance plus interest and amortization of debt). The current medium term frameworks for the seven Central American countries almost uniformly assume improved primary balances over the next five years (Table 1.6), and in most cases assume surpluses of 1–2 per cent of GDP.[17] At the same time, the gross financing requirement is projected to average 6 per cent of GDP in 2002 for the five non-HIPC eligible countries, declining to 4.2 per cent in 2007. Although much of current debt service is on multilateral or bilateral debt, the rapid increase in private market financing illustrated in Table 1.1 means that, in the future, these countries will be increasingly vulnerable to shifts in market sentiment.
- Related, but also distinct from this, is market confidence in the prevailing exchange rate. In the nondollarized countries, the large bulk (80–90 per cent) of total public debt is denominated in foreign

Table 1.6 Central America: primary fiscal balances and gross fiscal financing requirements, 2002–07

	2002	2003	2004	2005	2006	2007
Costa Rica						
Primary balance	1.8	1.9	2.0	2.0	2.1	2.2
Gross financing requirement	4.7	4.9	4.9	4.6	4.3	4.0
Dominican Republic						
Primary balance	0.5	0.8	1.2	1.2	1.2	1.2
Gross financing requirement	3.0	3.0	2.2	2.1	3.7	2.3
El Salvador						
Primary balance	−1.7	−1.0	−0.6	−0.4	0.6	0.5
Gross financing requirement	5.8	4.6	4.1	3.9	3.5	3.2
Guatemala						
Primary balance	1.0	1.6	1.7	1.7	1.7	1.7
Gross financing requirement	5.4	4.7	4.5	4.9	6.6	7.3
Honduras						
Primary balance	−3.3	−1.4	−1.1	−0.9	−1.1	−0.8
Gross financing requirement	9.9	8.7	8.4	7.7	7.4	6.0
Nicaragua						
Primary balance	1.1	0.8	1.5	2.0	1.3	1.2
Gross financing requirement	18.5	9.6	10.1	2.8	2.6	2.4
Panamá						
Primary balance	2.9	3.3	4.8	4.8	4.6	4.4
Gross financing requirement	10.9	6.7	5.1	4.8	8.5	4.3

Source: Fund staff estimates.

currencies, implying a significant vulnerability of public debt service (and debt stocks) to a depreciation in the exchange rate.

Stock operations that arise from the need to assume various contingent liabilities

The Central American countries are vulnerable to this through weak public banks, underfunded or implicit deposit guarantee schemes, quasi-fiscal losses in the central banks, and underfunded pension schemes. The size and the likelihood of such liabilities being incurred are, by their nature, difficult to assess. Over the past four years, the annual average size of this factor was 1.4 per cent of GDP in the non-HIPC countries in our sample. In recent banking crises, the fiscal cost from this factor alone has been substantially higher: in Ecuador, México, Indonesia, Korea, and Thailand, the total amount of public sector bonds issued to rescue failing banks have ranged between 17 and 38 per cent of GDP, and the interest cost of carrying these bonds between 1 and 4 per cent of GDP.

An important point in this context is that these adverse shocks rarely occur as isolated incidents; on the contrary, Hausmann (2002) finds that they tend to be positively correlated with each other.

Limited policy flexibility

Limited policy flexibility would constrain the authorities' ability to adjust fiscal policy to various shocks. These vulnerabilities would include:

- *A narrow tax base and low yield of the tax system.* This is reflected in the ratio of tax revenues to GDP, which ranges between 10 and 15 per cent (Table 1.7).[18] Moreover, the elasticity of taxes to GDP is at or below unity, in particular in El Salvador, Nicaragua, and Panamá (Table 1.8). To the extent that nominal GDP is a reasonable proxy for the tax base, the implication is that actual tax collections are – at best – barely able to keep up with growth in the tax base. Indeed, only the Dominican Republic and Guatemala have managed consistent increases in tax revenues in real terms (albeit starting from low levels); most of the fiscal adjustment that has taken place in the region since 1995 has been through expenditure cuts (see Table 1.7).
- *A high degree of revenue earmarking.* An estimated 20–30 per cent of revenue earmarking in these countries, implies that there is a substantial 'leakage' of any tax increase into automatic expenditure increases.
- *A tendency toward a procyclical fiscal policy stance.* A tendency toward a procyclical fiscal policy is noted for Latin American in general in Gavin *et al.* (1996) and IMF (2002), and illustrated in Figure 1.1 for the Central American countries.[19] While the reasons

Table 1.7 Central America: fiscal sector developments (in per cent of GDP)

	1995	1996	1997	1998	1999	2000	2001
Costa Rica							
Total revenues	31.6	31.5	30.6	30.3	28.4	30.3	32.8
Tax revenues	12.3	12.6	12.5	12.6	11.9	12.3	13.3
Nontax revenues	19.3	18.9	18.1	17.7	16.4	18.0	19.6
Total expenditures	33.3	33.9	31.7	31.4	30.6	32.8	35.0
Current expenditures	29.1	29.6	27.1	26.9	26.2	28.3	31.0
of which: interest	4.3	4.6	3.8	3.2	3.6	3.6	4.0
Capital expenditures	4.2	4.2	4.6	4.5	4.3	4.5	4.0
Primary balance	2.7	2.2	2.7	2.0	1.4	1.0	1.8
Non-financial public sector balance	−1.6	−2.4	−1.2	−1.2	−2.2	−2.6	−2.2
Dominican Republic							
Total revenues	15.8	15.0	17.2	16.9	16.6	17.0	16.7
Tax revenues	13.4	12.9	14.7	15.0	14.7	14.8	15.9
Nontax revenues	2.4	2.1	2.6	2.0	1.9	2.2	0.9
Total expenditures	20.9	22.2	24.2	24.0	24.5	23.9	21.7
Current expenditures	18.4	19.7	21.7	21.5	22.0	21.4	19.2
of which: interest	1.3	1.2	0.9	0.9	0.9	0.9	0.9
Capital expenditures	2.5	2.5	2.5	2.5	2.5	2.5	2.5
Primary balance	−3.7	−6.0	−6.0	−6.2	−7.0	−6.0	−4.1
Non-financial public sector balance[1]	−5.1	−7.2	−6.9	−7.1	−7.9	−6.9	−5.0
El Salvador							
Total revenues	20.9	21.4	19.7	16.8	17.1	18.0	17.6
Tax revenues	11.3	10.6	10.3	10.1	10.4	10.2	10.5
Nontax revenues	9.6	10.8	9.3	6.7	6.7	7.8	7.1
Total expenditures	19.6	21.1	19.3	18.6	18.8	20.3	21.5
Current expenditures	15.3	16.4	15.4	14.9	15.6	17.0	18.2
of which: interest	1.6	1.8	1.6	1.5	1.4	1.5	1.5
Capital expenditures	4.3	4.7	3.8	3.7	3.2	3.3	3.2
Primary balance	1.5	−0.7	−0.2	−1.1	−1.4	−1.5	−2.9
Non-financial public sector balance[2]	−0.1	−2.5	−1.8	−2.6	−2.8	−3.1	−4.3
Guatemala[3]							
Total revenues	8.6	9.2	9.4	9.7	10.5	10.5	11.0
Tax revenues	7.9	8.7	8.8	8.7	9.3	9.5	9.7
Nontax revenues	0.7	0.5	0.5	0.9	1.1	0.9	1.3
Total expenditures	9.5	9.4	10.1	11.9	13.3	12.4	13.8
Current expenditures	6.8	6.7	6.2	7.3	8.1	8.6	9.6
of which: interest	1.2	1.2	0.8	1.1	1.3	1.2	1.4
Capital expenditures	2.7	2.7	3.9	4.6	5.2	3.7	4.2
Primary balance	1.3	2.3	0.9	−0.4	−1.4	−0.4	−0.9

Table 1.7 Continued

	1995	1996	1997	1998	1999	2000	2001
Non-financial public sector balance	0.1	1.1	0.2	−1.5	−2.8	−1.6	−2.3
Honduras							
Total revenues	32.1	31.8	31.7	35.3	38.7	39.5	38.6
Tax revenues	18.0	16.8	16.9	19.0	20.0	19.1	19.6
Nontax revenues	5.7	5.2	6.0	6.4	8.3	10.7	9.5
Total expenditures	35.0	34.0	33.3	33.0	37.8	37.4	41.3
Current expenditures	22.8	23.7	23.7	23.3	24.8	26.0	28.4
of which: interest	5.6	5.0	3.7	3.2	3.1	2.4	2.7
Capital expenditures	12.2	10.3	9.6	9.7	13.0	11.4	12.9
Primary balance	3.9	2.4	2.2	5.2	3.1	3.5	−1.1
Non-financial public sector balance[1]	−1.6	−2.5	−1.5	1.9	0.0	1.1	−3.8
Nicaragua							
Total revenues	34.7	35.6	36.7	37.0	32.6	31.8	30.3
Tax revenues	26.8	27.4	30.0	31.7	30.9	30.1	28.8
Nontax revenues	7.9	8.2	6.7	5.4	1.7	1.6	1.6
Total expenditures	39.8	40.1	39.8	38.1	45.7	44.4	48.1
Current expenditures	27.3	28.5	28.8	27.0	27.4	27.5	33.1
of which: interest	4.8	3.6	5.9	4.7	4.5	4.4	7.7
Capital expenditures	12.5	11.7	10.9	11.0	18.3	16.9	15.0
Primary balance	−1.8	−3.4	1.8	4.4	−0.9	−2.2	−4.6
Non-financial public sector balance[1]	−6.6	−7.1	−4.0	−0.4	−5.3	−6.6	−12.3
Panamá							
Total revenues	29.2	28.0	28.7	28.4	29.0	28.8	27.7
Tax revenues	12.5	12.1	12.1	12.1	12.6	11.2	10.2
Nontax revenues	16.7	15.9	16.6	16.3	16.4	17.6	17.5
Total expenditures	29.0	27.5	28.9	31.3	30.4	29.5	30.2
Current expenditures	25.6	23.7	24.5	25.0	25.6	25.8	26.8
of which: interest	5.0	3.1	3.5	3.5	4.6	4.8	4.9
Capital expenditures	3.4	3.8	4.3	6.3	4.8	3.7	3.4
Primary balance	5.2	3.5	3.3	0.6	3.3	4.1	2.4
Non-financial public sector balance	0.2	0.5	−0.2	−2.9	−1.4	−0.7	−2.5

Notes

[1] Before grants.

[2] Discrepancies in the NFPS balance data are due to netting operations out within the government.

[3] Data refer to the Central Government only.

Sources: National authorities; and Fund staff estimates.

Table 1.8 Central America: revenue and expenditure elasticities (in per cent)

	1996	1997	1998	1999	2000	2001	Average
Costa Rica							
Total revenues	0.995	0.972	0.990	0.937	1.067	1.085	1.008
Tax revenues	1.018	0.998	1.007	0.947	1.028	1.079	1.013
Nontax revenues	0.980	0.955	0.978	0.929	1.096	1.089	1.005
Total expenditures	1.019	0.936	0.991	0.972	1.074	1.066	1.010
Dominican Republic							
Total revenues	0.950	1.148	0.982	0.982	1.021	0.986	1.011
Tax revenues	0.964	1.140	1.021	0.982	1.005	1.071	1.031
Nontax revenues	0.874	1.200	0.761	0.979	1.138	0.406	0.893
Total expenditures	1.063	1.088	0.995	1.020	0.974	0.909	1.008
El Salvador							
Total revenues	1.021	0.920	0.857	1.012	1.055	0.981	0.974
Tax revenues	0.933	0.975	0.980	1.028	0.985	1.030	0.988
Nontax revenues	1.125	0.867	0.721	0.989	1.164	0.917	0.964
Total expenditures	1.075	0.912	0.967	1.012	1.079	1.055	1.017
Guatemala							
Total revenues	1.067	1.017	1.032	1.084	1.000	1.050	1.042
Tax revenues	1.103	1.010	0.989	1.069	1.023	1.020	1.036
Nontax revenues	0.663	1.144	1.737	1.214	0.818	1.357	1.156
Total expenditures	0.984	1.081	1.178	1.115	0.931	1.113	1.067
Honduras							
Total revenues	0.991	0.996	1.114	1.097	1.021	0.975	1.032
Tax revenues	0.932	1.005	1.124	1.055	0.952	1.029	1.016
Nontax revenues	0.913	1.158	1.066	1.290	1.286	0.884	1.100
Total expenditures	0.971	0.979	0.993	1.144	0.989	1.104	1.030
Nicaragua							
Total revenues	1.028	1.029	1.009	0.880	0.975	0.955	0.979
Tax revenues	1.024	1.094	1.055	0.976	0.975	0.955	1.013
Nontax revenues	1.042	0.812	0.802	0.313	0.975	0.969	0.819
Total expenditures	1.009	0.991	0.957	1.202	0.971	1.085	1.036
Panamá							
Total revenues	0.958	1.026	0.990	1.021	0.992	0.962	0.992
Tax revenues	0.965	0.998	1.002	1.041	0.889	0.912	0.968
Nontax revenues	0.952	1.047	0.982	1.007	1.071	0.994	1.009
Total expenditures	0.948	1.049	1.085	0.971	0.970	1.024	1.008

Sources: National authorities; and Fund staff estimates.

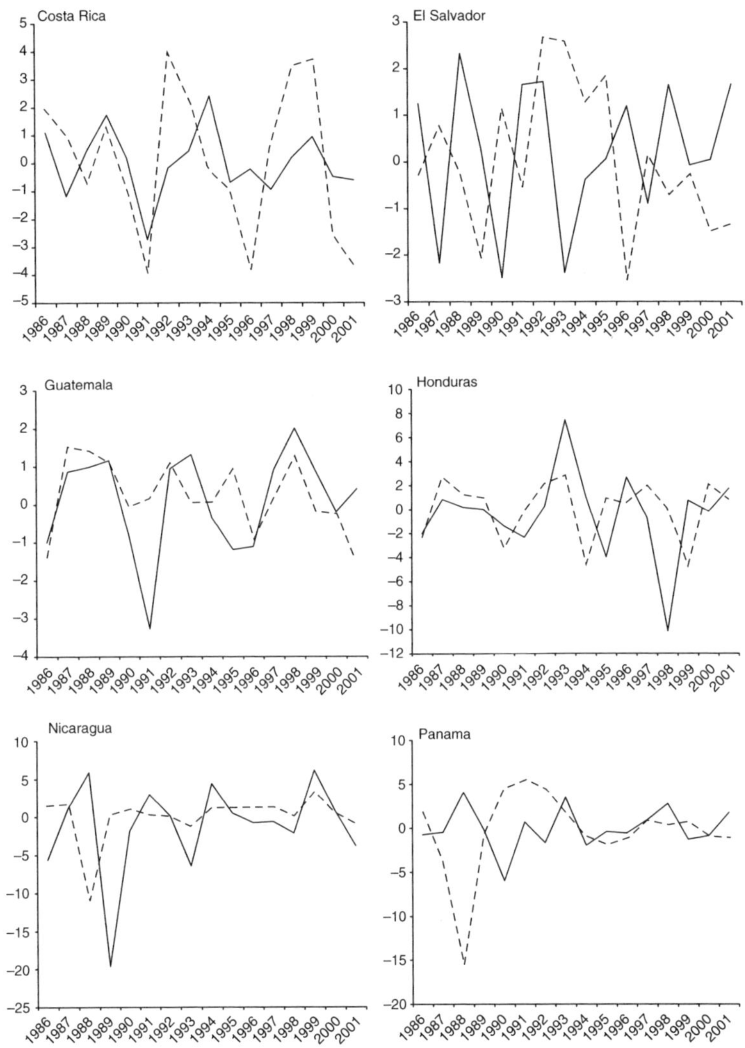

Figure 1.1 Central America: fiscal impulse and capacity utilization, 1986–2001

Source: Fund staff estimates.

for this procyclicality are not always clear, the implication is relatively straightforward: by effectively disabling the automatic stabilizers, it tends to amplify the impact of any of the above shocks to the economy.

A reflection of the last three points is the general deterioration in the fiscal stance between 1995 and 2001; the primary balance has worsened by an average of 2.6 percentage points of GDP over this period, with particularly strong deterioration in El Salvador, Guatemala, Honduras, Nicaragua, and Panamá.

How would adverse shocks impact on the need for fiscal adjustment?

Some important and intuitive messages would seem to emerge from the discussion thus far. One is that adverse shocks to these economies, from domestic or external sources, are and will continue to be, a 'fact of life'. Moreover, the ability to counteract these shocks is, to some extent, inversely related to the level of public debt and to the size of the economy. The corollary is simply that small, open economies, such as those in Central America, can generally sustain a lower debt level than larger economies.

This section will discuss some simple, partial equilibrium simulations to illustrate two points:[20] (i) how adverse shocks would impact on the long-term debt-to-GDP ratio if fiscal policy was completely 'passive' (i.e. no above-the-line fiscal adjustment in response to the shock); and (ii) what would be the fiscal adjustment necessary to fully offset the shocks (i.e. in the sense that the long-term debt-to-GDP ratio were the same as in a scenario without any shock). To avoid a cumbersome comparison of multiple medium-term scenarios for each of the seven different countries, the assessment of the impact of shocks will be done for a 'representative' Central American country – that is, with the relevant features equal to a rough 'average' of the five non-HIPC countries in the region. The main assumptions regarding this 'representative' country and the baseline scenario, that is, the scenario with no shocks, are summarized in Box 1.1.[21]

Four different adverse shocks will be simulated separately on this 'representative' country, each shock assumed to have a duration of

Box 1.1 Key assumptions for 'representative' country

Initial position:	
Total public debt	50 per cent of GDP
Share of gross debt denominated in foreign currencies[1]	90 per cent
Baseline assumptions:	
Domestic annual inflation rate	6 per cent
Foreign annual inflation rate	2.5 per cent
Real depreciation (i.e. annual nominal depreciation of 3.4 per cent)	0 per cent
Domestic interest rate (nominal)	14 per cent
Foreign interest rate (nominal)[2]	11 per cent
Annual real GDP growth rate	3–4.5 per cent
Annual primary fiscal surplus	1.2 per cent of GDP

[1] It is also assumed that the shares of domestic- and foreign-denominated debt in total debt remain constant at current levels.
[2] This interest rate implies a spread on about 600 basis points over current US Treasuries. This is somewhat on the high side relative to what countries in the region have obtained in recent years (300–500 basis points), but not so much that it biases the results.

two years, and to impact the economy in 2003 and 2004:

- *Interest rates* are assumed to increase by 5 percentage points in nominal terms, both on the foreign and domestic side;
- *Real growth* is assumed to decline by 2 percentage points, which is slightly below one standard deviation of average growth in the five countries between 1995 and 2001;
- *Real depreciation* of 5 per cent, which translates to a nominal depreciation of 8.6 per cent;
- *Stock adjustment* equal to 2 percentage points of GDP in each of the two years.

The results of these shocks are summarized in Table 1.9. When fiscal policy remains entirely passive, with no adjustment to the shocks, the end-period debt stock would be higher than in the

Table 1.9 Fiscal adjustment and debt dynamics under adverse shocks (in per cent of GDP)

	Year	Baseline	Higher interest rate	Lower growth	Real depreciation	Assumption of contingent liabilities
Primary balance with	2002	1.20	1.20	1.20	1.20	1.20
full contemporaneous	2003	1.20	3.21	1.90	3.23	3.20
adjustment to shock	2004	1.20	3.22	1.90	3.24	3.20
	2005	1.20	1.20	1.20	1.21	1.20
Debt level no adjustment	2001	50.00	50.00	50.00	50.00	50.00
to shock	2015	50.94	57.95	53.34	55.01	65.87

Source: Fund staff estimates.

baseline: 3.3 percentage points higher with a lower growth shock, 5–8 percentage points higher with the higher interest or real depreciation shocks, and a full 16 percentage points higher under the stock adjustment scenario (Table 1.9, lower panel). The first three of these shocks (lower growth, higher interest rates, or real depreciation) increase the interest service term $b(r - g)+b^*(r^* - g + \hat{e})$ in equation (2). This increased interest service in the two 'shock years' will be financed by additional debt in those two years, which – in turn – will require further interest service in future years. However, the stock increase of 4 percentage points of GDP early on will effectively quadruple over the simulation period because the additional interest obligation created by assuming this amount of contingent liabilities will be financed by additional borrowing, which will create further interest obligations, and so on.

The contemporaneous fiscal adjustments necessary to fully offset the shocks are substantial and very similar for three of the shocks – the higher external interest rate, the real depreciation, and the stock adjustment due to contingent liabilities.[22] All would require the primary surplus to increase by about 2 percentage points of GDP in the two years of the shock (i.e. increase to about 3.2 per cent of GDP). After that, the fiscal position could revert to its baseline level, and the end-period ratio of public debt to GDP would be identical to the baseline. The lower growth shock would require a far milder adjustment, by about 0.7 percentage points of GDP in the two 'shock years'.

The end-period impact on debt levels of some of these shocks, without any fiscal adjustment, may initially seem moderate. However, two points need to be kept in mind: (i) the size of the shocks discussed above are also quite moderate; and (ii) shocks often occur in tandem, for example, a severe terms-of-trade shock that adversely affects growth and fiscal revenues may cause foreign investors to increase their perception of country risk and thus result in an increase in interest rates. In new Fund guidelines for this type of sensitivity analysis, it is recommended that individual shocks be calibrated to two standard deviations from historical averages, that combinations of shock be calibrated to one standard deviation each, and that a stock adjustment shock be calibrated to 10 percentage points of GDP. Since, to a first approximation, the impacts of the different shocks in the above simulations are additive, it follows that a two-standard deviation deterioration in the growth rate (4 per cent) would result in an end-period debt ratio of 6.5 percentage points of GDP higher than in the baseline, and a combination of the higher interest rate and real depreciation shock would result in an end-period debt ratio about 13 percentage point of GDP higher. The fiscal adjustment necessary to offset either a larger shock or a combination of shocks would, of course, also be correspondingly higher, for example, a fiscal adjustment of about 4 percentage points of GDP in the case of a combined interest/exchange rate depreciation shock.

Would fiscal rules be useful?

The discussion above raises the question of whether some form of fiscal rule, placing legal or statutory restrictions on the conduct of fiscal policy, and in particular on the policy response to shocks, would be a helpful instrument.

Such fiscal rules are currently applied, or are under consideration, in a wide range of countries. Their purpose is to address a perceived bias toward fiscal deficits and continued public debt accumulation, and thus to improve the credibility of the authorities' commitment to a disciplined fiscal policy.[23] The current rules generally fall within three main categories:

- Balanced-budget or deficit rules, which place a limit on either the annual or the medium-term fiscal position, either through the overall balance or through the structural deficit;
- Borrowing rules, which place limits on government borrowing from the central bank and/or other domestic sources;
- Debt rules, which place some form of limit on gross or net government debt in relation to GDP.

As examples, Canada, the Netherlands, New Zealand, and Japan all have some form of deficit rule; Indonesia, CFA franc zone countries, and many countries in Latin America have some form of borrowing rule; Panamá has recently implemented a debt rule; and the European Union imposes a combination of all three categories of rules (over the business cycle) on its member countries.

The main advantages of fiscal rules are that they would reduce or possibly eliminate a tendency toward a deficit-bias in a discretionary fiscal policy stance. Moreover, if applied consistently and transparently, such rules would – over time – improve the credibility of fiscal policy and the access to and the terms of financing of the public sector. The main potential downside of the fiscal tightening implied by such rules is that – if applied rigidly and without supporting institutional reforms – they are likely to result in circumvention and 'creative accounting' practices which eventually will undermine rather than strengthen credibility.[24]

To avoid this downside, some basic criteria have been suggested for a 'good' fiscal rule (Kopits (2001) and Drazen (2002)): (i) it should be operationally simple to facilitate monitoring and control of compliance; (ii) it should be growth-oriented, in that it should be designed to avoid undue cuts in public investment and social safety net provisions; (iii) its legal status should be such that it is difficult to change or amend; (iv) it should be supported by procedural reforms, in particular reforms geared toward enhancing transparency in public sector accounting practices and timely provisioning of fiscal data; and (v) the rule should be sufficiently flexible, with 'escape clauses' to accommodate the impacts of unforeseen shocks. While all these criteria are important, the last has been emphasized since it involves a delicate trade-off. A rule that is too rigid, without escape clauses, may make it impossible to comply with over the long term, and hence fail to instill the credibility that is the purpose of the rule. A rule that is too flexible may, on the other hand, increase the possibilities for circumventing it, and thus also fail to instill the credibility of the authorities' commitment to fiscal discipline.

In the following, we shall sidestep these criteria, and examine how two specific fiscal rules would impact on the scenarios discussed in the previous section. The two rules are:

- *A balanced fiscal position rule*, that is, zero overall deficit in each year starting in 2002, with a primary surplus in each year that equals the interest obligations on public debt;
- *A debt rule*, which limits on the growth of the public debt stock to 80 per cent of the growth in nominal GDP. Since nominal GDP grows by 9.2–10.8 per cent annually in the baseline discussed above (increasing over time as real growth increases), this is tantamount to requiring the ratio of public debt to GDP to decline by 1.7–1.9 per cent annually.

It is intuitively clear that both fiscal rules would be useful in reducing the long-term ratio of debt to GDP. Under the *balanced fiscal position* rule, net borrowing requirements are zero, so the debt ratio will decline as nominal debt is amortized and nominal GDP grows. To accomplish the balanced position would, however, require a higher primary surplus than in the baseline discussed above, about 1.2 percentage points of GDP higher in the first few years, then falling to about 0.2 percentage points higher at the end of the simulation period (Table 1.10). With this higher primary surplus, the end-period ratio of public debt to GDP would decline to 38.5 per cent, which is 11.5 percentage points below the baseline discussed in the previous section. To facilitate the discussion, we will refer to this scenario as 'the baseline with a balanced fiscal position rule'. Similarly, *the debt rule* defines, in itself, the decline in the debt ratio, and with the particular parameters chosen here would require a path of the primary surplus almost identical to that under the balanced position rule; initially 1.2 percentage points of GDP higher than in the baseline without a fiscal rule, but with the difference gradually declining to about 0.2 percentage points. This is then 'the baseline with a debt rule'.

The broader question of 'Would fiscal rules be useful in protecting against shocks?' has an ambiguous answer. It is positive in the sense that these rules would, by definition, eliminate any discretion in the policy response to the shocks, that is, whether and by how much to adjust the primary surplus. As such, these rules would protect the debt stock from rising in the event of an adverse shock. However, under these two rules the size of the required fiscal adjustment in response to shocks is significant.

Relative to the two new baselines, with the fiscal rules incorporated, the impact of a higher interest rate, a real depreciation, and lower growth, would be fairly similar to those above; a contemporaneous increase in the primary surplus of about 2 percentage points with the former two shocks, and an increase of about 0.7 percentage points for lower growth. The 'stock adjustment' shock would generate different responses under these two rules; the balanced rule would require the primary surplus to increase only to accommodate the interest on the additional debt, not the full stock increase, whereas under the debt growth rule the whole stock operation would need to be offset. Consequently, the balanced rule would require a much smaller but a sustained adjustment throughout the simulation

Table 1.10 Debt dynamics under adverse shocks with fiscal rules (in per cent of GDP)

	Year	Baseline	Higher interest rate	Lower growth	Real depreciation	Assumption of contingent liabilities
Primary balance under						
1. Balanced budget rule	2002	2.39	2.39	2.39	2.39	2.39
	2003	2.19	4.14	2.86	4.13	2.19
	2004	2.15	4.06	2.81	4.05	2.25
	2005	2.04	2.04	2.04	2.04	2.25
	2006–10	1.79	1.79	1.79	1.79	1.98
	2011–15	1.49	1.49	1.49	1.49	1.67
2. Debt growth rule	2002	2.37	2.37	2.37	2.37	2.37
	2003	2.14	4.10	2.67	4.09	4.14
	2004	2.09	4.01	2.62	4.00	4.09
	2005	1.97	1.97	1.99	1.97	1.97
	2006–10	1.69	1.69	1.70	1.69	1.69
	2011–15	1.35	1.35	1.36	1.35	1.35
Debt level under						
1. Balanced budget rule	2001	50.0	50.0	50.0	50.0	50.0
	2015	38.5	38.5	38.5	38.5	42.5
2. Debt growth rule	2001	50.0	50.0	50.0	50.0	50.0
	2015	40.3	40.3	40.5	40.3	40.3

Source: Fund staff estimates.

period, and the debt growth rule would require a one-off full adjustment to the stock increase.

Relative to the baseline with no rule, the required fiscal adjustment to, for example, an interest rate shock is now almost 3 percentage points of GDP; quite formidable compared to the adjustments previously undertaken in the region.[25]

Some issues for further consideration

The chapter opened by making the general point that a country has reason to be concerned about the potential burden of its public debt, even if the debt is at relatively moderate levels, if it is vulnerable to adverse shocks and has limited flexibility to respond to these shocks. The subsequent sections have highlighted the sources of such shocks, including the importance of contingent liabilities, and the considerable strain such shocks could put on fiscal adjustment if the country aimed at keeping its ratio of public debt to GDP constant over the medium term.

Several topics deserve further discussion:

- The fiscal adjustment to a shock could be stretched out over three–four years. That would be a reasonable strategy if: (i) the shocks were temporary, as they are defined here; and (ii) if such shocks were rare phenomena, occurring only with long intervals between them. In practice, however, it is difficult to discern whether a shock may be temporary or permanent (the recent decline in coffee prices being a possible example), and Central America is clearly a region where various shocks are frequent phenomena (although not always of the adverse kind). In that environment, a more gradual fiscal adjustment would run the risk of not completing one round of adjustment before the next shock occurs. Although a full, contemporaneous adjustment may not be necessary or desirable, it would nonetheless seem prudent to err on the side of a shorter rather than a longer adjustment period to a shock.
- *The absence of adequate cushions* of foreign exchange reserves to confront such shocks (with the exception of Panamá). Such cushions could be built up through restrictive fiscal (and monetary)

policies, especially during the cyclical peaks, and would help in reducing the vulnerability to shocks and allow the adjustment to be more gradual. This point would be particularly important in El Salvador, which effectively has relinquished the use of monetary and/or exchange rate policies to counteract such shocks.

- *Effective structural policies* can better enable a country to carry a certain debt burden. Such policies would normally be geared toward lowering domestic interest rates (through deepening domestic capital markets and securing a viable banking system) and increasing economic growth (e.g. through increasing labor market flexibility and lowering barriers to trade, among others). It follows directly from equation (2) that, other things equal, this would lower the interest servicing burden. Moreover, structural fiscal reforms would typically be aimed at increasing the buoyancy of the tax system and reducing revenue earmarking, both of which would allow for a more effective use of automatic stabilizers and a countercyclical fiscal policy.
- *Some structural policies may result in additional pressure on the fiscal position*, at least within the time horizon being discussed here. This would hold true for trade liberalization, which would tend to reduce fiscal revenues, and poverty reduction programs, which will tend to increase expenditures. In order to allow such reforms to go forward without increasing the public sector borrowing requirement, restraint will be necessary in other aspects of fiscal policy.
- *Debt management* is clearly important to the degree of vulnerability of the economy to various shocks. In particular, a large (or increasing) share of total debt on short maturities (which implies a need for frequent roll-overs), a 'bunching' of maturities, a large (or increasing) share of total debt on variable interest rates and a large (or increasing) share of domestic debt denominated in foreign currencies are all factors that add to vulnerability. An active debt management policy will therefore be a helpful supplement to regular fiscal adjustment.

Appendix 1.1. The accounting framework

The accounting framework underpinning the calculations used in this paper are based on an approach developed in Anand and van Wijnbergen (1989). The starting point is the in-period budget constraint of the nonfinancial public sector:

$$D + i \cdot B + i^* \cdot B^* \cdot E = \dot{B} + \dot{B}^* \cdot E \tag{1}$$

where D is the primary fiscal balance, i (i^*) is the nominal interest rate on domestic (foreign) debt, B (B^*) is the stock of domestic (foreign) debt, E is the nominal exchange rate, and a '•' over a variable indicates its change over time, i.e. ∂x/∂t. Equation (1) therefore indicates that the fiscal balance of the nonfinancial public sector – the primary balance plus interest cost on domestic and foreign debt – can be financed either by increasing the stock of domestic or foreign debt.

This can be expressed as ratios to GDP by dividing through by PY where P is the GDP deflator and Y is real GDP, and inserting the following relationships:

$$\dot{b} = \left(\frac{\dot{B}}{PY}\right) = \frac{\dot{B}}{PY} - b(\pi + g)$$

$$\dot{b}^* = \left(\frac{\dot{B}^*E}{PY}\right) = \frac{\dot{B}^*E}{PY} - b^*(\pi + g - \hat{E})$$

$$\hat{E} = \frac{\dot{E}}{E} = \hat{e} - \pi^* + \pi$$

where π is rate of inflation in the GDP deflator P and g is the rate of growth of real GDP. By defining the real rate of interest on domestic debt as $r = i - \pi$ and similarly the real interest rate on foreign debt as $r^* = r^* - \pi^*$ and rearranging, this yields:

$$d + b(r - g) + (b^* - n^*)(r^* - g + \hat{e}) = \dot{b} + \dot{b}^* \tag{2}$$

For the purpose of the calculations presented here, equation (2) is converted to discrete time by defining:

$$\dot{b} = b_t - b_{t-1}; \quad r = \frac{(1 + i)}{(1 + \pi)} - 1$$

and similarly for $\dot{b}^*$ and r^*, where π^* would be change in the US GDP deflator.

One additional simplifying assumption for the projections discussed in Sections 6 and 7 is that the shares of domestic- and foreign-currency denominated debt in total debt remain constant at their current levels, that is:

$$b = \alpha\Gamma, \quad \text{and} \quad (b^* - n^*) = (1 - \alpha)\Gamma, \quad \text{where } \Gamma = b + (b^* - n^*),$$

which means that equation (2) can be simplified to:

$$d + \lambda\Gamma = \dot{\Gamma} \qquad (3)$$

where $\lambda = \alpha r + (1 - \alpha)(r^* + \hat{e}) - g$.

Notes

1. For the purpose of this paper, the region encompasses Costa Rica, Dominican Republic, El Salvador, Guatemala, Honduras, Nicaragua, and Panamá.
2. Since 1998 both Costa Rica and El Salvador have raised about US$1 billion in Eurobonds, amounting to 6.5 per cent and 7.2 per cent of 2001 GDP respectively, at spreads of 300–400 basis points over US Treasuries. El Salvador is expected to approach the markets for an additional US$700 million through end-2003. Guatemala has raised a total of almost US$500 million (2.4 per cent of 2001 GDP) since 1997 at somewhat higher spreads, and the Dominican Republic raised US$500 million in September 2001; 2.3 per cent of GDP that year.
3. In contrast to the conventional accounting of public investment as above-the-line expenditure (thus increasing the deficit) and privatization receipts as below-the-line financing (and thus not decreasing the deficit).
4. An additional source of uncertainty in the case of petroleum reserves is the estimate of undiscovered reserves.
5. In principle, the NFPS deficit can also be financed through money creation and seigniorage, which would reduce the direct borrowing requirement. However, since two of the countries in the sample are dollarized, and several others have restrictions on government borrowing from the central bank – thus reducing the possibility of excessive monetary financing – we will disregard this element in the following.
6. Equation (2) is frequently used as a starting point for deriving various 'sustainability indicators', such as the primary balance necessary to maintain a constant ratio of debt to GDP (see Blanchard *et al.* (1990) and Chalk and Heming (2000)). Although useful in some contexts, this approach will not be pursued here, mainly because it does not address the more fundamental question of whether a constant (or even a declining) debt ratio may still be 'too high', given the vulnerabilities of a given economy.

7. Additional sources of possible discrepancies between above-the-line net borrowing requirements and changes in the debt-to-GDP ratios would be: (i) inaccuracies in data and measurement errors; (ii) revaluation of domestic debt unrelated to exchange rate changes; (iii) arrears; and (iv) the issue of money for financing of budgetary deficits.
8. The ratio of the current value of debt stock to GDP may be misleading for Honduras and Nicaragua, both eligible for debt relief under the HIPC initiative. More meaningful is the ratio of net present value of debt (i.e. future debt service, discounted at market interest rates) to GDP, which, in 2001, would be about 50 per cent for Honduras and about 175 per cent for Nicaragua. In addition, it is widely acknowledged that official statistics in Nicaragua underestimate GDP by a significant margin; forthcoming revisions to GDP data can be expected to bring the ratio of NPV of debt to GDP below 100 per cent.
9. The concept of 'interest service' used here is the sum of the last two terms on the left-hand side of (2): the ratio of domestic debt to GDP multiplied by the difference between the real domestic interest rate and the GDP growth rate *plus* the ratio of external debt to GDP multiplied by the difference between the external real interest rate, the GDP growth rate, and the rate of real appreciation/depreciation.
10. In the remainder of the chapter, I will refer to this residual as 'stock operations' while recognizing that – as a residual – it also captures measurement issues and flow operations as discussed in note 8.
11. A more indirect channel would be that a potential debt overhang implies a high marginal tax on external creditors and therefore discourages foreign investment.
12. One would expect that a country can sustain a higher level of external debt to GDP as its export-to-GDP ratio increases. When a correction is made for differing export-to-GDP ratios, this study finds that the threshold level of debt typically increases by 5–10 percentage points, that is, to 40–50 per cent for relatively open economies.
13. In addition, the political violence prior to the presidential elections in 1994 contributed to a climate of uncertainty.
14. It is also instructive to note that, for example, in México, the gross public debt ratio to GDP had been declining for several years prior to the 1994 crisis.
15. Of course, countries with high private external debt may be vulnerable to external shocks even though public debt is moderate.
16. 'Effective' defined as actual domestic interest obligations divided by the level of domestic debt. Domestic interest rates have come down significantly in El Salvador after dollarization was implemented at the beginning of 2001.
17. These medium-term frameworks are generally developed by Fund staff in consultation with country authorities.
18. In Honduras and Nicaragua the ratios are significantly higher, most likely reflecting a significant underestimation of GDP, and thus an overestimation of indicators measured as ratios to GDP.

19. Figure 1.1 uses a fairly standard methodology and illustrates the correlation between the fiscal impulse (that is, the change in the cyclically adjusted fiscal balance from one year to the next) and cyclical swings (measured as the deviation between actual and trend GDP, where a Hodrick-Prescott filter is used to derive the underlying trend GDP).
20. It is worth reiterating that these sensitivity simulations are partial equilibrium in that, for example, the response to import demand to a growth shock or the response of exports and imports to a real depreciation, are not taken into account.
21. The baseline assumes a primary surplus of 1.2 per cent of GDP every year, and, by construction, that the ratio of public debt to GDP remains practically constant at 50 per cent throughout the simulation period, which runs from 2001 to 2015.
22. Implicit in the calculation of the impact of higher interest rates is an assumption that the entire stock of debt is on floating rates. In practice, a substantial share of debt in Central America is on fixed rates, and the impact would thus generally be smaller than indicated here. However, how much smaller would be different between the countries in the region. The country potentially most vulnerable to interest rate shocks is Costa Rica, which has above 20 per cent of GDP in domestic public debt; much of it with a short tenor. An abrupt increase in foreign interest rates, which would quickly translate to higher domestic interest rates, would therefore rapidly result in increased gross financing needs, which again could have an adverse impact on market assessment of Costa Rican country risk.
23. A number of related political-economy explanations have been suggested as the reasons for a possible deficit bias (Drazen (2002) and Hausmann (2002)): (i) a 'deficit illusion', where economic agents overestimate the value of today's fiscal expenditures but underestimate the associated future tax burden; (ii) a generational conflict over who should pay to reduce the deficit (i.e. a variant of a free rider problem); (iii) a 'common pool' problem, where government expenditures benefit specific (and powerful) constituencies while tax revenues have a broader base; and (iv) electoral budget cycles, where politicians are inclined to raise expenditures prior to elections but not to reduce them again afterwards.
24. For a more comprehensive review of fiscal rules, see Kopits and Symansky (1998).
25. The largest one-period improvement in the primary balance since 1995 among the non-HIPC countries was in the Dominican Republic in 2001, with an increase of 1.9 percentage points. Honduras and Nicaragua implemented larger increases in 1997/98.

References

Anand, R. and S. van Wijnbergen (1989) 'Inflation and the Financing of Government Expenditure: an Introductory Analysis with an Application to Turkey', *The World Bank Economic Review*, Vol. 3, No. 1, pp. 17–38.

Blanchard, O., J. C. Chouraqui, R. Hagemann, and Nicola Sartor (1990) 'The Sustainability of Fiscal Policy: New Answers to an Old Question', *OECD Economic Studies*, No. 15.

Buti, M. and G. Giudice (2002) 'EMU's Fiscal Rules: What Can and Cannot Be Exported', *Mimeo*. Paper for Conference on Rules-Based Fiscal Policy in Emerging Market Economies.

Chalk, N. and R. Hemming (2000) 'Assessing Fiscal Sustainability in Theory and Practice', *IMF Working Paper, WP/00/81*.

Drazen, A. (2002) 'Fiscal Rules From a Political Economy Perspective', *Mimeo*. Paper for Conference on Rules-Based Fiscal Policy in Emerging Market Economies.

Edwards, S. (2002) 'Debt Relief and Fiscal Sustainability', *NBER Working Paper No. 8939*.

Fischer, S. (2001) 'Farewell to the IMF Executive Board', Address given on August 30, 2001.

Fischer, S. and W. Easterly (1990) 'The Economics of the Government Budget Constraint', *The World Bank Research Observer*, Vol. 5, No. 2, pp. 127–44.

Gavin, M., R. Hausmann, R. Perotti, and E. Talvi (1996) 'Managing Fiscal Policy in Latin America and the Caribbean: Volatility, Procyclicality, and Limited Creditworthiness', *IDB Working Paper No. 13*.

Hemming, R. and M. Petrie (2000) 'A Framework for Assessing Fiscal Vulnerability', *IMF Working Paper, WP/00/52*.

Hausmann, R. (2002) 'Unrewarded Good Fiscal Behavior: The Role of Debt Structure', *Mimeo*. Paper for Conference on Rules-Based Fiscal Policy in Emerging Market Economies.

International Monetary Fund (2002) 'World Economic Outlook', May.

International Monetary Fund (2002) 'Assessing Sustainability', *Mimeo*.

Kopits, G. and S. Symansky (1998) 'Fiscal Policy Rules', *Occasional Paper No. 162, IMF*.

Kopits. G. (2001) 'Fiscal Rules: Useful Policy Framework or Unnecessary Ornament'? *IMF Working Paper, WP/01/145*.

—— (2002) 'Fiscal Policy Under High Capital Mobility' *Mimeo*. Paper for Conference on Rules-Based Fiscal Policy in Emerging Market Economies.

Pattillo, C., H. Poirson, and L. Ricci (2002) 'External Debt and Growth', *IMF Working Paper, WP/02/69*.

Spaventa, L. (1987) 'The Growth of Public Debt. Sustainability, Fiscal Rules, and Monetary Rules', *IMF Staff Papers*.

Van Wijnbergen, S., R. Anand, A. Chhibber, and R. Rocha (1990) '*External Debt, Fiscal Policy, and Sustainable Debt in Turkey*', John Hopkins University Press.

2

Tax Reform: Trends and Possibilities

Janet G. Stotsky and Asegedech WoldeMariam

Introduction

Central America's economic performance improved markedly in the 1990s.[1] But there remain many challenges for this region, especially in strengthening the public finances and revenue yields. Achieving and maintaining a sound fiscal position is essential for macroeconomic stability and for creating the appropriate conditions for sustained economic growth. Key issues are to reform the system of taxation to achieve a sound structure that is buoyant in generating revenue, distorts economic decisions as little as possible, and achieves the degree of redistribution that is consistent with equity goals. Because Central American countries are small, open economies, another goal is harmonization of their tax systems with each other to better enable producers to compete with the surrounding, larger neighbors, such as México or Colombia, and to avoid harmful tax competition for scarce resources such as capital and skilled labor. Harmonization can also facilitate tax and customs administration. Harmonization of the domestic tax system is complementary to harmonization of trade regimes, through efforts such as those made by the Central American Common Market.

Central American tax systems are modern in their orientation, especially now that every country has a value-added tax (VAT). However, there remain a number of significant challenges for countries in the region with regard to tax policy. First, revenue collections and tax productivities in many countries are still relatively weak. The causes underlying this weakness appear to be a combination of tax policies that have eroded tax bases as well as continuing weaknesses in tax and customs administration. Second, harmonization of taxes on domestic goods and services, primarily VAT and excises, would enhance efforts at strengthening both revenue collections and tax productivity. The European Union (EU) model could usefully be adapted to Central America. Third, property taxes and other, more locally based charges or taxes are currently minimal but could contribute to strengthening both the budget and efforts at fiscal decentralization.

General principles of tax reform

The most important economic principles underlying sound tax reform are:

- The tax system should be efficient in that private consumption, saving, production, and investment decisions should differ as little as possible from what they would be in the absence of taxes. However, in the presence of market imperfections, such as externalities some distorting taxes may improve efficiency and enhance growth. The tax system should thus support efforts to increase economic growth.
- The tax system should be fair or equitable in the distribution of the tax burden. Vertical equity implies that those with greater ability to pay tax should pay a larger proportion of their income or wealth in taxes while horizontal equity implies that those with equal ability to pay tax should pay the same proportion in taxes.
- The tax system should facilitate tax administration and reduce taxpayer compliance costs.
- The tax system should be stable, often with phasing in of significant changes, to ensure that taxpayers can make rational economic decisions. It should also match tax instruments to tax objectives.
- The tax system should be transparent and rules-driven, with scope for discretion on the part of administrators minimized, to reduce uncertainty and the incentive for corruption. The legal framework should be clear and applied in a uniform manner.

Efficiency considerations suggest that, for a given revenue requirement, the degree to which economic decisions are altered by taxes should be minimized, unless the purpose is to address externalities (distortions not taken into account by the market) and other market imperfections. This implies that tax bases should be broad-based and the tax rate should be as low as possible to achieve revenue goals. Income taxes should have relatively few tax rate brackets and corresponding rates, and few deductions or allowances. VATs are best levied at one rate, and should have few exemptions. Only exports should be subject to zero rating. Luxury or excise taxes serve certain purposes, like discouraging certain activities (e.g. excise taxes on alcohol or cigarettes) or adding progressivity to indirect taxes (e.g. excise taxes on cars) but should not apply to a wide range of activities.

In addition, efficiency considerations mean that production decisions should not be distorted in the presence of externalities and other market imperfections. Tax incentives, such as tax holidays, should not be used to encourage particular activities because such incentives tend to distort economic decisions and lead to revenue losses that require higher tax rates overall to achieve revenue goals.

Equity considerations suggest that taxes should be based on taxpayers' ability to pay, though it is also appropriate to base tax payments on the principle that those who benefit from a public service should pay for it. Achieving equity goals based on ability to pay requires reliance on a broad measure of income, which is the best indicator of underlying ability to pay, or else consumption, which is closely related to income but excludes the saving component. An income tax can be made more progressive through a schedule of increasing marginal tax rates (the tax rate applied to each bracket of income), or through a general allowance or one for family members and high expenses on necessities, such as medical care. Similarly, a VAT can be made more progressive by exempting certain goods or taxing them at a lower than standard rate, such as basic foodstuffs largely consumed by poorer households. A few luxury excises and targeted spending in the budget can also help achieve the desired progressivity of the fiscal structure.

The goal of administrability requires that the tax system be simple (or as simple as necessary to account for the complexity of economic decision making). This goal can be accomplished by using final withholding for certain forms of income tax, making the tax system schedular to some extent, and relying on a limited number of rates under the different taxes. Finally, the goals of stability and transparency require that tax laws and regulations be clear and comprehensive. Judicial reform is critical in this regard. Tax liabilities should be determined in accordance with the tax law and not negotiated. The tax administration should have sufficient powers to enforce the tax laws. Taxpayers should have recourse through the legal system to challenge or clarify the tax laws.

Structure of tax system in Central America

Central American countries have modern tax systems. However, they still differ in certain respects. One notable feature of Central American tax systems is the variation in the overall revenue and tax revenue to GDP ratio (Tables 2.1 and 2.2).[2] The average tax yield for Central American countries differs little from the average tax yield for South America despite the lower average level of income in Central America (Figure 2.1). Whether Central American countries should strengthen their revenues depends on the purposes for which that revenue would be spent, for example, on worthwhile government programs or to reduce budget deficits rather than on propping up or subsidizing poorly run parts of the public sector or on public expenditures with little social value. Many of these countries have faced significant fiscal imbalances, and this has led to pressures to increase the revenue yield.

Between 1990–94 and 1995–99, tax revenues to GDP rose on average in Central America from 14.5 per cent of GDP to 16.5 per cent of GDP, paralleled by a similar change in total revenues to GDP and by an increase in tax revenue in South America. Notably, all countries in Central America experienced an increase in the tax revenue to GDP ratio between these periods.[3] Two countries, Nicaragua and Panamá, finished the period with a tax revenue to GDP ratio above 20 per cent, with Nicaragua's tax revenue to GDP ratio increasing from 17.6 per cent in 1990–94 to 23.9 per cent in 1995, the latest year for which data were available.[4] Guatemala has the weakest revenue share, largely reflecting prolonged civil conflict, though it also improved the tax revenue to GDP ratio from 7.4 per cent to 8.9 per cent, from 1990–94 to 1995–99, still short of its goal of 12 per cent, as agreed to in the Peace Accords.

Central American tax systems rely on diverse sources of revenue, including the major categories of domestic taxes on goods and

Table 2.1 Consolidated central government: tax structure for Latin American countries, 1990–94 (in per cent of GDP)

	Sample size	Total revenue	Tax revenue	Other revenue	Taxes on income, profits, and capital gains			Social Security taxes	Payroll taxes	Domestic taxes on goods and services			International trade taxes			Property taxes
					Total	*Of which:* Individual	*Of which:* Corporate			Total	*Of which:* General sales, turnover, or VAT	*Of which:* Excises	Total	*Of which:* Import duties	*Of which:* Export duties	
Latin America																
Argentina[1]	1990–94	12.8	11.6	1.2	0.7	0.2	—	5.3	0.0	3.7	2.4	1.2	1.1	0.5	0.2	0.4
Bolivia	1990–94	15.3	9.9	5.4	0.7		0.4	1.2	0.0	5.7	3.9	1.7	1.0	1.0	0.0	1.2
Brazil	1990–94	29.1	18.0	11.1	3.9	0.2	1.1	7.3	1.2	5.1	1.6	2.4	0.5	0.5	0.0	0.0
Chile	1990–94	22.2	18.4	3.8	3.8	—	—	1.6	0.0	10.0	8.1	1.9	2.2	—	—	0.0
Colombia[2]	1990–94	13.2	11.5	1.8	5.0	0.2	3.9	0.0	0.0	4.8	4.0	0.7	1.6	1.5	0.1	0.0
Costa Rica	1990–94	20.2	17.5	2.7	1.9	1.5	0.5	5.7	0.0	6.3	3.6	2.4	3.6	2.8	0.7	0.1
Dominican Republic	1990–94	14.6	13.2	1.4	2.4	1.1	1.3	0.6	0.0	3.9	—	3.1	6.1	5.7	0.0	0.1
Ecuador[2]	1990–94	16.3	15.5	0.8	9.3	—	7.9	0.0	0.0	3.9	3.1	0.8	2.0	1.7	0.0	0.2
El Salvador[2]	1990–94	10.6	9.8	0.8	2.2	0.9	1.3	0.0	0.0	5.1	3.8	1.1	1.9	1.6	0.3	0.6
Guatemala[2]	1990–94	8.7	7.4	1.3	1.7	0.2	1.4	0.0	0.0	3.6	2.5	1.0	1.7	1.7	0.0	0.1
Honduras	—	—	—	—	—	—	—	—	—	—	—	—	—	—	—	—
Mexico	1990–94	15.1	13.5	1.6	5.0	—	—	1.8	0.0	8.4	3.0	1.5	1.1	1.0	0.0	0.0
Nicaragua	1990–94	19.1	17.6	1.5	2.2	—	—	2.2	0.0	8.5	2.1	6.4	3.6	3.6	0.0	0.2
Panama	1990–94	31.3	21.4	9.9	5.5	0.3	1.9	6.2	0.0	5.3	2.1	2.2	3.3	3.1	0.2	0.5
Paraguay	1990–94	13.1	9.3	3.8	1.3		1.3	0.0	0.1	3.5	1.7	1.4	2.1	1.8	0.0	0.8
Peru	1990–94	14.6	13.4	1.2	1.6	0.4	1.1	1.6	0.3	7.4	3.9	3.5	1.7	1.5	0.2	0.5
Uruguay	1990–94	27.2	25.7	1.6	1.8	0.5	1.3	8.0	0.2	8.9	5.5	3.1	1.8	1.5	0.1	1.3
Venezuela	1990–94	20.2	15.9	4.3	11.2	—	—	0.9	0.0	1.8	0.6	0.6	1.8	1.7	—	0.3
Unweighted regional average[3]		17.9	14.7	3.2	3.6	0.5	1.9	2.5	0.1	5.6	3.2	2.1	2.2	1.9	0.1	0.4
Central America																
Costa Rica	1990–94	20.2	17.5	2.7	1.9	1.5	0.5	5.7	0.0	6.3	3.6	2.4	3.6	2.8	0.7	0.1
Dominican Republic	1990–94	14.6	13.2	1.4	2.4	1.1	1.3	0.6	0.0	3.9	—	3.1	6.1	5.7	0.0	0.1
El Salvador[2]	1990–94	10.6	9.8	0.8	2.2	0.9	1.3	0.0	0.0	5.1	3.8	1.1	1.9	1.6	0.3	0.6
Guatemala[2]	1990–94	8.7	7.4	1.3	1.7	0.2	1.4	0.0	0.0	3.6	2.5	1.0	1.7	1.7	0.0	0.1
Honduras	—	—	—	—	—	—	—	—	—	—	—	—	—	—	—	—
Nicaragua	1990–94	19.1	17.6	1.5	2.2	—	—	2.2	0.0	8.5	2.1	6.4	3.6	3.6	0.0	0.2
Panama	1990–94	31.3	21.4	9.9	5.5	0.3	1.9	6.2	0.0	5.3	2.1	2.2	3.3	3.1	0.2	0.5
Unweighted regional average[3]		17.4	14.5	2.9	2.7	0.8	1.3	2.5	0.0	5.5	2.8	2.7	3.4	3.1	0.2	0.3

Notes

[1] Total tax revenue shown is net of tax revenue transferred back to subcentral levels of government due to revenue sharing agreements.

[2] Budgetary central government.

[3] For each revenue classification, only countries for which data are available are included in the calculation.

Sources: *Government Finance Statistics* (IMF); *International Financial Statistics* (IMF); and *World Economic Outlook* (IMF).

Table 2.2 Consolidated central government: tax structure for Latin American countries, 1995–99 (in per cent of GDP)

	Sample size	Total revenue	Tax revenue	Other revenue	Taxes on income, profits, and capital gains			Social Security taxes	Payroll taxes	Domestic taxes on goods and services			International trade taxes			Property taxes
					Total	*Of which:* Individual	*Of which:* Corporate			Total	*Of which:* General sales, turnover, or VAT	*Of which:* Excises	Total	*Of which:* Import duties	*Of which:* Export duties	
Latin America																
Argentina[1]	1995–98	13.6	12.5	1.1	1.8	0.6	1.2	4.0	0.0	5.4	3.7	1.6	0.9	0.8	0.0	0.3
Bolivia	1995–99	17.3	13.9	3.4	1.1	—	1.1	1.9	0.0	8.0	6.0	1.9	1.1	1.1	0.0	1.5
Brazil	1997	24.5	19.8	4.7	3.9	0.3	1.5	8.6	1.2	5.4	2.1	1.9	0.6	0.6	0.0	0.0
Chile	1995–99	22.9	19.0	3.9	4.1	—	—	1.4	0.0	10.6	8.5	2.1	1.9		—	0.0
Colombia[2]	1995–99	12.0	10.3	1.6	4.2	0.2	3.9	0.0	0.0	5.0	4.5	0.5	1.0	1.0	0.0	0.1
Costa Rica	1995–99	20.3	17.9	2.4	2.4	1.7	0.5	5.7	0.0	7.7	4.8	2.5	1.9	1.5	0.2	0.1
Dominican Republic	1995–98	16.3	14.9	1.4	2.6	1.5	1.0	0.6	0.0	5.6	—	4.7	5.9	5.5	0.0	0.1
Ecuador[2]	—	—	—	—	—	—	—	—	—	—	—	—	—	—	—	—
El Salvador[2]	1995–99	11.7	11.1	0.6	3.2	1.3	1.9	0.0	0.0	6.2	5.5	0.6	1.5	1.5	0.0	0.1
Guatemala[2]	1995–99	9.2	8.9	0.3	2.0	0.2	1.1	0.0	0.0	5.2	3.8	1.1	1.5	1.5	0.0	0.0
Honduras	—	—	—	—	—	—	—	—	—	—	—	—	—	—	—	—
Mexico	1995–98	14.6	12.6	2.0	4.4	—	—	1.8	0.0	8.4	3.0	1.5	0.6	0.6	0.0	0.0
Nicaragua	1995	25.8	23.9	2.0	2.8	—	—	3.3	0.0	10.9	2.9	7.6	5.3	5.3	0.0	0.0
Panama	1995–98	33.4	22.5	10.9	6.3	0.3	2.0	5.7	0.0	—	—	—	0.1	—	0.1	0.5
Paraguay	—	—	—	—	—	—	—	—	—	—	—	—	—	—	—	—
Peru	1995–99	17.2	14.9	2.4	3.4	1.2	2.2	1.4	0.5	8.5	6.4	2.1	1.7	1.7	0.0	0.0
Uruguay	1995–99	28.6	26.2	2.4	3.5	1.4	2.0	8.3	0.2	10.7	7.4	3.0	1.0	0.9	0.0	1.5
Venezuela	1995–99	18.8	13.7	5.1	5.9	—	—	0.6	0.0	5.7	4.5	0.7	1.6	1.6	—	0.3
Unweighted regional average[3]		19.1	16.1	2.9	3.4	0.9	1.7	2.9	0.1	7.4	4.8	2.3	1.8	1.8	0.0	0.3
Central America																
Costa Rica	1995–99	20.3	17.9	2.4	2.4	1.7	0.5	5.7	0.0	7.7	4.8	2.5	1.9	1.5	0.2	0.1
Dominican Republic	1995–98	16.3	14.9	1.4	2.6	1.5	1.0	0.6	0.0	5.6	—	4.7	5.9	5.5	0.0	0.1
El Salvador[2]	1995–99	11.7	11.1	0.6	3.2	1.3	1.9	0.0	0.0	6.2	5.5	0.6	1.5	1.5	0.0	0.1
Guatemala[2]	1995–99	9.2	8.9	0.3	2.0	0.2	1.1	0.0	0.0	5.2	3.8	1.1	1.5	1.5	0.0	0.0
Honduras	—	—	—	—	—	—	—	—	—	—	—	—	—	—	—	—
Nicaragua	1995	25.8	23.9	2.0	2.8	—	—	3.3	0.0	10.9	2.9	7.6	5.3	5.3	0.0	0.0
Panama	1995–98	33.4	22.5	10.9	6.3	0.3	2.0	5.7	0.0	—	—	—	0.1	—	0.1	0.5
Unweighted regional average[3]		19.4	16.5	2.9	3.2	1.0	1.3	2.5	0.0	7.1	4.2	3.3	2.7	3.1	0.1	0.1

Notes

[1] Total tax revenue shown is net of tax revenue transferred back to subcentral levels of government due to revenue sharing agreements.

[2] Budgetary central government.

[3] For each revenue classification, only countries for which data are available are included in the calculation.

Sources: *Government Finance Statistics* (IMF); *International Financial Statistics* (IMF); and *World Economic Outlook* (IMF).

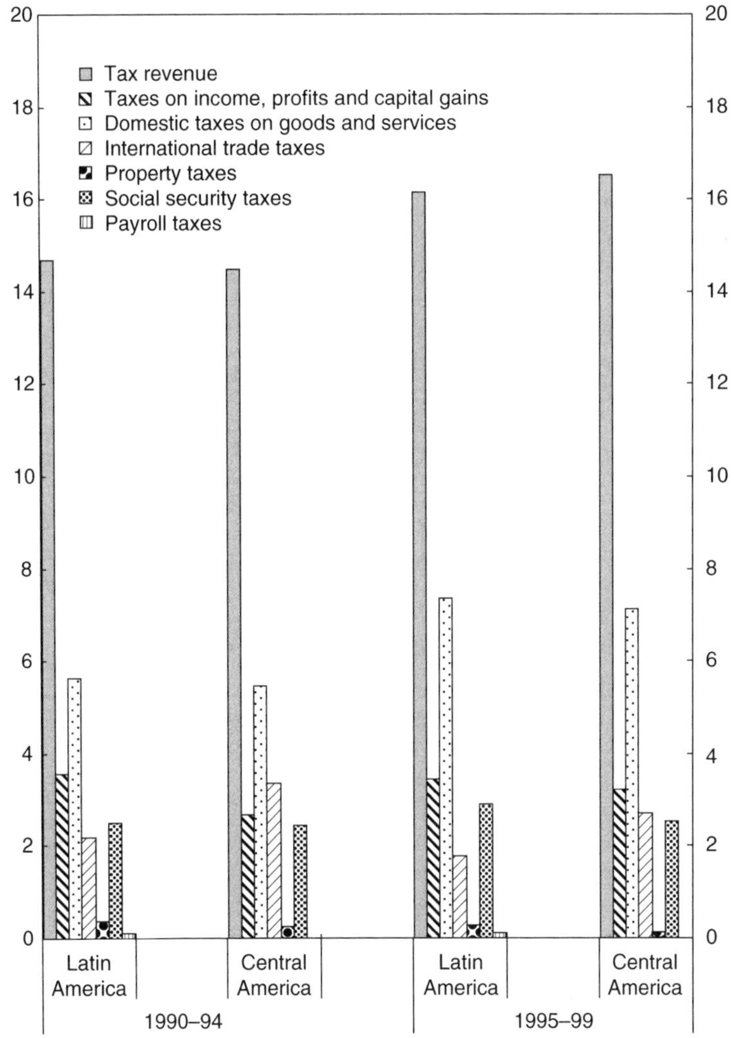

Figure 2.1 Latin American countries: tax revenue structure, 1990–94 and 1995–99 (in per cent of GDP)

Sources: *Government Finance Statistics* (IMF), *International Financial Statistics* (IMF), and *World Economic Outlook* (IMF).

services, taxes on income and profits, and international trade taxes (Tables 2.3 and 2.4). By virtue of the small size of Central American countries, most revenue is collected by the central government. Domestic taxes on goods and services, consisting of VAT, excises or selective sales taxes (sometimes applied to an extensive array of goods), and other transactions-type taxes, are the broadest and most robust source of tax revenue.[5] This component of tax revenues rose from 39.5 per cent of tax revenues to 48 per cent over the two periods, paralleling a similar rise in South America.

VAT is the main source of revenue from domestic goods and services in these countries, rising from 22.7 per cent of tax revenue to 32.8 per cent over the two periods. This growth in reliance on broad-based sales taxes is consistent with worldwide trends. These taxes are seen as a relatively administrable and efficient way to generate revenues. Excises are also an important revenue source in the region, generating on average 17.9 per cent of tax revenues in the earlier period and marginally increasing to 19 per cent in the latter. Although developed countries have seen a drop in reliance on excises in recent decades, this is less evident in developing countries, especially those where income taxes are weak.

Taxes on income and profits, consisting of personal income and enterprise income taxes, constitute another main source of tax revenue. In contrast to domestic consumption taxes, this component of taxation is relatively weak in most Central American countries, averaging only 19.2 per cent of tax revenues in the earlier period and rising to 20.3 per cent in the latter. These shares are a little lower than that in South America, though the trends diverged over the two periods, with the income tax share rising in Central America and dropping in the South American countries. Enterprise income taxes are the larger component of this revenue in Central America, though the gap between enterprise and personal income taxes as a share of tax revenue narrowed over the two periods, reflecting worldwide trends toward reduced reliance on enterprise income taxes and increased reliance on personal income taxes. The gap between enterprise and personal income taxes is much larger in South America, though it too narrowed over the two periods.

International trade taxes are a third major source of tax revenue in Central America, averaging 24.1 per cent of tax revenues in the earlier period and 21.1 per cent in the latter period. This decline offers

Table 2.3 Consolidated central government: tax structure for Latin American countries, 1990–94 (in per cent of tax revenue)

	Sample size	Total revenue	Tax revenue	Other revenue	Taxes on income, profits, and capital gains			Social Security taxes	Payroll taxes	Domestic taxes on goods and services			International trade taxes			Property taxes
					Total	*Of which:*				Total	*Of which:*		Total	*Of which:*		
						Individual	Corporate				General sales, turnover, or VAT	Excises		Import duties	Export duties	
Latin America																
Argentina[1]	1990–94	110.5	100.0	10.5	5.8	1.5	—	46.2	0.0	30.8	19.5	10.7	9.9	4.3	2.3	3.4
Bolivia	1990–94	154.8	100.0	54.8	7.3	—	3.8	12.4	0.0	56.5	38.6	17.3	10.1	10.1	0.0	12.5
Brazil	1990–94	162.0	100.0	62.0	21.9	1.2	5.8	40.4	6.8	28.2	8.7	13.2	2.6	2.6	0.0	0.0
Chile	1990–94	121.9	100.0	21.9	20.7	—	—	8.7	0.0	54.3	43.8	10.5	12.3	—	—	0.0
Colombia[2]	1990–94	115.8	100.0	15.8	43.6	2.3	39.5	0.0	0.0	41.5	35.1	6.2	13.9	13.2	0.7	0.0
Costa Rica	1990–94	115.4	100.0	15.4	11.0	8.3	2.6	32.5	0.0	35.8	20.6	13.7	20.5	15.8	3.6	0.7
Dominican Republic	1990–94	110.5	100.0	10.5	19.1	8.4	10.5	4.6	0.0	28.9	—	23.0	46.4	43.4	0.0	0.7
Ecuador[2]	1990–94	105.2	100.0	5.2	59.9	—	50.8	0.0	0.0	25.6	20.3	5.2	12.6	11.2	0.3	1.2
El Salvador[2]	1990–94	107.4	100.0	7.4	22.7	9.4	13.3	0.0	0.0	52.0	38.7	11.6	19.0	16.2	2.8	5.8
Guatemala[2]	1990–94	117.6	100.0	17.6	22.8	2.9	19.4	0.0	0.0	48.5	32.6	13.8	22.7	22.7	0.1	1.3
Honduras	—	—	—	—	—	—	—	—	—	—	—	—	—	—	—	—
Mexico	1990–94	111.9	100.0	11.9	37.4	—	—	15.8	0.7	57.4	22.3	12.0	7.8	7.7	0.0	0.0
Nicaragua	1990–94	109.8	100.0	9.8	13.7	—	—	11.9	0.0	47.1	12.0	35.0	20.6	26.2	0.0	1.4
Panama	1990–94	146.3	100.0	46.3	25.9	1.3	8.7	29.1	0.0	24.6	9.6	10.4	15.7	20.6	1.2	2.3
Paraguay	1990–94	141.3	100.0	41.3	13.7	—	13.7	0.0	1.5	37.2	18.7	14.9	22.4	14.4	0.0	9.0
Peru	1990–94	108.9	100.0	8.9	11.5	3.1	8.4	11.7	2.2	55.5	28.8	26.7	12.5	10.8	1.7	3.9
Uruguay	1990–94	106.0	100.0	6.0	7.1	1.8	4.9	30.9	0.6	35.0	21.7	12.2	7.2	7.3	0.2	5.0
Venezuela	1990–94	127.1	100.0	27.1	69.5	—	—	5.6	0.0	12.0	4.4	3.6	11.7	5.9	—	1.9
Unweighted regional average[3]		121.9	100.0	21.9	24.3	4.0	15.1	14.7	0.7	39.5	23.5	14.1	15.8	14.5	0.9	2.9
Central America																
Costa Rica	1990–94	115.4	100.0	15.4	11.0	8.3	2.6	32.5	0.0	35.8	20.6	13.7	20.5	15.8	3.6	0.7
Dominican Republic	1990–94	110.5	100.0	10.5	19.1	8.4	10.5	4.6	0.0	28.9	—	23.0	46.4	43.4	0.0	0.7
El Salvador[2]	1990–94	107.4	100.0	7.4	22.7	9.4	13.3	0.0	0.0	52.0	38.7	11.6	19.0	16.2	2.8	5.8
Guatemala[2]	1990–94	117.6	100.0	17.6	22.8	2.9	19.4	0.0	0.0	48.5	32.6	13.8	22.7	22.7	0.1	1.3
Honduras	—	—	—	—	—	—	—	—	—	—	—	—	—	—	—	—
Nicaragua	1990–94	109.8	100.0	9.8	13.7	—	—	11.9	0.0	47.1	12.0	35.0	20.6	26.2	0.0	1.4
Panama	1990–94	146.3	100.0	46.3	25.9	1.3	8.7	29.1	0.0	24.6	9.6	10.4	15.7	20.6	1.2	2.3
Unweighted regional average[3]		117.8	100.0	17.8	19.2	6.1	10.9	13.0	0.0	39.5	22.7	17.9	24.1	24.1	1.3	2.0

Notes
[1] Total tax revenue shown is net of tax revenue transferred back to subcentral levels of government due to revenue sharing agreements.
[2] Budgetary central government.
[3] For each revenue classification, only countries for which data are available are included in the calculation.

Sources: *Government Finance Statistics* (IMF); *International Financial Statistics* (IMF); and *World Economic Outlook* (IMF).

Table 2.4 Consolidated central government: tax structure for Latin American countries, 1995–99 (in per cent of tax revenue)

	Sample size	Total revenue	Tax revenue	Other revenue	Taxes on income, profits, and capital gains			Social Security taxes	Payroll taxes	Domestic taxes on goods and services			International trade taxes			Property taxes
					Total	*Of which:* Individual	*Of which:* Corporate			Total	*Of which:* General sales, turnover, or VAT	*Of which:* Excises	Total	*Of which:* Import duties	*Of which:* Export duties	
Latin America																
Argentina[1]	1995–98	108.9	100.0	8.9	14.4	4.5	9.9	32.1	0.0	43.1	30.0	12.5	7.1	6.2	0.2	2.4
Bolivia	1995–99	125.9	100.0	25.9	7.8	—	7.8	13.6	0.0	57.2	43.1	13.9	7.9	7.9	0.0	10.8
Brazil	1997	123.8	100.0	23.8	19.9	1.6	7.6	43.7	6.1	27.2	10.6	9.7	3.0	3.0	0.0	0.2
Chile	1995–99	120.4	100.0	20.4	21.4	—	—	7.6	0.0	55.6	44.5	11.1	10.1	—	—	0.0
Colombia[2]	1995–99	115.9	100.0	15.9	40.2	2.1	38.1	0.0	0.0	48.7	43.5	5.1	9.8	9.8	0.0	1.1
Costa Rica	1995–99	113.4	100.0	13.4	13.4	10.0	2.9	31.6	0.0	43.3	26.6	13.8	10.7	8.5	1.3	0.3
Dominican Republic	1995–98	109.1	100.0	9.1	17.7	10.3	6.9	4.3	0.0	37.3	—	31.3	39.8	36.8	0.0	0.7
Ecuador[2]	—	—	—	—	—	—	—	—	—	—	—	—	—	—	—	—
El Salvador[2]	1995–99	105.4	100.0	5.4	28.6	11.9	16.8	0.0	0.0	56.1	49.7	5.6	13.4	13.3	0.0	1.1
Guatemala[2]	1995–99	103.5	100.0	3.5	22.3	2.5	13.0	0.0	0.0	57.8	42.8	12.3	17.5	17.4	0.0	0.2
Honduras	—	—	—	—	—	—	—	—	—	—	—	—	—	—	—	—
Mexico	1995–98	115.9	100.0	15.9	34.9	—	—	14.6	0.0	66.5	23.7	12.2	4.6	4.6	0.0	0.0
Nicaragua	1995	108.2	100.0	8.2	11.8	—	—	13.8	0.0	45.6	12.0	31.9	22.2	45.5	0.0	0.0
Panama	1995–98	148.9	100.0	48.9	28.1	1.3	8.8	25.0	0.0	—	—	—	22.8	22.2	0.5	2.1
Paraguay	—	—	—	—	—	—	—	—	—	—	—	—	—	—	—	—
Peru	1995–99	115.9	100.0	15.9	23.2	8.2	15.0	9.5	3.3	57.0	43.0	14.0	11.1	11.1	0.0	0.0
Uruguay	1995–99	109.4	100.0	9.4	13.6	5.5	7.7	31.7	0.6	40.7	28.3	11.4	3.9	6.7	0.0	5.6
Venezuela	1995–99	137.4	100.0	37.4	41.9	—	—	4.4	0.0	41.7	32.6	5.6	12.0	3.5	—	2.8
Unweighted regional average[3]		117.5	100.0	17.5	22.6	5.8	12.2	15.5	0.7	48.4	33.1	13.6	13.0	14.0	0.2	1.8
Central America																
Costa Rica	1995–99	113.4	100.0	13.4	13.4	10.0	2.9	31.6	0.0	43.3	26.6	13.8	10.7	8.5	1.3	0.3
Dominican Republic	1995–98	109.1	100.0	9.1	17.7	10.3	6.9	4.3	0.0	37.3	—	31.3	39.8	36.8	0.0	0.7
El Salvador[2]	1995–99	105.4	100.0	5.4	28.6	11.9	16.8	0.0	0.0	56.1	49.7	5.6	13.4	13.3	0.0	1.1
Guatemala[2]	1995–99	103.5	100.0	3.5	22.3	2.5	13.0	0.0	0.0	57.8	42.8	12.3	17.5	17.4	0.0	0.2
Honduras	—	—	—	—	—	—	—	—	—	—	—	—	—	—	—	—
Nicaragua	1995	108.2	100.0	8.2	11.8	—	—	13.8	0.0	45.6	12.0	31.9	22.2	45.5	0.0	0.0
Panama	1990–98	148.9	100.0	48.9	28.1	1.3	8.8	25.0	0.0	—	—	—	22.8	22.2	0.5	2.1
Unweighted regional average[3]		114.8	100.0	14.8	20.3	7.2	9.7	12.5	0.0	48.0	32.8	19.0	21.1	23.9	0.3	0.7

Sources: *Government Finance Statistics* (IMF); *International Financial Statistics* (IMF); and *World Economic Outlook* (IMF).

Notes

[1] Total tax revenue shown is net of tax revenue transferred back to subcentral levels of government due to revenue sharing agreements.

[2] Budgetary central government.

[3] For each revenue classification, only countries for which data are available are included in the calculation.

a sharp contrast with the other components of revenue, but is fully consistent with worldwide trends toward trade liberalization and reduced reliance on international trade taxes. Although in principle international trade taxes may be levied on both imports and exports, most revenues are collected on imports. The share of export taxes practically vanished by the latter period, while the share of import duties only declined slightly.

Two final sources of revenues are social security taxes, which fell from 13 per cent of tax revenues in 1990–94 to 12.5 per cent in 1995–99[6] and property taxes, which are relatively small but also fell over this period. The first trend is at variance with general worldwide trends, which have seen an increased reliance on social security taxes, especially to provide social insurance and pension annuities to aging workforces.

Central America offers an interesting contrast with the Caribbean. The tax ratio in the Caribbean is for the most part higher than in Central America, averaging more than 20 per cent of GDP (Itam *et al.*, 2000). The difference is most pronounced in the area of income tax. This may reflect a combination of cultural traditions and attitudes toward the public sector or a different administrative emphasis. The greater formalization of the labor market in the Caribbean compared to Central America and the greater ease of compliance in small islands at customs borders may also contribute to stronger tax bases.

Domestic taxes on goods and services

Domestic taxes on goods and services are the mainstay of collections in most developing countries. The VAT is the key component of these revenues (Ebrill *et al.*, 2001). All countries in Central America have a VAT, with the date of introduction ranging from 1975 for Nicaragua and Costa Rica to 1992 for El Salvador. The standard rate of VAT varies across countries (Table 2.5 and Figure 2.2) but has tended to rise over time, increasing the dominance of this form of revenues. At introduction, the rates ranged from 3 to 10 per cent, averaging 6.7 per cent, but in 2001, the rates ranged from 5 to 13 per cent, averaging 11.7 per cent.[7] Over time, the variation in VAT rates across these countries has declined, even with the introduction of multiple rates in some countries. As of 2001, all countries, except Nicaragua and Panamá had a

Table 2.5 Cross-country comparisons: value-added tax rates, 1994, 1997, and 2001[1] in per cent

	Date VAT introduced or proposed	**At introduction**	**1994**	**1997**	**2001**	**VAT revenue productivities (latest year)[2]**
Latin America						
Argentina	Jan. 1975	**16**	**18**; 26; 27[3]	**21**; 27	10.5; **21**; 27	0.30
Bolivia	Oct. 1973	5; **10**; 15	**14.92**[4]	**14.92**	**14.92**	0.43
Brazil[5]	Jan. 1967	**15**	**20.5**; 22.0 33.3	**20.5**; 22.0 33.3	**20.5**; 22.0;.33.3	—[6]
		15	7.5; 13.6	7.5; 13.6	7.5; 13.6	
Chile	Mar. 1975	8; **20**	**18**	**18**	**18**	0.58
Colombia	Jan. 1975	4; 6; **10**	8; **14**; 20; 35; 45	8; 15; **16**; 20; 35; 45.6	**16**; 20; 35; 45; 60	0.32
Costa Rica	Jan. 1975	**10**	**8**	**8**	**13**	0.45
Dominican Republic	Jan. 1983	**6**	**6**	**8**	**12**	0.31
Ecuador	Jul. 1970	**4**; 10	**10**	**10**	**12**	0.42
El Salvador	Sept. 1992	**10**	**10**	**13**	**13**	0.49
Guatemala	Aug. 1983	**7**	**7**	**10**	**12**	0.42
Honduras	Jan. 1976	**3**	**7**; 10	**7**; 10	**12**; 15	0.55
Mexico	Jan. 1980	**10**	**10**	**15**	10; **15**	0.28
Nicaragua	Jan. 1975	**6**	5; 6; **10**	5; 6; 10; **15**	5; 6; **15**	0.60
Panama[7]	Mar. 1977	**5**	**5**; 10	**5**; 10	**5**; 10	0.52
Paraguay	Jul. 1993	**12**	**10**	**10**	**10**	0.51
Peru	Nov. 1972	2; 3; 7; **15**; 25	**18**	**18**	**18**	0.42
Uruguay	Jan. 1968	5; **14**	12; **22**	14; **23**	14; **23**	0.31
Venezuela[8]	Oct. 1993	**10**	**10**	**16.5**	**14.5**	0.31
Unweighted regional average[9]		**10.2**	**12.1**	**13.8**	**14.7**	0.42

Central America						
Costa Rica	Jan. 1975	**10**	**8**	**8**	**13**	0.45
Dominican Republic	Jan. 1983	**6**	**6**	**8**	**12**	0.31
El Salvador	Sept. 1992	**10**	**10**	**13**	**13**	0.49
Guatemala	Aug. 1983	**7**	**7**	**10**	**12**	0.42
Honduras	Jan. 1976	**3**	**7**; 10	**7**; 10	**12**; 15	0.55
Nicaragua	Jan. 1975	**6**	5; 6; **10**	5; 6; 10; **15**	5; 6; **15**	0.60
Panama	Mar. 1977	**5**	**5**; 10	**5**; 10	**5**; 10	0.52
Unweighted regional average[9]		**6.7**	**7.6**	**9.4**	**11.7**	0.48

Notes

[1] Rates shown in bold type are so-called effective standard rates (tax exclusive) applied to goods and services not covered by other especially high or low rates. Some countries zero rate a few goods and exports.

[2] VAT revenue as a per centage of final consumption expenditure, divided by the VAT standard rate. This is often termed the 'c-efficiency' ratio.

[3] Supplementary VAT rates of 8 per cent and 9 per cent on noncapital goods imports; through 'catch-up', these can revert to 18 per cent retail.

[4] Effective rate (legislated tax-inclusive rate is 13 per cent).

[5] Tax exclusive equivalent rates to tax inclusive rates. Top line are rates 17, 18, and 25 on intra-state trade and bottom line are rates 7 and 12 on inter-state trade.

[6] No calculation is made because the VAT is a state-level tax.

[7] The rate of cigarettes and alcoholic beverages is 10 per cent.

[8] Venezuela was the last country to introduce a VAT in October 1993, had removed it by March 1994, but reintroduced it soon thereafter.

[9] Only standard rates.

Sources: *Corporate Taxes: Worldwide Summaries* (PricewaterhouseCoopers); *Taxation in Latin America* (IBFD); and *International Tax Summaries: A Guide for Planning and Decisions* (Coopers & Lybrand International Tax Network).

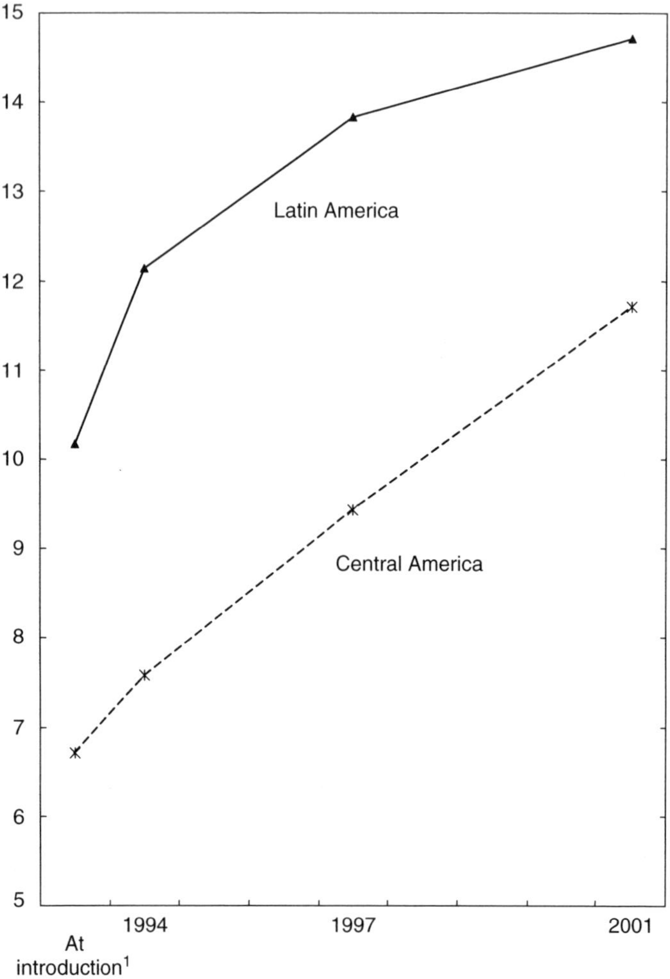

Figure 2.2 Latin American countries: value-added tax rates, from introduction, 2001 (in per cent)

Note: [1] Because of various dates of introduction, the x-axis is not drawn to scale in this region.
Sources: *Corporate Taxes: Worldwide Summaries* (PricewaterhouseCoopers); *Taxation in Latin America* (IBFD); and *International Tax Summaries: A Guide for Planning and Decisions* (Coopers & Lybrand International Tax Network).

standard VAT rate of 12 or 13 per cent. Nicaragua's was 15 per cent and Panamá's 5 per cent. In comparison to South America, the average VAT rate in Central America is lower. The average rate in South America rose from 12.4 per cent at introduction (varying dates by country) to 16.6 per cent in 2001. This rate is still relatively low compared to developed countries, but is close to the average in the Anglophone Caribbean of 15 per cent (e.g. Jamaica, Trinidad and Tobago, and Barbados).

In several countries, the VAT is levied at two or more rates. In some cases, a higher rate applies to certain luxury goods and in others a lower rate applies to certain necessities. Honduras and Panamá use a higher luxury rate, applied in both cases to a limited set of goods. Nicaragua uses two lower rates and is the only country in the region that uses more than two rates. Although many countries with VATs, inside and outside of Latin America, use multiple rate VATs, including those with more than two rates, it is generally thought advisable to limit the number of VAT rates to a single rate, as unlike in the income tax, administrative complexity grows more than proportionately to the number of rates, and may impair collections as well as lead to excessive distortion in economic decisions. Many of the more recently introduced VATs have only a single rate.

VAT revenue productivity is difficult to measure. One commonly used measure, termed the 'c-efficiency' ratio, is defined as VAT revenue as a share of domestic consumption (both private and public) divided by the standard VAT rate, and offers some standardization of measurement of the revenue productivity across countries. It averaged about 0.48 in Central America, higher than the ratio of 0.39 in South America in the latest year for which data are available (Table 2.6). In Central America there has been a decline in the average VAT productivity in the past few years, after increasing for several years before that. The pattern of change, however, is uneven across the region, with El Salvador and Nicaragua improving VAT productivity, Panamá remaining stable, and Costa Rica, the Dominican Republic, Guatemala, and Honduras experiencing a decline. A declining VAT productivity, if sustained, should be a source of serious concern. Declining productivity overall likely reflects base erosion through legislative changes or reduced tax compliance, though the reasons in any particular country require careful scrutiny. There are, however, several shortcomings of this measure. First, it tends to be biased in countries with multiple rates, given that the calculation is

Table 2.6 Cross-country comparisons: value-added revenue productivities[1]

	1994	**1997**	**Latest year data available**
Latin America			
Argentina	0.45	0.40	0.30
Bolivia	0.38	0.52	0.43
Brazil[2]	—	—	—
Chile	0.58	0.58	0.58
Colombia	0.36	0.35	0.32
Costa Rica	0.58	0.76	0.45
Dominican Republic	0.51	0.43	0.31
Ecuador	0.43	0.50	0.42
El Salvador	0.51	0.43	0.49
Guatemala	0.39	0.43	0.42
Honduras	0.55	0.65	0.55
Mexico	0.33	0.28	0.28
Nicaragua	0.28	0.48	0.60
Panama	0.50	0.52	0.52
Paraguay	0.49	0.53	0.51
Peru	0.41	0.45	0.42
Uruguay	0.28	0.43	0.31
Venezuela	0.33	0.46	0.31
Unweighted regional average	0.43	0.48	0.42
Central America			
Costa Rica	0.58	0.76	0.45
Dominican Republic	0.51	0.43	0.31
El Salvador	0.51	0.43	0.49
Guatemala	0.39	0.43	0.42
Honduras	0.55	0.65	0.55
Nicaragua	0.28	0.48	0.60
Panama	0.50	0.52	0.52
Unweighted regional average	0.48	0.53	0.48

Notes

[1] VAT revenue as a per centage of final consumption expenditure, divided by the VAT standard rate.

[2] No calculation is made because the VAT is a state-level tax.

Sources: *Corporate Taxes: Worldwide Summaries* (PricewaterhouseCoopers); *Taxation in Latin America* (IBFD); and *International Tax Summaries: A Guide for Planning and Decisions* (Coopers & Lybrand International Tax Network). Revenue and consumption data are from *Government Finance Statistics* (IMF); *International Financial Statistics* (IMF); and *World Economic Outlook* (IMF).

based on a standard rate. Countries with multiple rates in which there are luxury rates higher than the standard rate tend to score better on productivity because the higher revenue is attributed to a lower standard rate, while countries in which there are lower rates than the standard rate tend to score worse, although the dramatic improvement in Nicaragua's VAT productivity belies this observation. Second, countries that limit input tax credits for a substantial number of goods or services generate higher revenues, even at the cost of some loss of efficiency of the tax. This would be measured as an improvement in revenue productivity, without taking into account the loss of efficiency. Third, any mismeasurement of final consumption expenditure (likely reflecting a mismeasurement of GDP) would also translate into a mismeasurement of the VAT productivity. With these qualifications in mind, the differences in VAT revenue productivity across the Central American countries are striking, ranging from a high of 0.60 in Nicaragua to a low of 0.31 in the Dominican Republic in the latest period. This variation suggests that there may be some systematic differences in both the structure of the tax (the degree to which the base captures domestic consumption) and the effectiveness of administration of the tax.

Central American VATs share some characteristics in common, including that they are invoice and destination based, as in the EU and in most other countries with a VAT. The VAT base tends to be eroded by an excessive number of zero rated and exempt items.[8] Zero-rated items should generally be limited to exports while exempt items should be limited to many (or most) educational, medical, and social services, as well as financial intermediation, housing rentals, and a few other goods and services. Several Central American countries have reasonably well-structured VATs, with broad bases and moderate tax rates. El Salvador, in particular, provides a good model of a VAT adopted in the 1990s, with a broad base and a single rate. Costa Rica's VAT is hampered by an excessive degree of denial of input tax credits, which leads to cascading. Central American VATs have scope to broaden the tax base. In particular, exemptions for the agricultural sector and food, for capital goods, and for certain services, such as public events, and special exemptions for investors erode the tax base. Several countries made progress in the 1990s in limiting the scope of VAT exemptions, thus strengthening collections and the structure of the tax.

Excises are a useful supplement to VATs and other broad-based sales taxes. Excises typically apply to tobacco, alcohol, and petroleum, but may also apply to other goods, such as motor vehicles or consumer durables. Excise tax rates tend to vary considerably from one country to another, and the manner in which they are levied – whether ad valorem or unit-based – also tends to vary (Table 2.7). They also tend to be changed frequently, making it difficult to keep track of the particular excise tax rates in any one country. Because the effective rate of unit-based excise taxes depends on the price of the goods to which they are applied, it is also more difficult to compare them across countries. Excise tax rates may be quite high, and hence, they may enable a country to avoid levying multiple rates under the VAT. However, in general, it appears that excise tax rates in Central America are not high, by an international comparison or compared to some South American countries. There would appear to be scope to increase excises on both tobacco and alcoholic beverages in several of these countries.

Taxes on income and profits and taxes on wealth

Taxes on income and profits are also an important component of revenues. Income taxes are less standardized in comparison to VAT, and hence, across any group of countries – even those linked by geography or tradition – there is likely to be substantial variation in income taxes. In Central America, as in most developing countries, more revenue is generated by taxes on enterprise income than by taxes on personal income. The same basic principles underline the ideal structure of the income tax as with the VAT. The tax is best levied on a broad base and at moderate rates. However, personal income taxes accommodate multiple rates, through the use of a graduated schedule, more easily than the VAT.

Both enterprise and personal income tax rates tended to decline for about a decade from the mid-1980s to the mid-1990s, but have since stabilized (Table 2.8 and Figure 2.3). In Central America, the top rate of the enterprise income tax averaged 43.3 per cent in 1986, declining to 28.4 per cent in 1997, and then roughly stabilizing at this level through the most recent year. The current average rate reflects relatively little overall variation in the rate, with Honduras having the highest top rate of 35 per cent and three countries having the lowest top rate of 25 per cent.[9] A few countries with multiple rates either

Table 2.7 Central Latin American countries: excise tax summary[1]

	Costa Rica 30 Mar. 1996	Dominican Republic 31 Mar. 1999	El Salvador July 2001	Guatemala 31 Dec. 2000	Honduras	Nicaragua	Panamá 30 Sept. 1998
Taxes on alcoholic beverages							
Beer	—	25 per cent	20 per cent	10.00 per cent	—	34 per cent	B. 1.325 per liter
Champagne	—		20 per cent on alcoholic beverages. Alcoholic beverages and beer (C0.05 for each 1 per cent of alcohol per liter)		—	37 per cent	
Wine	—	35 per cent		4.18 per cent	—	37 per cent	B. 005 per liter[2]
Vermouth Wine	—			4.18 per cent	—	37 per cent	
Brandy	—				—	37 per cent	
Whisky	—	45 per cent			—	36 per cent	
Rum	—	35 per cent			—	36 per cent	
Vodka	—	45 per cent			—	36 per cent	
Distilled alcoholic	—			10.60 per cent	—	30 per cent	
Other	—			10.60 per cent	—	43 per cent	Spirits B. 0.035 per degree of alcoholic strength per liter
Taxes on nonalcoholic beverages						(tasas per gallon) 37 per cent	
Sparkling wine	—			4.18 per cent	—	9 per cent	
Refreshment drinks	—				—	22 per cent	
Soft drinks	—	RD$0.05 per bottle			—	37 per cent	
Cider	—			2.09 per cent	—	—	
Mineral water	—				—	11.5 per cent	
Plain or sweetened carbonated	—		10 per cent	0.20 per cent	—		5 per cent[3]
Taxes on liquid combustibles and natural gas		Prices (RD$ per gallon)[4]		(Rates per gallon)		(Rates US$ per gallon)	(Rates per gallon)
Gasoline(regular)	—			Q 3.65	—	0.6955	B. 0.60
Gasoline (premium)	—	36.10		Q 3.70	—	0.6985	
Diesel	—	41.56		Q 1.30	—	0.5415	B. 0.25
Kerosene	—	23.91		Q 0.50	—	0.4224	B. 0.13
Avtur	—	22.4			—	0.9017	
Fuel oil	—	18.60		Q 0.55 (Bunker C)	—	0.1888	B. 0.15
Solvent and turpentine	—	17.17			—	0.0	
Aircraft gasoline	—			Q 2.00	—	—	
Gas oil	—			Q 1.30	—	0.0	

Table 2.7 Continued

	Costa Rica 30 Mar. 1996	Dominican Republic 31 Mar. 1999	El Salvador July 2001	Guatemala 31 Dec. 2000	Honduras	Nicaragua	Panamá 30 Sept. 1998
Liquid petroleum gas	—			Q 0.50	—	0.0	
Crude oil used as fuel	—			Q 0.50	—	0.0	
Other fuel derived from petroleum	—			Q 0.50	—	0.0	
Asphalt	—			Q 0.50	—		B. 0.08
Taxes on tobacco[5]							
Cigarettes	—	50 per cent	39 per cent	Machine produced tobacco 100 per cent, Imported tobacco 100 per cent, Imported raw tobacco per kg – Q. 0.50 (produced in Central America), Imported raw tobacco per kg – Q. 1.30 (produced in other countries), Guatemalan cut pipe tobacco per kg – Q. 1.00	—	39 per cent	32.5 per cent of the consumer sales price
Cigars	—	25 per cent			—		
Other	—				—		
Taxes on match boxes	—	RD$0.0033 per box of 15–30 matches; RD$0.01 on boxes of 30 matches or more			—	—	
Taxes on motor vehicles	—	Various			—	35 per cent	
Taxes on services							
Electric energy	—				—	15 per cent	
Telephone	—	12 per cent[6]			—	15 per cent	
Taxes on airline tickets (International flights)		12 per cent			—	6 per cent US$25 per passenger	
Taxes on airport fees	—	US$10 per passenger[7]			—	15 per cent	
Taxes on hotel rooms	—				—	—	
Taxes on the sales of tickets for	—	RD$0.01 per ticket with			—	15 per cent	

public performance and for sport events		price of RD$0.20 or lower, 7 per cent on the value of tickets with higher prices; and RD$0.05 per ticket for sport events 10 per cent					
Taxes on hotel	—	12 per cent			—	15 per cent	
Taxes on insurance premiums	—				—	15 per cent	2 and 5 per cent – Risk insurance premiums, 7 per cent – fire insurance
Taxes on agriculture	(in per cent) Banana 1 Coffee 1 Meat 1 Cattle 8 Banana package export duty – US$0.30 per case				—	—	

Notes

[1] '—' where the countries have not reported the figures.

[2] B. 0.05 per liter on each alcoholic beverage not classified as wine, where the alcoholic content does not exceed 20 per cent proof by volume, except beer.

[3] 6 per cent, syrups or concentrate used in the production of carbonated beverages.

[4] Prices in effect on 8 May 2002. Resolution 112-00 allows for prices to be adjusted periodically for, inter alia, changes in the consumer price index, world oil prices, and the official exchange rate, but in practice, adjustments have been infrequent.

[5] Tax on tobacco, per centage applied to the taxable base, which is no less than 44 per cent of the retail price, which the manufacturer or importer must suggest and report to the superintendency of tax administration, net of value-added tax in Guatemala.

[6] Tax on long distance communication services at home and abroad, which includes radio, cable, telegraph, and satellites.

[7] Exemption on diplomatic travelers.

Currency and exchange rates:
Costa Rica: Colones per US dollar, January 1996, period average = 196.23
Dominican Republic: Pesos per US dollar, January 2002, period average = 17.310
El Salvador: Colones per US dollar, January 2002, end of period = 8.750
Guatemala: Quetzales per US dollar, January 2002, period average = 7.8829
Honduras: Lempiras per US dollar, January 2002, period average = 15.9727
Nicaragua: Gold Cordobas per US dollar, January 2002, period average = 13.88
Panama: Balboas per US dollar, January 2001, end of period = 1.00.

Source: Country documents tax summary tables.

Table 2.8 Enterprise income tax rates, 1986, 1992, 1997–2002 (in per cent of taxable income)

	1986	1992	1997	1998	1999 or 2000[1]	2001 or 2002[2]
Latin America						
Argentina	33.0	20.0	33.0	35.0	35.0	35.0
Bolivia	30.0	40.0	25.0	25.0	25.0	25.0
Brazil[3]	35.0	25.0–30.0	15.0–25.0	15.0–25.0	15.0	15.0
Chile[3]	10.0–37.0	15.0–35.0	15.0–35.0	15.0–35.0	15.0	15.0
Colombia[3]	40.0	30.0	35.0	35.0	35.0	35.0
Costa Rica[3]	10.0–50.0	30.0	30.0	30.0	30.0	30.0
Dominican [5] Republic[4,5]	10.0–46.0	10.0–46.0	25.0	25.0	25.0	25.0
Ecuador[3]	20.0–40.0	25.0–44.4	25.0	25.0	15.0–25.0	15.0–25.0
El Salvador[4]	2.5–30.0	25.0	25.0	25.0	25.0	25.0
Guatemala	5.0–42.0	12.0–34.0	25.0	30.0	30.0	31.0
Honduras[3,6]	3.0–40.0	15.0–35.0	15.0–30.0	15.0–35.0	15.0–35.0	15.0–35.0
Mexico	42.0	35.0	34.0	34.0	35.0	35.0
Nicaragua[4]	45.0	35.5	30.0	30.0	30.0	25.0
Panama[6]	20.0–50.0	27.5–45.0	30.0–34.0	30.0–34.0	30.0	30.0
Paraguay[3]	30.0–40.0	25.0–30.0	25.0–30.0	25.0–30.0	25.0–30.0	25.0–30.0
Peru[3]	20.0–40.0	30.0	30.0	30.0	30.0	30.0
Uruguay[6]	30.0	30.0	30.0	30.0	30.0	30.0
Venezuela	18.0–67.7	20.0–67.7	15.0–34.0	15.0–34.0	15.0–34.0	15.0–34.0
Unweighted regional average	12.6–41.0	17.8–35.7	19.2–29.7	19.2–30.4	17.5–28.6	17.5–28.3

Central America						
Costa Rica[3]	10.0–50.0	30.0	30.0	30.0	30.0	30.0
Dominican Republic[4,5]	10.0–46.0	10.0–46.0	25.0	25.0	25.0	25.0
El Salvador[4]	2.5–30.0	25.0	25.0	25.0	25.0	25.0
Guatemala	5.0–42.0	12.0–34.0	25.0	30.0	30.0	31.0
Honduras[3,6]	3.0–40.0	15.0–35.0	15.0–30.0	15.0–35.0	15.0–35.0	15.0–35.0
Nicaragua[4]	45.0	35.5	30.0	30.0	30.0	25.0
Panama[6]	20.0–50.0	27.5–45.0	30.0–34.0	30.0–34.0	30.0	30.0
Unweighted regional average	8.4–43.3	16.1–35.8	22.5–28.4	30.0–29.9	15.0–29.3	15.0–28.7
OECD average[7]	28.7–42.8	21.5–37.3	22.4–33.5	22.9–33.7	23.8–32.9	22.9–31.8
Canada[4]	46.0	38.0	38.0	38.0	38.0	38.0
United States	15.0–34.0	15.0–34.0	15.0–35.0	15.0–35.0	15.0–35.0	15.0–35.0

Notes

1 The data, unless otherwise indicated, present the tax rates in effect at January 1, 2000.

2 The data, unless otherwise indicated, present the tax rates in effect at January 1, 2001.

3 Data are for 1999 in column '1999 or 2000'.

4 Data are for 1998 in column '1999 or 2000'.

5 Data are for 1999 in column '2001 or 2002'.

6 Data are for 2000 in column '2001 or 2002'.

7 Excluding Mexico.

Sources: *International Bureau of Fiscal Documentation* (IBFD); 'European Taxation', 'Taxes and Investment in Asia and the Pacific', and 'Taxation in Latin America' (Loose-leaf; Amsterdam); and *Corporate Taxes, Worldwide Summaries* (PricewaterhouseCoopers).

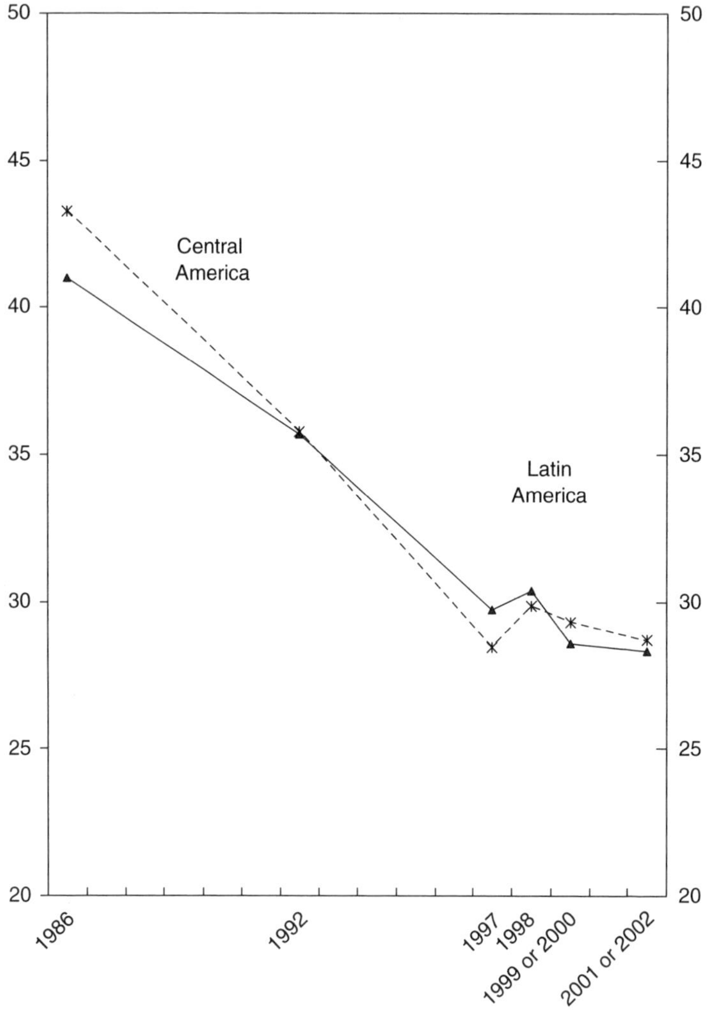

Figure 2.3 Latin American countries: enterprise income tax rates, 1986–2002 (per cent of taxable income)

Sources: *Corporate Taxes: Worldwide Summaries* (PricewaterhouseCoopers); and *Taxation in Latin America* (IBFD).

eliminated this feature or else narrowed the gap between the bottom and top rates, which improved the structure and administrability of the tax.

The trend in South America is similar to that for Central America. In Organization for Economic Cooperation and Development (OECD) countries, the top rate also continued to drop through the present, though there has been more stability in the United States and Canada. Overall, a comparison of these three groups of countries show considerable convergence of enterprise income tax rates at a level with a top rate around 30 per cent on average. Some stabilization in enterprise income tax rates after a point is not surprising given the need to preserve revenue yield, though the relative stability of revenue suggests that some base broadening has occurred during the period in which rates were being reduced.

Although this comparison is limited to enterprise income tax rates, other features of the enterprise income tax, such as depreciation schedules, loss carry forward provisions, special incentives, and the like are also quite critical in determining the eventual income tax burden. For instance, several countries offer free trade zones or special incentives, including Costa Rica, Guatemala, Honduras, Nicaragua, and Panamá. The Dominican Republic has recently revoked all tax incentive laws for new investments. Although free trade zones and special incentives are quite common in developing countries, they are generally an inefficient way to provide incentives for additional investment, as they lead to greater administrative complexity, forgone revenue, which requires higher tax rates on others, distorted economic decisions, and an inequitable burden of taxes, depending on whether investments qualify (Zee *et al.*, 2002). Income tax exemptions may be in violation of World Trade Organization rules. A preferred manner of providing incentives to investment is through generous depreciation allowances (including accelerated depreciation) and loss carry forward provisions, and possibly some limited investment tax credits.

As with VAT, it is possible to measure enterprise income tax productivity by taking the ratio of enterprise income tax to GDP divided by the standard income tax rate (Table 2.9).[10] The most striking feature of this table is the low productivity in all these countries. In Central America, the ratio rose from 0.040 in 1994 to 0.049 in 1997

Table 2.9 Cross-country comparisons: enterprise income tax revenue productivities[1,2]

	1994	1997	Latest year data available
Latin America			
Argentina	0.036	0.038	0.043
Bolivia	0.010	0.050	0.059
Brazil	0.044	0.060	0.060
Chile	—	—	—
Colombia	0.131	0.119	0.114
Costa Rica	0.016	0.017	—
Dominican Republic	0.037	0.041	0.044
Ecuador	0.260	—	—
El Salvador	0.051	0.067	0.078
Guatemala	0.033	0.040	0.037
Honduras	—	—	—
Mexico	—	—	—
Nicaragua	—	—	—
Panama	0.062	0.080	0.049
Paraguay	—	—	—
Peru	0.056	0.086	0.061
Uruguay	0.055	0.062	0.076
Venezuela	—	—	—
Unweighted regional average	0.066	0.060	0.062
Central America			
Costa Rica	—	—	—
Dominican Republic	0.037	0.041	0.044
El Salvador	0.051	0.067	0.078
Guatemala	0.033	0.040	0.037
Honduras	—	—	—
Nicaragua	—	—	—
Panama	0.062	0.080	0.049
Unweighted regional average	0.046	0.057	0.052

Notes

1 Enterprise tax revenue as a per centage of GDP, divided by the upper level of the enterprise rate.

2 For some countries, revenue data were not available and hence no tax productivity could be calculated.

Sources: *Government Finance Statistics* (IMF), *International Financial Statistics* (IMF); *World Economic Outlook* (IMF); *Corporate Taxes: Worldwide Summaries* (PricewaterhouseCoopers); *Taxation in Latin America* (IBFD); and *International Tax Summaries: A Guide for Planning and Decisions* (Coopers & Lybrand International Tax Network).

and 0.053 in the most recent year. South America experienced the opposite trend, with this ratio, which was significantly higher in 1994, then falling so that it remains higher than in Central America, though the gap between the two narrowed over this period. Among Central American countries, El Salvador had the highest ratio, and Guatemala the lowest. Panamá's sharp decline in recent years is also noteworthy.

Trends in personal income tax rates are similar in many respects to those for enterprise income tax rates (Table 2.10 and Figure 2.4). All countries in Central America levy personal income taxes with graduated rates but the number of rate brackets, the income level at which the brackets apply, and the coverage of income – labor and capital income – varies from country to country, making precise comparisons difficult except by taking a representative taxpayer in each country and comparing their tax burden. The personal income tax may take on a more or less global nature depending on the extent of coverage. Where coverage of different forms of income is broadest and the treatment of different forms of income most similar, the tax takes on a more global nature, consistent with worldwide trends and personal income taxes in developed countries. However, even the most developed countries retain some schedular elements to their personal income taxes. All Central American personal income taxes are global in the sense that one set of graduated rates applies to labor and some other forms of income, but they differ in the extent of coverage of nonlabor income.

In Central America, the top and bottom bracket rates fell on average over the same period of time, leveling off at the end of this period, as with corporate rates. The current average range is 10.3–27.3 per cent. Again, there is relatively little variation in the rates across Central America. The highest top rate is in Guatemala, where it is 31 per cent. The top rate in the other countries is either 25 or 30 per cent. The lowest rate is either 10 or 15 per cent, except in Panamá, where it is 2 per cent. The top rate is lower than in both South America and the OECD, while the bottom bracket is intermediate these two groups. A few South American countries, such as Bolivia and Colombia, have adopted flat rates of personal income tax, though at very different rates – Bolivia at 13 per cent and Colombia at 35 per cent.

Table 2.10 Personal income tax rates, 1985, 1992, 1997–2002 (per cent of taxable income)

	1985 or 1986[1]	**1992**	**1997**	**1998**	**1999 or 2000[2]**	**2001 or 2002[3]**
Latin America						
Argentina	16.5–45.0	15.0–30.0	6.0–33.0		9.0–35.0	9.0–35.0
Bolivia	30.0	10% flat rate	13% flat rate	13% flat rate	13% flat rate	13% flat rate
Brazil[4]	0.0–60.0	10.0–25.0	15.0–25.0	15.0–25.0	15.0–27.5	15.0–27.5
Chile[4]	0.0–57.0	5.0–50.0	5.0–45.0	5.0–45.0	5.0–45.0	5.0–45.0
Colombia[4]	49.0	5.0–30.0	35% flat rate	35% flat rate	35% flat rate	35% flat rate
Costa Rica[4]	5.0–50.0	10.0–25.0	10.0–25.0	10.0–25.0	10.0–25.0	10.0–25.0
Dominican Republic[5,6]	2.0–73.0	3.0–70.0	3.0–70.0	15.0–25.0	15.0–25.0	15.0–25.0
Ecuador[4]	19.0–40.0	10.0–25.0	10.0–25.0	10.0–25.0	0.0–15.0	5.0–25.0
El Salvador[5]	3.0–60.0	10.0–30.0	10.0–30.0	10.0–30.0	10.0–30.0	10.0–30.0
Guatemala	11.0–48.0	4.0–34.0	15.0–30.0	15.0–25.0	15.0–25.0	15.0–31.0
Honduras[4,7]	3.0–40.0	12.0–40.0	9.0–40.0	10.0–30.0	10.0–25.0	10.0–25.0
Mexico	3.0–55.0	3.0–35.0	3.0–35.0	3.0–40.0	3.0–40.0	3.0–40.0
Nicaragua[5]	15.0–50.0	8.0–35.5	10.0–30.0	10.0–30.0	10.0–30.0	10.0–25.0
Panama[7]	13.0–56.0	3.5–56.0	4.0–30.0	4.0–30.0	2.0–30.0	2.0–30.0
Paraguay[4,8]	5.0–30.0	—	—	—	—	—
Peru[4,9]	0.0–49.0	6.0–37.0	15.0–30.0	15.0–30.0	15.0–30.0	15.0–20.0
Uruguay[10]	0.7–3.0	0.7–3.0	0.7–3.0	0.7–0.3	1.0–6.3	1.0–6.0
Venezuela	12.0–45.0	10.0–30.0	6.0–34.0	6.0–34.0	6.0–34.0	6.0–34.0
Unweighted regional average	7.2–49.2	7.2–33.3	8.4–32.5	9.2–29.2	8.4–27.7	8.7–27.7

Central America						
Costa Rica[4]	5.0–50.0	10.0–25.0	10.0–25.0	10.0–25.0	10.0–25.0	10.0–25.0
Dominican Republic[5,6]	2.0–73.0	3.0–70.0	3.0–70.0	15.0–25.0	15.0–25.0	15.0–25.0
El Salvador[5]	3.0–60.0	10.0–30.0	10.0–30.0	10.0–30.0	10.0–30.0	10.0–30.0
Guatemala	11.0–48.0	4.0–34.0	15.0–30.0	15.0–25.0	15.0–25.0	15.0–31.0
Honduras[4,7]	3.0–40.0	12.0–40.0	9.0–40.0	10.0–30.0	10.0–25.0	10.0–25.0
Nicaragua[5]	15.0–50.0	8.0–35.5	10.0–30.0	10.0–30.0	10.0–30.0	10.0–25.0
Panamá[7]	13.0–56.0	3.5–56.0	4.0–30.0	4.0–30.0	2.0–30.0	2.0–30.0
Unweighted regional average	7.4–53.9	7.2–41.5	8.7–36.4	10.6–27.9	10.3–27.1	10.3–27.3
OECD average[11]	22.2–52.8	16.8–44.1	15.8–43.6	16.1–43.1	15.0–43.0	16.0–41.2
Canada[5]	25.0–34.0	17.0–29.0	17.0–29.0	17.0–29.0	17.0–29.0	16.0–29.0
United States	18.0–50.0	15.0–31.0	15.0–39.6	15.0–39.6	15.0–39.6	15.0–39.6

Notes

1 The average shown is a joint average of the two year.
2 The data, unless otherwise indicated, present the tax rates in effect at 1 January 2000.
3 The data, unless otherwise indicated, present the tax rates in effect at 1 January 2001.
4 Data are for 1999 in column '1999 or 2000'.
5 Data are for 1998 in column '1999 or 2000'.
6 Data are for 1999 in column '2001 or 2002'.
7 Data are for 2000 in column '2001 or 2002'.
8 In the case of Paraguay, the personal income tax in 1985/86 was restricted to CEOs, and was eliminated thereafter.
9 In 2002 the upper tax rate was incremented to 27 per cent.
10 No income tax is levied on personal income in Uruguay, except for tax on income derived from agricultural activities and tax on commissions.
11 Excluding Mexico.

Sources: *International Bureau of Fiscal Documentation* (IBFD); 'European Taxation', *Taxes and Investment in Asia and the Pacific;* and *Taxation in Latin America* (Loose-leaf, Amsterdam); and *Individual Taxes, Worldwide Summaries* (PricewaterhouseCoopers).

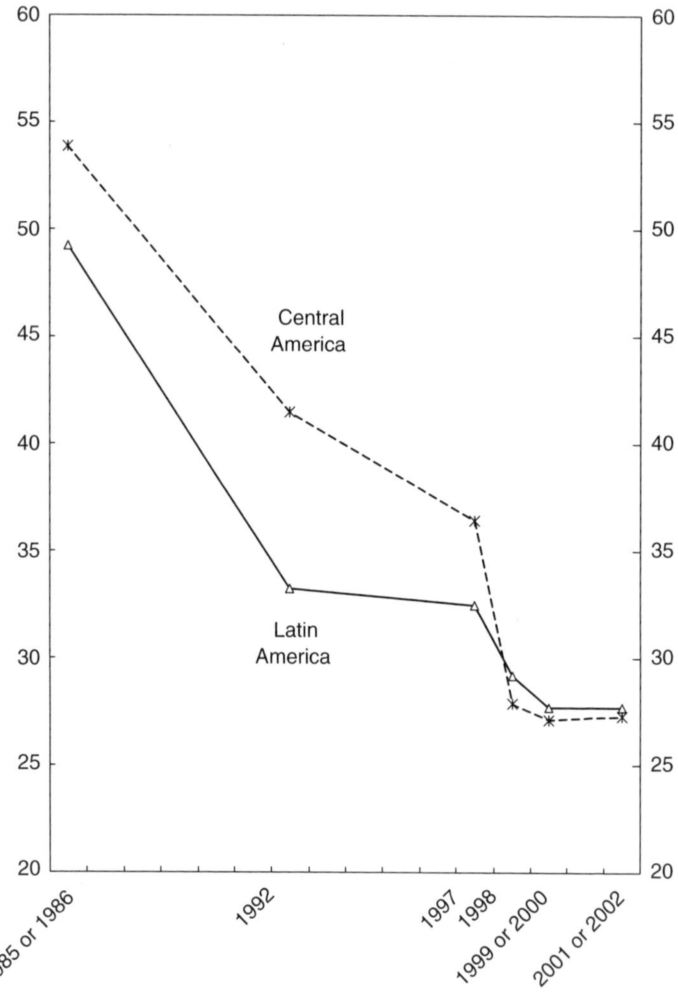

Figure 2.4 Latin American countries: personal income tax rates, 1985–2002 (per cent of taxable income)

Sources: *Individual Taxes: Worldwide Summaries* (PricewaterhouseCoopers); and *Taxation in Latin America* (IBFD).

For comparative purposes, Table 2.11 presents information on the basic exemption level and the income level at which the top bracket applies for these countries over the same period, measured in terms of multiples of per capita GDP in each country. In Central America, the personal exemption level has risen and then fluctuated up and down with no clear direction of change in recent years around a value of about three or a little more than three times per capita GDP. There is considerable variation across the countries, with the lowest in Costa Rica at 0.8 times per capita GDP and the highest in Nicaragua at 7.7 times per capita GDP. The average level is a somewhat higher than in South America, and is much higher than in developing countries on average, where this figure usually ranges from 1 to 2, and in developed nations, where it is usually well under 1. The exemption level is an important determinant of the degree of progressivity of the personal income tax, as it not only removes low income households entirely from liability to the tax, it also reduces the average (as opposed to marginal tax rate) on others, with a disproportionate effect of lowering the average rate on lower incomes. Typically, the exempt level tends to decline relative to per capita GDP as a country becomes wealthier because a larger proportion of the population has a level of resources that enables it to more comfortably afford this tax. This high level of basic exemption would contribute to the relatively small number of personal income taxpayers in Central America.

The income level at which the upper bracket applies exhibits the opposite trend, first falling and then fluctuating up and down with no clear tendency around 30 or a little less than 30 times per capita GDP. Again, there is considerable variation across the countries, with the lowest level in Costa Rica, with 3.7 times per capita GDP and the highest in Nicaragua, with 61.2 times per capita GDP. The decline in the income level at which the upper bracket applies implies some increase in progressivity of the tax in the middle range of income, though perhaps some reduction in progressivity in the upper range of income.

A desirable feature of an income tax is that the highest tax bracket of the personal income tax and the corporate income tax should be roughly the same, to avoid distorting the form of economic activities. This rough equivalence is achieved in several Central American countries. And in the others, the differences are not that large.

Table 2.11 Personal income tax: exemption level and upper income bracket, 1985 or 1986, 1991, and 1997–2001 (multiples of per capita GDP)

	Personal exemption level							Upper income bracket						
	1985 or 1986	1991	1997	1998	1999	2000	2001	1985 or 1986	1991	1997	1998	1999	2000	2001
Latin America														
Argentina	0.8	0.5	1.2	1.2	1.3	1.3	1.4	21.4	13.7	14.5	14.4	25.5	15.5	16.5
Bolivia	1.0	0.5	—	—	—	—	—	10.1	0.5	—	—	—	—	—
Brazil	0.3	1.2	2.1	2.0	1.8	1.7	1.5	10.1	2.8	4.2	4.1	3.7	3.3	3.1
Chile	0.2	2.3	0.1	0.1	0.1	0.1	0.1	2.8	22.6	1.3	1.3	1.2	1.2	1.2
Colombia	0.0	0.4	2.7	4.9	5.0	4.4	4.1	20.5	25.3	12.0	12.9	13.1	11.7	16.6
Costa Rica	1.2	2.9	1.1	1.1	0.6	0.8	0.8	1.4	5.3	5.6	5.4	3.1	4.1	3.7
Dominican Republic	1.1	0.2	0.1	3.4	2.9	2.6	2.3	413.5	74.3	34.3	8.4	7.3	6.5	5.8
Ecuador	0.4	2.9	1.8	2.8	1.9	0.9	2.4	29.2	35.8	22.7	34.4	23.4	11.3	8.3
El Salvador	—	2.3	1.4	1.3	1.3	1.2	1.2	171.7	32.5	12.7	12.2	11.8	11.4	11.0
Guatemala	0.9	2.3	6.3	5.8	5.6	5.3	5.0	356.0	31.7	17.5	16.0	15.6	14.7	22.5
Honduras	0.0	6.9	5.2	4.4	—	3.9	3.6	600.4	686.8	103.4	88.8	—	39.1	36.0
Mexico[1]	0.7	0.2	0.1	0.1	0.1	0.1	0.1	21.3	11.7	5.0	5.3	44.2	36.8	44.0
Nicaragua	1.7	—	6.6	6.2	4.7	8.3	7.7	56.9	9.9	47.4	44.4	33.9	49.9	61.2
Panama	0.3	0.5	0.9	0.9	0.9	0.9	0.9	89.0	97.8	63.1	61.1	59.9	58.9	57.8
Paraguay	0.5	—	—	—	—	—	—	10.4	—	—	—	—	—	—
Peru	—	—	2.6	2.7	2.8	2.8	2.9	—	—	20.1	20.9	21.8	21.5	22.3
Uruguay	—	—	—	—	—	—	—	—	—	—	—	—	—	—
Venezuela	—	—	0.0	0.0	0.0	0.0	0.0	—	—	0.0	0.0	0.0	0.0	0.0

Unweighted regional average[2]	0.6	1.8	2.1	2.5	2.1	2.3	2.3	121.0	75.0	24.2	22.0	18.9	19.0	20.7
Central America														
Costa Rica	1.2	2.9	1.1	1.1	0.6	0.8	0.8	1.4	5.3	5.6	5.4	3.1	4.1	3.7
Dominican Republic	1.1	0.2	0.1	3.4	2.9	2.6	2.3	413.5	74.3	34.3	8.4	7.3	6.5	5.8
El Salvador	—	2.3	1.4	1.3	1.3	1.2	1.2	171.7	32.5	12.7	12.2	11.8	11.4	11.0
Guatemala	0.9	2.3	6.3	5.8	5.6	5.3	5.0	356.0	31.7	17.5	16.0	15.6	14.7	22.5
Honduras	0.0	6.9	5.2	4.4	—	3.9	3.6	600.4	686.8	103.4	88.8	—	39.1	36.0
Nicaragua	1.7	—	6.6	6.2	4.7	8.3	7.7	56.9	9.9	47.4	44.4	33.9	49.9	61.2
Panama	0.3	0.5	0.9	0.9	0.9	0.9	0.9	89.0	97.8	63.1	61.1	59.9	58.9	57.8
Unweighted regional average[2]	0.9	2.5	3.1	3.3	2.7	3.3	3.1	241.3	134.0	40.6	33.8	21.9	26.3	28.3

Notes

[1] Allowance equals 12 months minimum wage in zone of residence (13 months with Christmas bonus). The data provided correspond to the Federal District in 1997.

[2] Average are taken over the set of countries for which data for 1997, 1991, and 1985 or 1986 are available.

Sources: IMF *Government Finance Statistics* (IMF); *World Economic Outlook* (IMF); *International Bureau of Fiscal Documentation* (IBFD); 'Taxation in Latin America' (Loose-leaf, Amsterdam); and *Individual Taxes, Worldwide Summaries* (PricewaterhouseCoopers); and other similar sources.

To strengthen collections of income tax and the structure of the tax it is important to define and administer the tax over as broad a base of labor and related labor income as possible. Although all countries in Central America define the tax base to include income from wages and salaries, in most countries income from bonuses, and fringe benefits (in the form of housing allowances, car allowances, which can be both in kind and in cash) are not fully taxed. This favorable treatment creates inequities between taxpayers who earn these kinds of income and those who do not, which disproportionately benefits higher income employees and those working for larger enterprises, who tend to earn this income. It also encourages employers to provide remuneration in these forms, even though most employees would prefer cash outright to allowances or in-kind benefits, that may distort their consumption decisions. Although there has been some movement to limit the tax favored treatment of these forms of remuneration, there is still scope for further broadening of the base. Cross crediting of the VAT against income tax is a practice found in Latin America. This cross crediting does not serve a useful purpose, as it confounds the nature of the two taxes – the income tax and the VAT, and adds to administrative complexity, weakening compliance with both taxes.

In many countries, especially developed ones, corporate income is usually taxed twice – at the level of the firm and at the level of the individual once it is paid out in the form of dividends or capital gains. Because interest paid on debt is normally deductible, income from corporate debt is taxed only once at the level of the individual. Provisions of the personal income tax with respect to income from dividends, interest on bonds, and capital gains are thus critical in determining the ultimate tax burden on owners of corporate capital. Countries differ in the manner in which they try to relieve the burden of double taxation on corporate income. Central American countries use a classical system, but because capital income is lightly taxed in general, the double tax issue would seem of minor importance at this point.

In developing countries, apart from wage and salary income, the next largest source of income tax revenue is usually from taxation of interest. Central American countries exhibit a range of practices with respect to taxation of dividends and interest income. This treatment is favorable compared to most developed countries and would be favorable compared to most developing countries as well. For instance, in El Salvador, interest received from financial institutions is not taxable to individuals. Also, to avoid double taxation, dividends paid by corporations that are subject to corporate tax are not taxable to individuals. In Honduras, interest and dividends are taxed at flat rates of 5 and 15 per cent, respectively, by a final withholding tax. Guatemala, in contrast, taxes interest and dividends at a flat rate of 10 per cent but exempts dividends on which corporate income tax has been paid. The Dominican Republic exempts interest income but taxes dividends at standard rates. Nicaragua exempts interest from bank deposits and dividend income, though other investment income is taxable. Panamá taxes interest income with a 10 per cent withholding tax and dividends at a 10 per cent rate, except dividends on bearer shares, which are taxed at 20 per cent. Costa Rica taxes only interest income with a 15 per cent withholding tax on bearer documents except those registered with the local stock exchange, which are taxed at 8 per cent.

In developing countries, owing to the underdeveloped state of domestic financial markets, capital gains taxation generally comprises a relatively small part of income tax revenue, though it can be useful as a device to avoid conversion of other forms of taxable income into untaxable capital gains income. In most countries of Latin America, the treatment of capital gains is the same as for other forms of income, and this has been relatively stable over time (Table 2.12). However, in a few countries in Central America, capital gains have received preferential treatment. In Costa Rica and the Dominican Republic, this income is exempt from income tax, while in El Salvador and Guatemala it is taxed at a favorable rate. In Honduras and Nicaragua it is taxed at normal rates, while in Panamá it is taxed on the basis of the gross sales price. Developed countries, in contrast, also exhibit a wide range of practices with respect to capital gains income, though the tendency is to tax it at a preferential rate but not exempt it altogether. This tax is rarely based on the gross sale price, as this turns the tax into a turnover-type tax rather than a capital gains tax. The choice of filing unit is another area of variation in income tax laws. Except Panamá, which most likely drew upon the US model, Central American countries require individual filing. Panamá requires joint filing for married couples but allows them to opt for individual filing, where advantageous. Most developing

Table 2.12 Latin American countries: treatment of capital gains, 1980, 1991, 1997, and 2001 (rate in per cent of capital gains, unless otherwise indicated)

	1980	**1991**	**1997**	**2001**
Argentina	15[1]	Normal[2]	Normal[2]	Normal[2]
Bolivia	Normal	Exempt	Exempt	Exempt
Brazil	Normal	Normal	Normal	Normal
Chile	Normal	Normal	Normal	Normal
Colombia	Normal	Normal	Normal	Normal
Costa Rica	Normal	Exempt	Exempt	Exempt
Dominican Republic	Exempt	Exempt	Exempt	Exempt
Ecuador	8[1]	Normal	Normal	Normal
El Salvador	6.8–21.5	5–15[1]	5–20[1]	5–20[1]
Guatemala	Normal	Normal	15 per cent	10 per cent
Honduras	Normal	Normal	Normal	Normal
Mexico	Normal	Normal	Normal	Normal
Nicaragua	Exempt	1–15[1]	Normal	Normal
Panama	2 per cent of price	2 per cent of price	2 per cent of price	2 per cent of price
Paraguay	5[1]	5[1]	5[1]	5[1]
Peru	Normal	Normal	Exempt	Exempt
Uruguay[3]	Normal	Normal	Normal	Normal
Venezuela	Normal	Normal	Normal	Normal

Notes
[1] Less than normal corporate tax rate.
[2] 'Normal' throughout the table indicates that the prevailing income tax rate is applicable.
[3] Except for capital gains on property in rural areas, which are exempt from tax.

Sources: *Corporate Taxes: Worldwide Summaries* (PricewaterhouseCoopers); *Taxation in Latin America* (IBFD); and *International Tax Summaries: A Guide for Planning and Decisions* (Coopers & Lybrand International Tax Network).

countries use individual filing, primarily for administrative reasons. However, even in developed countries, the trend has been toward adoption of individual filing and away from joint or family concepts of filing. With individual filing, a key issue is how to allocate joint income, such as investment income, and deductions or allowances for children. In some countries, this allocation is at the option of the taxpayers while in others it is automatically attributed to the husband (and less often, to the higher earner in the couple). In Europe and in some developing countries, there has been a movement in recent years toward greater gender neutrality in this aspect of the tax system, with the allocation either being determined on a formulaic basis (e.g. split between the two individual returns) or allocated to the higher earner.

Withholding tax rates on foreign remittances of corporate income are also important characteristics of an income tax, especially from the point of view of foreign investors. These taxes typically apply to dividends, interest, and royalties, but may also apply to management fees and other components of capital and labor income (Table 2.13). As with other income tax rates in Central America, after rising in the late 1980s and early 1990s, there is some downward trend evident in these rates in the 1990s to the present, though it is most pronounced for dividends and royalties. Interest tax rates exhibited relatively little change. For South America, rates declined in the early period and have risen recently for interest and royalties.

Some tax systems supplement income taxes with a tax on net worth or assets. This tax can take one of several forms, including a tax on gross assets or net assets (or net worth), or on only a subset of assets, such as fixed assets (usually applied to businesses) or real estate (Table 2.14). This type of tax is often seen as a complement to an income tax, as a type of minimum tax, when the base of the income tax is eroded excessively by exemptions or low compliance. Also, in some countries with persistently high inflation but no general correction to business balance sheets for inflation, the income tax base can become eroded, if businesses are able to take large nominal deductions for interest. If assets yield a uniform rate of return, an asset tax set at an appropriate rate can, in fact, mimic an income tax. For instance, if assets typically yield a return of 10 per cent, then an income tax of 30 per cent is equivalent to an assets tax of 3 per cent. However, in practice, assets do not yield a uniform return across sectors, or assets, or over time. Several Central American countries use this tax, including Costa Rica, Guatemala, Honduras, Nicaragua, and Panamá. El Salvador had such a tax but revoked it. In general, these taxes do not yield a substantial amount of revenue, and appear to be widely evaded.

The property tax has, in some countries, been used as an important component of local revenues because the tax base is relatively immobile. Property taxation has the potential to be a more significant source of revenue all over Central America, especially that component directed at residential and commercial real estate, as opposed to

Table 2.13 Withholding taxes on foreign remittances, 1986, 1992, 1997, and 2001 per cent of remittance

	1986			1992			1997			2001		
	Dividends	Interest	Royalties	Dividends	Interest	Royalties	Dividends	Interest	Royalties	Dividends	Interest	Royalties
Latin America												
Argentina	17.5[1]	15.8	36.0[2]	20.0	14.4	25.2	—	13.2	23.1	—	15.05 or 35.0	21 or 28
Bolivia	25.0	25.0	25.0	10.0	10.0	—	13.0	—	—	13.0	—	—
Brazil	25.0	25.0	25.0	25.0	25.0	25.0	0.0[3]	15.0[3]	15.0	0.0[3]	15.0[3]	10–15
Chile	40.0	40.0	40.0	35.0	40.0	40.0	35.0	40.0	40.0	35.0	5.0–40.0	5–40
Colombia	40.0	40.0	—	—	—	—	7.0	—	7.0	7.0	—	7
Costa Rica	15.0	10.0	20.0	15.0	15.0	25.0	15.0	15.0	25.0	15.0	15.0	25
Dominican Republic	20.0	20.0	20.0	35.0	35.0	35.0	30.0	30.0	30.0	25.0	25.0[4]	25
Ecuador	—[5]	—[6]	40.0	36.0	—	36.0	20.0	—	33.0	25.0	—	33
El Salvador	22.0	22.0	22.0	—	—	—	—	—	—	—	—	—
Guatemala	12.5	10.0[7]	25.0	12.5	25.0[7]	34.0	12.5	20.0[7]	30.0	0.0[8]	10.0[9]	30
Honduras	15.0	5.0	10.0	15.0	5.0	35.0	15.0	5.0	35.0	10.0	10.0	—[10]
Mexico	55.0	24.8[11,12]	31.5	none	20.2[13]	23.8	Nil	11.5[14,15]	26.0[16,17,18]	5.0	15.0	—[19]
Nicaragua	20.0	—	—	—	35.0	35.0	—	30.0	20.0	—	25.0	25
Panama	10.0	—	50.0[20]	10.0	6.0	45.0[20]	10.0	6.0	34.0[20]	10.0	6.0	30
Paraguay	10.0	30.0	30.0	10.0[21]	30.0	30.0	5.0	35.0	35.0	5.0	35.0	35
Peru	30.0	1.0; 40.0[17]	55.0[22]	10.0	1.0; 37.0[17]	28.0[23]	Nil	1.0; 30.0[17]	30.0	Nil	1.0; 5.0; 30.0[17,24]	30[25]
Uruguay	—	—	30.0	—	—	—	—	—	30.0	—	—	30
Venezuela	20.0	20.0	—	—	—	15.0	—	5.0	5.0	—	5.0	5
Unweighted regional average	23.6	23.4	30.6	19.5	22.9	30.9	14.8	19.7	26.1	12.5	20.5	25.6
Central America												
Costa Rica	15.0	10.0	20.0	15.0	15.0	25.0	15.0	15.0	25.0	15.0	15.0	25.0
Dominican Republic	20.0	20.0	20.0	35.0	35.0	35.0	30.0	30.0	30.0	25.0	25.0[4]	25.0
El Salvador	22.0	22.0	22.0	—	—	—	—	—	—	—	—	—
Guatemala	12.5	10.0[7]	25.0	12.5	25.0[7]	34.0	12.5	20.0[7]	30.0	0.0[8]	10.0[9]	30.0
Honduras	15.0	5.0	10.0	15.0	5.0	35.0	15.0	5.0	35.0	10.0	10.0	—[10]
Nicaragua	20.0	—	—	—	35.0	35.0	—	30.0	20.0	—	25.0	25.0
Panama	10.0	—	50.0[20]	10.0	6.0	45.0[20]	10.0	6.0	34.0[20]	10.0	6.0	30.0
Unweighted regional average	16.4	13.4	24.5	17.5	20.2	34.8	16.5	17.7	29.0	12.0	15.2	27.0

Notes

[1] Pertains to dividends in cash or kind, other than stock dividends. The beneficiary must be identified: otherwise, the rate is 22.25 per cent. Dividends and remittances of branch profits in excess of 12 per cent of registered investments are subject to a special remittance tax ranging from 15 per cent to 25 per cent.

[2] Services derived from agreements ruled by the Foreign Technology Law: (a) technical assistance, technology, and engineering – 27 per cent (45 per cent on assumed profit of 60 per cent); (b) cession of right or licenses for inventions, patents, exploitation, and others – 36 per cent (45 per cent on assumed profit of 80 per cent); and (c) nonregistered agreements – 45 per cent (profit of 100 per cent is assumed).

[3] These rates have been established as of January 1 1996. Treaty rates in excess of those in force for nontreaty countries are automatically reduced. Payments of income to nonresidents in nontreaty countries that tax income at less than 20 per cent are subject to withholding tax at 25 per cent.
[4] Payments on interest (loans) to foreign financial institutions are subject to a withholding tax of 15 per cent.
[5] Taxes on dividends are withheld at the basic tax rate with surcharges. If the dividends are paid from undistributed profits of prior years, credit is allowed for the tax already paid on such profits by the company.
[6] No withholding required on interest remitted or credited abroad on loans. A special tax of 0.5 per cent to 2 per cent on the portion of the loans payable up to two years is levied (only once) at the time loans are registered at the Central Bank of Ecuador. If the loan is due after two years, the special tax is not payable.
[7] Interest on cash foreign-source loans brought into the country is not subject to withholding taxes.
[8] Tax on income shown by partial closure of accounts or computation of presumed liquidation of operations at the end of each quarter.
[9] Tax on 5 per cent of overall gross income earned during the corresponding quarter of the preceding year (5 per cent of the 30 per cent income tax rate = 1.5 per cent).
[10] Royalties are taxed as ordinary income and are included in the taxpayer's gross income.
[11] The withholding taxes are an average of different interest and royalties rates.
[12] Interest payments to nonresidents are exempt from Mexican income tax in the case of (a) loans to the federal government; (b) fixed-rate loans for five or more years, by duly registered financial institutions; and (c) certain securities and bank acceptances issued in foreign currency.
[13] Interest payments to nonresidents are exempt from Mexican income tax for (a) loans to the federal government; and (b) loans for three or more years by duly registered financial entities that promote exports by special financing; (c) these gains are taxable as interest; (d) when royalties are paid for the use of patents in connection with the technical assistance required for their use under the same contract, both the licensing fee and amounts paid for the technical assistance will be subject to the lower 15 per cent rate; (e) the nonresident taxpayer may elect to pay at the regular corporate tax rate on net profit if he has a resident representative and advises the customer accordingly. The latter, then, makes no withholding.
[14] Interest payments to nonresidents are exempt from Mexican income tax in the case of: (a) loans to the federal government; and (b) loans for three or more years by duly registered financial entities that promote exports by special financing; (c) preferential loans granted or guaranteed institutions by foreign financial entities to authorized to receive tax-deductible donations in Mexico, provided that these institutions are properly registered and use the funds for purposes consistent with their status.
[15] The election is available only if the payee is a resident taxpayer of a country that has signed an income tax treaty with Mexico and the treaty is in force.
[16] 35 per cent income tax must be withheld on payments made to foreign persons or entities located in low-tax jurisdictions.
[17] When these payments involve items on which tax must be withheld at either the 15 per cent or the 35 per cent rate, the tax must be calculated by applying the applicable rates to the payments made for each of the corresponding items; when no distinction can be made, the 35 per cent rate must be applied to the total payment. The 1 per cent rate applies in case of banking concesional loans, otherwise the other rate applies.
[18] The alienation (even as a capital contribution) of drawings, models, plans, formulas procedures is treated as an authorization for their use; accordingly, the corresponding amount is taxed at the 15 per cent rate.
[19] Royalties paid to residents are subject to tax as ordinary income and are normally included in the taxpayer's gross income.
[20] Upper enterprise income tax rates are used; however, the rates of royalties or technical assistance fees paid is subject to withholding tax at corporate or individual tax rates, depending on the recipient.
[21] Taxable income is determined as gross rentals less depreciation computed as provided by law.
[22] Under certain circumstances, exemptions are granted.
[23] Payments for transfer of technology or for information regarding commercial, industrial, or scientific knowledge are deemed to be royalties.
[24] Under certain circumstances, exemptions are granted.
[25] Payments for transfer of technology or for information regarding commercial, industrial, or scientific knowledge are deemed to be royalties.

Sources: *Corporate Taxes: Worldwide Summaries* (PricewaterhouseCoopers); *Taxation in Latin America* (IBFD); and *International Tax Summaries: A Guide for Planning and Decisions* (Coopers & Lybrand International Tax Network).

Table 2.14 Net worth or assets tax, 1986, 1992, 1998, 2000, and 2001 (in per cent)

	1986	1992	1998	2000	2001
Argentina	1.5 on net worth[1]	2 on gross assets	1.0 on assets	1.0 on assets	1.0 on assets
Bolivia	—	3 on net worth	3 on net worth	3 on net worth	3 on net worth
Brazil	—	—	—	—	—
Chile	—	—	—	—	—
Colombia	8 on net worth	7 on net worth	—	—	—
Costa Rica	0.36–1.17 on fixed assets	0.36–1.17 on fixed assets	1.0 on assets	1.0 on assets	1.0 on assets
Dominican Republic	—	—	—	—	—
Ecuador	0.15 on assets	0.15 on net worth[2]	0.15 on net worth[2]	0.15 on net worth[2]	0.15 on net worth[2]
El Salvador	0.1–1.4 on net worth	0.9–2 on assets	—	—	—
Guatemala	0.3–0.8 on real estate[3]	0.3–0.9 on real estate[3]	1.5 on assets	1.5 on assets	0.2–0.9 on real estate[3] 3.5 on assets[4]
Honduras	—	—	1.0 on assets	0.5 on assets	0.25 on assets[5]
Mexico	—	2 on gross assets[1]	1.8 on assets[1]	1.8 on assets[1]	1.8 on assets[1]
Nicaragua	1.0 on real estate[3]	1.5–2.5 on net worth	1.0 on real estate	1.0 on real estate	1.0 on real estate
Panamá	1.0 on net worth[6]	1.0 on net worth[6]	1.0 on net worth[6]	1.0 on net worth[6]	1.0 on net worth[6]

Paraguay	1.0 on real estate[3]	1.0 on real estate[3]	1.0 on real estate[3]	1.0 on real estate[3]	1.0 on real estate[3]
Peru	1.0–2.5 on net worth	2.0 on net worth	0.5 on assets[7]	Nil	Nil
Uruguay	2.8 on net worth	2.0 on net worth	1.5–3.5 net worth	1.5–3.5 net worth	1.5–3.5 net worth
Venezuela	—	—	1.0 on assets[1]	1.0 on assets[1]	1.0 on assets[1]

Notes

[1] Minimum corporate income tax; can be credited against normal corporate tax. In Mexico, the income tax can be credited against the gross assets tax in order to avoid the foreign investors' problem of crediting against tax liability in the home country.

[2] One per cent of assets as income tax advance payment.

[3] The base is real estate. The tax, however, is conceived not as a property tax but as an additional corporate tax.

[4] There is no net worth tax in Guatemala. However, the tax levied at rate of 3.5 per cent on assets or 2.25 per cent on gross income declared in the preceding annual income tax return.

[5] Honduras does not have a business net worth tax. However, levied on fixed assets exceeding HNL 750 000 which are held by companies at the end of the tax period.

[6] This tax has the form of a license to do business. The maximum tax amount is PAB 20,000 per year.

[7] Minimum corporate income tax; can be credited against normal corporate tax.

Sources: *Corporate Taxes*: *Worldwide Summaries* (PricewaterhouseCoopers); *Taxation in Latin America* (IBFD); and *International Tax Summaries*: *A Guide for Planning and Decisions* (Coopers & Lybrand International Tax Network).

natural resources. There are two essential elements to running a successful property tax: having an accurate cadastre of property and an accurate and up-to-date assessment of property value. Until these elements are in place, it is unlikely that the property tax could yield substantially greater revenues. For now, given the administrative limitations (and the small size of the countries) in Central America, it may be more productive to levy the property tax at the federal level.

Administrative issues

Central American tax systems are extending the tools necessary for adequate enforcement of the tax law. These steps include the expansion and improvement of withholding taxes; implementation of self-assessment and improved audit selection and conduct; and computerization. One important step was taken by Guatemala in 1998 with the formation of an autonomous tax administration agency under the ministry of finance, which led to distinct improvements in productivity. However, the establishment of large taxpayers units is another measure that is underway in some countries but should be reinforced and extended to all the countries as it has been an essential component of success in improving collections from large taxpayers in many developing countries.

Recent unpublished estimates suggest that evasion of the VAT may be approximately 40 per cent of revenue in several Central American countries. Although not unusual for developing countries – and even some developed countries – such high rates of evasion suggest that there is considerable scope for strengthening collections through general administrative practices, such as audit, and improvements in the structure of the tax, which would make it easier to administer.

In general, there is a need to adopt rules (and supporting regulations) in the income tax, in particular, to deal with cross-border issues, such as transfer pricing, thin capitalization (excessive use of debt to remove earnings from a country through high interest deductions), and other devices used by multinational corporations. Over time, as the complexity of Central American economies grow, there may be a need to deal with issues, such as taxation of groups and the tax treatment of corporation reorganizations. So far, these issues are largely absent in Central American income tax laws.

Because wealthy individuals may keep a large proportion of their wealth abroad, it is not only important to both extend the jurisdiction of the tax system to global income but also to develop the tools and relationships with other countries to uncover income from assets held abroad. Strengthening income taxation of the self-employed is another challenge but also a critical one, and may require greater clarity in whether taxpayers owe liability under the enterprise income tax or personal income tax. Better enforcement of income taxation for both wealthy individuals and the self-employed would make a significant contribution toward improving the equity of the tax system and strengthening collections.

Regional tax harmonization

International issues have become increasingly important in tax policy reform in recent years. The Central American countries could likely gain by greater integration of their tax systems. The movement toward a common market implies that there would also be freer movement of tax bases (Keen, 1993). In Central America, the emphasis of regional tax harmonization has first entailed movement toward more uniform tariffs and the elimination of internal tariffs. Moving beyond those goals, harmonization of domestic tax systems would also be beneficial to Central American countries, given their natural links and their small size. In this regard, harmonization of domestic taxes on goods and services should be a priority. As tariffs converge, countries could be tempted to use domestic taxes to gain advantages with regard to their neighbors. However, there do appear to be some promising trends underway in Central America. Already, the trends point toward convergence of VAT rates. One goal might be to aim for a single rate of 15 per cent, as in the Caribbean. Similarly, harmonization of excises should be on the agenda, though here, it might be more useful to set certain minimum rates, as in the EU, rather than a single set of rates, given the importance of having flexibility in excise rates for meeting immediate budgetary needs and the recognition that there are different levels of administrative control over excises. Over time, however, as the common market takes shape, it may be more important to have greater convergence in excises.

Some convergence of income tax rates also appears to be taking place, and greater harmonization of income taxes – especially tax incentives – should be a medium-term goal. It is important that Central American countries modernize their income tax with appropriate anti-avoidance legislation, such as in the area of transfer pricing, to ensure that multinational companies do not take advantage of differences in enterprise income tax legislation and practices to shift profits from one jurisdiction to a less highly taxed jurisdiction in Central America or elsewhere.

Looking to the future

Tax policy reform in Central America should continue to emphasize the importance of strengthening domestic tax systems by relying on a broad range of taxes, including domestic consumption and income taxes, and broadening the tax bases to permit revenue goals to be achieved with moderate tax rates, which will reduce tax-induced distortions in economic behavior and disincentives to domestic and foreign investment, and enhance compliance. Important principles underlying these reforms are that tax policies should be based on clear and transparent tax legislation and administrative regulations, and administration should support the implementation of tax policies by the establishment and maintenance of modern and professional tax administrations based on the rule of law. The best tax policy is formed in an environment in which the tax authorities facilitate public discussion of reform. Globalization will continue to reduce barriers to cross-border trade and investment continue, making it thus more imperative that countries adopt policies and practices that do not deviate significantly from regional and international norms. This will be all the more important in countries that have adopted a common market, as in Central America.

Taxes on domestic goods and services, such as the VAT, will continue to be the mainstay of domestic revenue systems in the foreseeable future. However, the broad-based taxes should be supplemented by excises, especially when limited in application to key goods, such as alcoholic beverages, tobacco products, and petroleum products. Trade taxes should continue to fall in importance, and eventually serve only limited trade policy purposes, as in developed countries, rather than revenue purposes. Income taxes need to be strengthened, mindful of the global competition for investments. Personal income taxes in particular, must reach out to encompass higher income tax-payers and those earning capital and other non-wage and salary income. Property taxation is an underused source of revenue and should also be strengthened, with this revenue possibly being dedicated to local uses. Continuing improvement in administrative performance is essential.

Notes

1. In this chapter, Central America refers to Costa Rica, the Dominican Republic, El Salvador, Honduras, Guatemala, Nicaragua, and Panamá.
2. The data come from *Government Finance Statistics* (IMF); *International Financial Statistics* (IMF); and *World Economic Outlook* (IMF). Only years for which revenue data are available are included. These data are provided by the government to the IMF. For regional averages, the simple average is used.
3. GDP estimates in several Central American countries appear to be significantly underestimated, raising the measured tax to GDP ratio for these countries. However, if this mismeasurement is systematic, the trends in this ratio would still be meaningful, even if the precise level is not.
4. Although GDP tends to be understated in many developing countries, Nicaragua's and Honduras's GDP estimates are thought to be significantly understated, so that, if GDP were adjusted upward, the tax ratio would fall. There have recently been some revisions to Costa Rica's GDP series, which have been incorporated into the data presented in this chapter.
5. Domestic taxes on goods and services include taxes collected at the first stage on imports, as under the VAT and excises, since ultimately the tax is borne by domestic consumers (as these taxes are rebated on exports).
6. To some extent, the classification of taxes as social security taxes or payroll taxes is arbitrary in GFS.
7. The average is based on the standard rate of VAT, not a weighted average, if there are multiple rates. In these countries, the additional rate generally applies to only a limited set of goods.
8. Exemption does not necessarily lead to base erosion if there is cascading – exempt items, with VAT on inputs already built into their cost are later sold to a taxable producer, who cannot claim credit for tax on these inputs, hence the tax is levied on tax.
9. One country had a range of rates, so this was the top rate in that country.
10. The upper rate is used when there is a range, as it likely applies to the majority of enterprises.

References

Bird, Richard M. (1992) 'Tax Reform in Latin America: A Review of Some Recent Experiences', *Latin American Research Review*, Vol. 27 (January), pp. 7–36.

Ebrill, Liam, Michael Keen, Jean-Paul Bodin, and Victoria Summers (2001), *The Modern VAT*, Washington, DC.: International Monetary Fund.
Itam, Samuel, Simon Cueva, Erik Lundback, Janet Stotsky, and Stephen Tokarick (2000) 'Developments and Challenges in the Caribbean Region', *IMF Occasional Paper No. 201*, Washington, DC.: International Monetary Fund.
Keen, Michael (1993) 'The Welfare Economics of Tax Coordination in the European Community: A Survey', *Fiscal Studies*, Vol. 14 (May), pp. 15–36.
Shome, Parthasarathi (1999) 'Taxation in Latin America: Structural Trends and Impact of Administration', *IMF Working Paper 99/19*, Washington, DC.: International Monetary Fund.
Tanzi, Vito and Howell H. Zee (2000) 'Tax Policy for Emerging Markets: Developing Countries', *National Tax Journal*, Vol. 53 (June), pp. 299–322.
Zee, Howell H., Janet G. Stotsky, and Eduardo Ley (2002) 'Tax Incentives for Business Investment', *World Development*, Vol. 30 (September), pp. 1497–516.

3
Public Expenditure and Governance

Ana Corbacho and Hamid R. Davoodi

Introduction

After a weak performance during the so-called lost decade of the 1980s, the economies of Central America rebounded to varying degrees in the 1990s. The rebound was due to a number of factors, ranging from improvements in fiscal, monetary and exchange rate policies to an accelerating pace of structural reforms, expansion of the world economy and a more favorable terms of trade.

For the purpose of this chapter, Central America consists of seven countries: El Salvador, Costa Rica, Nicaragua, Honduras, Guatemala, Panamá, and the Dominican Republic.[1] These countries comprise a heterogeneous group with respect to many factors, including per capita income, political history, exposure to external shocks, and the pace of economic reforms. However, these countries are facing – albeit to differing degrees – similar challenges, including high inequality and poverty, that may require common solutions.

The chapter addresses three questions. First, what has been Central America's track record on fiscal adjustment, poverty and inequality, health and education outcomes, adequacy of social safety nets, and governance? Second, notwithstanding other factors at work, to what extent the observed track record can be traced to reforms in the areas of public expenditure and governance? This question attempts to get at the elusive issue of quality of public spending and governance by unbundling different aspects of reforms in these areas. Expenditure reforms covered in this paper cover public expenditure policies and management of public expenditure system, while quality of governance and institutions would address various dimensions of governance and the underlying public policy measures taken by the countries in the region to address governance concerns and improve quality of institutions. Third, should countries in Central America follow similar reforms in the area of expenditure and governance even though they may have markedly different track records and different economic conditions?

Economic growth, poverty, and inequality

It is widely recognized that sound expenditure policies, an effective expenditure management system and good governance, among other things, could reduce inequality and poverty and lead to higher growth. Higher growth would in turn have a favorable impact on poverty and perhaps on inequality. This section summarizes the track record on poverty and inequality and the relationship between these indicators and economic growth in the region and draws some policy implications.

Central American countries display diverse growth experiences and are at various stages of economic development. Growth experiences are driven by, among other things, external factors (e.g. hurricanes in Honduras, Nicaragua; terms of trade shocks), resolution of armed conflict in a number of countries in the region (e.g. Guatemala) and the underlying economic policies and quality of institutions.[2] Per capita income is the most widely used proxy for the stage of economic development and this could in part account for differences in the level and composition of government expenditure in the region. According to the World Bank's latest calculations (World Bank, 2002), Costa Rica has the highest per capita gross national income (GNI) among the seven countries, estimated at $7980 in 2000 purchasing power parity (PPP) terms, followed by the Dominican Republic and Panamá (Table 3.1).[3] Nicaragua has the lowest per capita gross national income at $2080 in 2000 PPP terms, followed by Honduras. On a PPP basis, Costa Rica's per capita income is almost three and a half times than that of Nicaragua. Using a slightly different criterion, the World Bank classifies Nicaragua as a low-income country, Panamá as an upper-middle-income country, and the remaining five as lower-middle-income countries.[4]

Table 3.1 Growth, inequality, and poverty

	Per capita gross national income[1] 2000 US$ PPP	Economic growth[2]		Growth elasticity of poverty[3]	Inequality[4]		Percentage share of income or consumption[5]				Percentage of population below						
											International poverty line					National[5]	
		1980s	1990s		Gini early 1990s	Gini late 1990s	Survey year (latest)	Gini	Bottom 20%	Top 20%	$2 a day early 1990s[6]	$2 a day late 1990s[6]	Survey year (latest)[5]	$1 a day[5]	$2 a day[5]	Survey year (latest)	National poverty line
Costa Rica	7 980	−0.4	2.4	−1.6	46.0	46.1	1997	45.9	4.5	51.0	34.2	30.5	1998	12.6	26.0	1992	22.0
El Salvador	4 410	−2.6	3.0	−1.5	50.5	55.9	1998	52.2	3.3	56.4	58.6	64.0	1998	21.0	44.5	1992	48.3
Guatemala	3 770	−1.9	1.3	−1.2	59.1	55.8	1998	55.8	3.8	60.6	—	—	1998	10.0	33.8	1989	57.9
Honduras	2 400	−0.8	0.3	−1.4	54.9	58.5	1998	56.3	2.2	59.4	75.9	74.9	1998	24.3	45.1	1993	53.0
Nicaragua	2 080	−4.2	0.1	−1.3	56.7	60.2	1998	60.3	2.3	63.6	70.7	72.7	—	—	—	1993	50.3
Panama	5 680	−0.5	3.1	−1.3	56.3	56.5	1997	48.5	3.6	52.8	47.8	38.1	1998	14.0	29.0	1997	37.3
Dominican Republic	5 710	0.9	2.9	−1.5	50.5	47.8	1998	47.4	5.1	53.3	—	34.6	1996	3.2	16.0	1998	28.6
Central America	4 576	−1.4	1.9	−1.4	53.4	54.4	as above	52.3	3.5	56.7	57.4	52.4	as above	14.2	32.4	as above	42.5
Latin America[4]	—	—	—	—	51.7	53.8	—	—	—	—	42.6	39.3	—	—	—	—	—
Latin America[5]	5 425	0.1	1.8	—	—	—	varies	52.5	3.0	56.6	—	—	as above	15.3	31.2	varies	32.1
High-income OECD countries[6]	25 771	2.2	2	—	—	—	varies	30.8	8.0	39.0	—	—	—		—	—	—
Sub-Saharan Africa	1 600	0.2	0.2	—	—	—	varies	47.4	4.8	52.9	—	—	varies	42.1	71.9	varies	45.6
Eastern Europe and Central Asia	6 670	2.3	−2.4	—	—	—	varies	33.3	7.8	41.3	—	—	varies	6	23.5	varies	28.7
World	7 928	0.8	0.9	—	—	—	varies	40.0	3.0	46.8	—	—	varies	26.1	47.0	varies	36.0

Notes

1 World Development Indicators (2002). Per capita gross national income uses US$ purchasing power parity (PPP) in 2000. See text for details.

2 IMF's *World Economic Outlook*. Economic growth is measured as growth in real per capita GDP in local currency.

3 This is Gini-Adjusted growth elasticity, defined as (1-initial Gini/100)* –3 where –3 is part of the growth elasticity that depends on initial Gini. The latter is Gini in early 1990s as shown. See Ravallion (2001) and the text for details on growth-adjusted elasticity.

4 Deininger and Squire (1996), Wodon and others (2000) and Szekely (2001). Definition of poverty and inequality from Szekely (2001) uses international PPP for per capita consumption in 1985 prices, except for measures based on national poverty lines.

5 *World Development Indicators* (2002). Definition of inequality measure uses per capita income for all Central American countries except for Nicaragua and Panama. Inequality measures have the same sample of 15 Latin American countries as sources indicated under[3].

6 Szekely (2001). Definition of poverty uses per capita consumption in international PPP in 1985 prices. OECD countries denotes the member countries of the Organization for Economic Cooperation and Development.

Source: All regional averages use arithmetic average. International poverty lines make it possible to compare poverty across countries by allowing for cross-country differences in prices using a common denominator, the purchasing power parity of a $1 or $2.

Stage of economic development has been the primary determinant of the type of access these countries have to the facilities of International Financial Institutions and regional banks. Of the seven countries, two (Nicaragua and Honduras) have access to International Monetary Fund's Poverty Reduction Growth Facility (PRGF) and World Bank's International Development Association (IDA) facility for borrowing under concessional terms.[5] As part of the eligibility requirement under these facilities, both countries have articulated their vision for poverty reduction in a public document known as the Poverty Reduction Strategy Paper (PRSP).[6] The IMF also lent to some Central America countries hit by hurricanes under its emergency assistance program (e.g. the Dominican Republic and Guatemala in 1998).

Poverty in Central America is higher than the rest of Latin America, but both regions have poverty rates that are well below sub-Saharan Africa and the world average. This situation has held throughout the 1990s. However, there is considerable heterogeneity among the countries in the region. Costa Rica and Honduras have had the lowest and highest poverty rates, respectively, throughout the period, with Costa Rica's poverty rate in the low 30s and Honduras' in the mid-1970s;[7] Nicaragua has the second highest poverty rate. Poverty rates in both Honduras and Nicaragua are similar to those of high poverty countries in sub-Saharan Africa. Although data coverage and comparability of poverty rates vary in general across countries and over time, the data set compiled for this chapter allows one to conclude with high certainty that in the late 1990s Central American countries can be classified into two poverty groups, based on either US$1 a day or US$2 a day definitions of poverty.[8] The group with higher poverty rates consists of Nicaragua, Honduras, and El Salvador; and that with lower poverty rates consists of the remaining four countries. On a US$2 a day definition, the higher- and lower-poverty groups have poverty rates in excess of 60 per cent and less than 40 per cent, respectively.

Inequality in Central America is higher than in Latin America, which is the regime with highest inequality in the world. These findings hold throughout the 1990s using different data sources, variety of inequality measures (Table 3.1), including the Gini coefficient and the income shares of the richest and the poorest in the population.[9] The poorer countries tend to be more unequal. For example, the simple correlation coefficient between per capita income in PPP US$

and the Gini coefficient of consumption in late 1990s among the seven countries is −0.84, with a *t*-statistic of −4.1. Among the seven countries, Nicaragua has the lowest per capita income and the highest poverty rate, whereas Costa Rica has the highest per capita income and the lowest inequality.

Poverty in Central America has declined on average in the 1990s while inequality has increased, but substantial heterogeneity remains across countries. By contrast, poverty, based on US$2 a day definition, in the rest of Latin America has declined by more.[10] However, by the end of the decade, Latin America's inequality had converged towards Central America's. Of the five Central American countries for which both the poverty headcount indexes and the Gini coefficients are available in the early and the late 1990s, Honduras is the only country in which poverty declined while inequality rose. In El Salvador and Nicaragua, poverty rates as well as inequality rose. In Panamá and Costa Rica, poverty fell while inequality remained the same.

Poverty and inequality are highly persistent over time and are highly correlated in Central America. In spite of the heterogeneity noted above, countries with high poverty and inequality at the start of the 1990s continued to experience high poverty and inequality at the end of the decade. For example, for five Central American countries with available data, the correlation coefficient between poverty at the beginning of the 1990s and the end of the 1990s is 0.96, with a *t*-statistic of 6.9.[11] The correlation coefficient for the Gini coefficient between the two time periods for the same countries is 0.88, with a *t*-statistic of 3.9.[12] Countries with high poverty also tend to have high inequality. For example, the correlation coefficient between poverty and inequality at the start of the decade is 0.54, with a *t*-statistic of 1.6; while that for the end of the decade is 0.72, with a *t*-statistic of 2.3. The implication of these findings is that policies that reduce poverty are likely to reduce inequality as well. As the following sections would show, improvement in quality of education and health for all, in general, and for the bottom end of the income distribution, in particular, are such policies.

High initial inequality may be a serious impediment to aggregate growth, and poverty reduction. Recent research suggests that high initial inequality can lower aggregate growth for several reasons, including failures in credit markets that limit investment in physical and human capital and its distribution (Knowles, 2001). Lower growth in turn reduces the rate of poverty reduction (Ravallion and Chen, 1997). This finding is an obvious cause for concern in Latin America as a whole and Central America in particular with its higher level of inequality. This finding may also help explain the relatively slow growth achieved, as well as the persistence of poverty in the 1990s.[13] Recent research also suggests that it is perhaps not initial income inequality, but asset or wealth inequality that may matter more for growth, and hence, for poverty reduction (Birdsall and Londoño, 1997).

High initial inequality may be an impediment to pro-poor growth as well. Previous research (Ravallion and Chen, 1997) found that for every 1 per cent increase in aggregate growth, the proportion of people living on less than US$1 day falls by as much 2.5 to 3 per cent. This result was thought to be independent of the initial distribution of income or consumption. However, some recent studies suggest that this elasticity declines with higher initial inequality (Ravallion, 1997, 2001). Therefore, in a country with high initial inequality, higher aggregate growth is needed to achieve the same reduction in poverty as in a country with low initial inequality. In other words, poverty is less responsive to growth in countries with high inequality. For Honduras, the growth elasticity is −1.4, instead of the average estimate of −2.5 or −3.[14] Similarly, reflecting the impact of initial inequality, growth elasticities in Central America vary from −1.2 (Guatemala) to −1.6 (Costa Rica).

The experiences of Costa Rica and Honduras reveal the interaction between initial inequality and pro-poor growth. Between the early and the late 1990s, poverty rates in Costa Rica and Honduras fell by about 4 and 1 per cent, respectively; while growth was 2.4 and 0.3 per cent, respectively. However, inequality in Honduras at the start of the decade was 54.9, almost nine points higher than that of Costa Rica. A much higher growth rate than 0.3 per cent per year is needed for Honduras to overcome its high initial inequality and achieve a higher rate of poverty reduction. For example, Honduras's growth rate in the 1990s would have had to be at least 8 per cent a year in order to achieve the same per cent reduction in poverty as Costa Rica experienced in the 1990s. Although growth in per capita income of this magnitude is implausible, the exercise does illustrate the adverse potential impact of high inequality. Of course, Honduras' actual growth and poverty performance in the 1990s was also worsened by the fact that its already high inequality at the start of the 1990s rose even further during the decade, pushing its inequality from being the fourth highest to the second highest by late 1990s. By contrast, Costa Rica's inequality remained the same.

Sustained growth, among other factors, is a prerequisite for poverty reduction. Central America's growth track record has been erratic and despite the turn around in the 1990s, growth has not been high enough to make a substantial impact on poverty. In fact, in marked contrast to many cross-country studies, which establish a high negative correlation between growth and changes in poverty, there is little correlation between aggregate growth and changes in poverty in the 1990s for the sample of five Central American countries with full data. As noted above, the interaction between poverty, inequality, and growth is highly complex, perhaps more for Central America than the rest of Latin America. Other factors are certainly at work, and some have been suggested above; some factors are structural in nature and require longer time for their implementation and for their full effects. There are also other factors that are more short run in nature. The next sections will address both sets of factors.

Level and composition of government spending

The fiscal adjustment achieved in the 1990s came about largely through expenditure reductions. Central government balances in the seven countries improved from a deficit of about 6 per cent of GDP in the 1980s to a deficit of about 3.5 per cent of GDP in the 1990s. This adjustment was achieved through lower expenditure (3.3 per cent of GDP), that was partly offset by lower revenues (0.8 per cent of GDP). Nicaragua, the country with the highest public sector deficit in Central America, recorded the largest adjustment, reducing its deficit from 17 per cent of GDP to about 11 per cent of GDP, followed by Honduras and Guatemala as they emerged from the aftermath of Hurricane Mitch and armed conflict, respectively.[15]

Despite the sizable fiscal adjustment, by the end of the decade, central government spending on wages and salaries is large by international standards and exceeds capital investment for almost all countries. Wages and salaries in Central America form the largest spending item; and are higher than the average for Latin America and for low income countries (Table 3.2). These observations are

Table 3.2 Economic classification of expenditure (Latest year for which data are available; group averages include Central American countries)[1] (As a percent of GDP)

	Costa Rica[2]	Dominican Republic[2]	El Salvador[2]	Guatemala[2]	Honduras[2]	Nicaragua[3]	Panamá[4]	Central America	Latin America
Total expenditure and net lending	15.7	18.2	18.6	12.4	23.7	39.3	22.8	21.5	22.8
Current expenditure	14.1	13.9	15.3	8.7	16.8	22.5	19.2	15.8	18.7
Goods and services	5.7	7.2	11.2	4.8	11.7	10.9	9.4	8.7	7.7
Wages and salaries	5.2	5.6	8.3	3.5	9.0	6.2	7.2	6.4	5.1
Other goods and services	0.5	1.6	2.8	1.3	2.7	4.7	2.2	2.3	2.2
Interest	3.6	0.9	1.5	1.0	1.7	4.4	4.7	2.5	3.3
Subsidies and transfers	4.7	3.4	2.6	2.6	3.4	7.2	5.1	4.1	7.6
Capital expenditures	1.6	4.3	3.3	3.8	5.5	16.7	3.6	5.5	3.8
Net lending	0.0	0.0	0.0	0.0	1.4	0.1	—	0.3	0.5
Sample size[5]	—	—	—	—	—	—	—	7	17

	Income groups					
	All	High-income	High-income non-OECD	Upper-middle income	Lower-middle income	Low-income
Total expenditure and net lending	29.2	34.0	36.2	32.1	25.7	24.9
Current expenditure	24.9	32.2	31.3	28.2	21.5	18.2
Goods and services	10.4	8.5	15.8	10.1	10.3	11.1
Wages and salaries	5.9	4.3	9.1	6.3	6.0	5.8
Other goods and services	4.4	4.1	6.7	3.7	4.3	5.2
Interest	3.6	3.8	3.2	3.6	3.6	3.3

Subsidies and transfers	11.2	19.8	12.3	14.1	7.7	4.5
Capital expenditures	4.3	2.0	4.2	3.8	4.4	6.7
Net lending	0.2	0.5	0.0	0.1	−0.2	0.4
Sample size[5]	79	15	4	19	24	17

	HIPCs			PRGF program/ eligible countries[4]
	All[2]	Completion Point[3]	Decision Point	
Total expenditure and net lending	25.0	23.5	26.5	25.7
Current expenditure	15.6	14.2	16.0	17.2
Goods and services	8.5	7.0	8.1	9.0
Wages and salaries	5.9	5.8	5.4	5.7
Other goods and services	2.7	1.3	2.7	3.3
Interest	2.8	0.9	3.4	2.7
Subsidies and transfers	2.2	3.1	2.5	3.5
expenditures	8.9	9.1	10.0	8.1
Net lending	0.3	0.1	0.3	0.3
Sample size[5]	35	5	21	45

Notes

[1] Latest year is mostly 1999 or 2000. For the Central American countries, latest year is 2000, except Panamá for which the latest year is 1999.

[2] Classified under lower-middle income group.

[3] Classified under low-income group.

[4] Classified under upper-middle income group.

[5] Refers to the sample of size of countries with data on total government spending. Sample size varies across expenditure categories. The components may therefore not sum to the total.

Source: GFS database; national authorities; and IMF staff estimates.

valid whether wages are expressed as a fraction of total central government spending or as a fraction of GDP. El Salvador and Honduras have the highest wage bill while Guatemala has the lowest one.[16] The two PRSP countries (Nicaragua and Honduras) spend more on transfers and subsidies than almost all other PRGF-eligible countries and all other HIPC countries.

On average, the current size of central government spending is low by international standards.[17] Over the 1990s, spending fell in some countries (Costa Rica, El Salvador, and Panamá), rose in others (Dominican Republic and Nicaragua) and was somewhat stable in two countries (Guatemala and Honduras). Part of this nonuniformity is due to drastic changes between the first and second half of the decade. Spending fell in the first half of the decade for five out of seven countries; and rose substantially in the second half for Honduras, Nicaragua, and Guatemala as these countries began dealing with the aftermath of hurricanes.

A growing body of literature has shown that *quality of fiscal adjustment matters; especially that low government consumption promotes long-run growth*. The distortionary taxation or deficit spending that tend to accompany high consumption seem to be the primary reasons for the negative impact on growth (Barro and Sala-I-Martin, 1995). Some new research on low-income countries in the 1990s (Gupta *et al.*, 2002) has shown that a high wage bill, which forms a sizable part of government consumption in many countries, reduces growth while capital investment and spending on operations and maintenance boosts growth. Further evidence from the same study shows that initial fiscal conditions matter for growth and that the composition of spending affects the sustainability of fiscal adjustment.

High capital investment and high spending on other goods and services appear to go hand in hand. This is consistent with the fact that capital investment implies recurrent costs for operations and maintenance if investment is to be used effectively. However, this observation may need further scrutiny since part of operations and maintenance involves labor (e.g. fixing roofs, potholes in streets), which is typically classified under wages and salaries. Calculating recurrent cost implications of capital investment is a challenging task. The policy lesson from many other countries is that low quality of public investment is often traceable to current and past low levels of operations and maintenance. Too often countries embark on new investments without recognizing that higher operations and maintenance are needed to realize the potential returns for the initial investment.

Investment in education and health

Investment in human capital is an important prerequisite for economic growth and development. Within human capital investments, education and health are considered primary factors contributing to economic performance. Not only are education and health individually important, they are also interrelated both within and across generations. More educated individuals usually make healthier choices that lead to more prolonged and productive lives, while healthier individuals have an easier time acquiring more learning skills and higher education levels. These choices, among other things, can influence dynamics of income distribution and poverty.

Education can both accelerate economic growth and promote equity. With respect to growth, education not only raises productivity, ceteris paribus, it also facilitates the development and adoption of new technologies. With respect to equity, better access to education for a larger segment of the population gives more people the opportunity to enjoy the benefits of productivity growth.

Investment in health also contributes to improved earnings capabilities. Improvement in health is considered both a central goal and an important outcome of development. The linkages among improvement in health status, poverty reduction and long-term economic growth are powerful. Especially in low-income countries, the burden of disease can represent a difficult barrier for economic growth (World Health Organization, 2001). From the perspective of an individual, good health increases productivity and, consequently, earnings.

Investment in health and education plays an important role in countries' PRSPs. For instance, Honduras' PRSP aims to strengthen 'the human capital of poor groups by improving access to basic education and health within a framework of equity and quality that would allow them to improve their employment opportunities and income.' The PRSP for Nicaragua also recognizes that investment in human capital will 'enhance ... productivity, income and welfare'.[18] Both PRSPs stress the need to expand access as well as improve quality of human capital. In Honduras, the PRSP even asserts that the crisis in the educational system is 'fundamentally a crisis of quality'. These PRSPs recognize that increased investment in health and education leads not only to higher income, but also to a higher quality of life. In addition, the benefits grow with each generation, as healthier, more educated families have wider reproductive choices, and opt to have fewer children and invest more in their education and health.

Provision of education

This section focuses on the provision of education in Central America. First, it summarizes some studies that quantify the impact of investments in education on economic performance. Second, it describes trends in average educational attainment in Central America and compares them with trends in other regions of the world. Finally, it analyzes indicators of the levels of resources invested in education across countries in the region and the outcomes these resources achieve.

Returns to investment in education

It is important to focus on education outcomes when analyzing the effectiveness of investment in education. The goal of education is not to ensure that students spend a particular number of years in classrooms, but rather that the right courses are taught and that students learn their lessons. For example, Hanushek and Kim (1995) find that labor force quality, measured through academic achievement in math and science, is strongly related to economic growth and has a larger effect than the more commonly used measure of average years of schooling. The problem is that it is much easier to measure, for instance, attendance rates than it is to measure academic performance.

An increase in education inputs is likely to lead to higher education outputs. In the United States, for instance, Card and Krueger (1996a and 1996b) find that differences in school resources between North and South Carolina help explain the earnings gap between blacks and whites in the two states.

An important issue in education policy, however, is how to assess the trade-off between the quality and quantity of inputs. Studies based on Texas schools have found that school characteristics can have powerful effects on academic achievement, *both* through teacher quality and smaller class sizes (Hanushek *et al.*, 1998). Krueger (2002), on the other hand, focuses primarily on the quantity of inputs, and estimates that a reduction in class size from 22 to 15 students in elementary schools in Tennessee has an internal rate of return of around 6 per cent. Also, students in small classes are likely to perform better on standardized tests at the eighth grade and are more likely to take college-entry exams.

The evidence on the quality vs. quantity debate is scarce for developing countries, but it seems to support the importance of both for earnings and academic achievement. Behrman and Birdsall (1983), using the average education of teachers as a proxy for quality, estimate returns to quality and quantity of educational inputs in Brazil and conclude that social return to quality even exceeds the social return to quantity. Case and Yogo (1999) find that reducing class size in South Africa can increase significantly returns to education for black men. They also find that schooling quality significantly affects educational attainment and probability of employment. Bedi and Marshall (1999) find that, for the case of Honduras, investment in teacher quality has a positive significant effect on student academic achievement, as do smaller class size and other classroom and school characteristics.

From almost any perspective, education is a good investment. Several studies have found a significant positive relationship between additional years of education and earnings. For instance, returns to education in Central America are 7 per cent at the primary level, 10 per cent at the secondary level, and 15 per cent at the tertiary level (Table 3.3). These estimates are very close to those of Latin America as a whole. The higher returns for higher levels of education can explain the large effect of education inequality on income inequality in Latin America (Inter-American Development Bank, 1998). However, it is important to remember that returns – both social and private – are difficult to measure. Moreover, the higher returns to higher levels of education are not generally found in OECD countries (see Table 3.3). An important issue to explore is whether the findings for Latin America stand up to closer scrutiny and, if they do, whether

Table 3.3 Returns to education for male workers (in percent)

	Latin American countries			
	Year	Primary	Secondary	Tertiary
Argentina	1999	5	8	17
Bolivia	1999	5	3	13
Brazil	1999	12	15	22
Chile	1998	7	12	24
Mexico	1998	7	10	15
Peru	2000	10	9	15
Uruguay	1998	9	9	15
	Central America			
Costa Rica	1998	6	6	19
Guatemala	1998	8	13	14
El Salvador	1998	5	8	20
Nicaragua	1998	9	13	15
Panamá	1999	6	8	16
Average Central America[1]		7	10	15
Average Latin America[1]		7	10	15
			Basic	Tertiary
Honduras[2]	1997	—	3	6
	OECD Countries			
	Year		Upper-secondary	Tertiary
United States	2000		16	15
Japan	2000		7	8
Germany	2000		11	9
France	2000		14	14
Italy	2000		11	7
United Kingdom	2000		15	19
Canada	2000		14	9
Denmark	2000		11	14
Netherlands	2000		8	12
Sweden	2000		6	11
Average OECD			11	12

Notes

[1] Excluding Honduras for primary and secondary education, and females.

[2] The estimates for Honduras are from Corbacho (2001), and include both males and females. The methdology and control variables may not be fully comparable to Duryea and Pages (2002).

Sources: Latin America: Duryea and Pages (2002) based on individual household surveys. Includes urban workers only. OECD Economic Outlook 70 (2001).

they reflect a relatively inefficient use of resources at lower levels of education.

Trends in educational attainment

Educational attainment is increasing in Central America. Progress was slow during the 1960s, accelerated between the 1970s and 1980s, and continued at a moderate pace during the 1990s. The average years of education in the adult population has doubled, from two and a half years in the 1960s to five years in 2000, and the percentage of population with no formal schooling has decreased from nearly 50 per cent in the 1960s to around 27 per cent in 2000 (Table 3.4).

Educational attainment in Central America still remains below the Latin American average despite the overall progress. The average level of education in Central America is one of the lowest in the world, after sub-Saharan Africa and South Asia. Also, other countries have been able to improve educational attainment at a much faster rate, even if starting from lower levels. For instance, the average years of education in South Korea and Singapore were lower than that of Costa Rica in the 1960s, but surpassed the level in Costa Rica during the 1980s (Barro and Lee, 2000).

Increase in the average educational attainment has been mostly achieved by promoting higher levels of education. The percentage of the population with complete primary education has remained fairly constant since the 1960s, while the percentage of the population with higher education has increased more than eight times. Among developing countries, Central America has currently the largest share of population with complete post-secondary schooling. Central America exhibits a polarized distribution of education, with a relatively low age of population with complete secondary education, but relatively large shares at initial and high levels of education (see Table 3.4).

Educational attainment is highly correlated with income in the region. Average attainment in Panamá exceeds the Latin American average by over two years. The Panamá case is followed by Costa Rica and Dominican Republic, and then El Salvador, Nicaragua, Honduras, and Guatemala. Costa Rica, in turn, has the lowest percentage of population in the region without any formal education (Table 3.5).

Gender discrepancies have generally declined in Central America. This is in line with the experience of the Latin American region as

Table 3.4 Educational attainment in Central America and other regions

	No schooling	Highest level attained (Percentage of the population aged 25 and over)						Average years of schooling
		First level		Second level		Post-secondary		
		Total	Complete	Total	Complete	Total	Complete	
Central America								
1960	48.6	44.1	12.5	5.9	1.9	1.5	1.0	2.5
1970	46.3	43.1	9.0	8.1	3.0	2.5	1.7	2.7
1980	36.7	48.4	12.3	10.1	4.2	4.8	3.3	3.5
1990	30.8	47.1	12.2	13.0	5.9	9.0	6.1	4.4
1995	28.3	47.8	12.3	13.5	6.0	10.5	7.2	4.7
2000	26.6	47.3	12.2	14.0	6.1	12.1	8.2	5.0
Latin America and the Caribbean								
1960	38.7	49.3	13.1	10.0	3.8	2.0	1.3	3.1
1970	35.7	50.9	17.4	10.9	4.5	2.6	1.7	3.5
1980	28.4	53.2	13.4	12.9	5.4	5.5	3.6	4.1
1990	20.6	53.9	15.5	16.6	7.0	8.9	5.8	5.0
1995	19.2	51.8	14.8	18.4	7.8	10.5	6.9	5.4
2000	17.7	50.6	14.4	19.9	8.4	11.8	7.7	5.7
All developing								
1960	68.0	26.2	8.3	5.1	1.9	0.8	0.5	1.8
1970	62.1	29.3	10.5	6.9	2.8	1.7	1.2	2.3
1980	55.7	28.0	8.6	13.0	5.3	3.2	2.2	3.1
1990	46.9	31.5	11.2	16.3	7.3	5.3	3.6	4.0
1995	41.8	33.5	11.9	18.3	8.2	6.3	4.3	4.5
2000	37.2	35.9	12.8	19.7	8.8	7.2	4.9	4.9
Advanced countries								
1960	6.5	53.6	31.5	32.2	13.4	7.5	4.3	7.0
1970	5.1	50.6	32.1	34.4	15.9	9.9	5.7	7.5
1980	5.3	35.1	17.9	43.2	24.4	16.4	9.4	8.7
1990	4.2	31.2	15.9	40.5	19.1	24.0	13.9	9.3
1995	4.0	28.7	14.9	41.4	19.4	25.9	15.0	9.6
2000	4.1	27.4	14.4	39.4	18.4	29.1	16.8	9.8
Middle East and North Africa								
2000	32.0	29.6	10.2	29.5	10.2	8.8	3.4	5.4
Sub-Saharan Africa								
2000	42.8	38.1	8.3	17.0	2.5	2.2	0.9	3.5
East Asia and Pacific								
2000	19.8	35.8	18.1	32.7	14.8	11.7	5.0	6.7
South Asia								
2000	45.2	28.2	10.0	22.9	7.0	3.7	2.0	4.6
Transitional Economies								
2000	2.2	32.4	20.2	51.6	17.4	13.9	9.4	9.7

Source: Barro and Lee (2000).

Table 3.5 Trends in educational attainment in Central American countries

	No schooling	Highest level attained (Percentage of the population aged 25 and over)						Average years of schooling
		First level		Second level		Post-secondary		
		Total	Complete	Total	Complete	Total	Complete	
Central America								
1960	48.6	44.1	12.5	5.9	1.9	1.5	1.0	2.5
1970	46.3	43.1	9.0	8.1	3.0	2.5	1.7	2.7
1980	36.7	48.4	12.3	10.1	4.2	4.8	3.3	3.5
1990	30.8	47.1	12.2	13.0	5.9	9.0	6.1	4.4
2000	26.6	47.3	12.2	14.0	6.1	12.1	8.2	5.0
Costa Rica								
1960	17.7	72.8	21.0	6.8	2.4	2.7	1.8	3.9
1970	20.6	68.7	12.1	7.6	2.9	3.1	2.1	3.6
1980	14.5	66.8	16.0	10.3	4.4	8.4	5.7	4.7
1990	10.8	62.2	14.0	13.2	5.5	13.8	9.4	5.6
2000	9.4	60.7	13.6	11.3	4.7	18.6	12.7	6.0
Dominican Republic								
1960	43.4	53.1	13.8	2.7	0.7	0.8	0.5	2.4
1970	40.1	45.9	4.3	12.1	2.5	1.9	1.3	2.9
1980	35.7	50.5	10.2	9.5	2.9	4.3	2.9	3.4
1990	28.8	51.0	11.2	11.2	4.0	9.0	6.1	4.3
2000	25.7	46.8	10.3	13.1	4.7	14.5	9.8	5.2
El Salvador								
1960	61.8	33.2	5.1	4.6	2.0	0.5	0.3	1.7
1970	54.2	37.9	8.0	6.0	2.5	1.9	1.3	2.3
1980	36.0	52.0	11.5	8.7	3.6	3.3	2.2	3.3
1990	37.1	45.9	10.2	9.8	4.0	6.3	4.3	3.6
2000	35.0	45.6	10.1	8.8	3.7	10.6	7.2	4.5
Guatemala								
1960	69.2	26.7	7.2	3.6	1.0	0.5	0.3	1.4
1970	68.4	26.9	6.2	3.7	1.1	1.0	0.7	1.5
1980	54.7	35.7	8.0	7.4	2.2	2.2	1.5	2.3
1990	52.9	35.9	8.0	6.7	2.0	4.4	3.0	2.6
2000	47.1	37.6	8.3	9.5	2.8	5.8	4.0	3.1
Honduras								
1960	60.9	34.9	6.9	3.5	1.6	0.6	0.4	1.7
1970	61.9	34.2	7.9	3.1	1.8	0.9	0.6	1.7
1980	49.0	44.4	8.6	4.8	2.8	1.8	1.2	2.3
1990	31.9	52.6	11.5	11.0	6.3	4.5	3.1	3.7
2000	25.9	57.0	12.4	10.6	6.0	6.5	4.4	4.1
Nicaragua								
1960	59.0	33.7	9.1	4.7	1.4	2.5	1.7	2.1
1970	53.9	34.6	7.9	6.9	2.0	4.5	3.1	2.6
1980	48.9	39.1	8.7	6.5	1.9	5.6	3.8	2.9

Table 3.5 Continued

	No schooling	Highest level attained (Percentage of the population aged 25 and over)						Average years of schooling
		First level		Second level		Post-secondary		
		Total	Complete	Total	Complete	Total	Complete	
1990	41.3	40.6	9.0	10.2	3.0	7.9	5.4	3.6
2000	31.7	43.0	9.5	16.5	4.8	8.9	6.0	4.4
Panamá								
1960	28.0	54.1	24.4	15.4	4.1	2.6	1.8	4.3
1970	24.9	53.5	16.4	17.4	8.4	4.2	2.9	4.6
1980	18.3	50.3	23.2	23.2	11.5	8.3	5.7	5.9
1990	12.9	41.6	21.6	28.7	16.2	16.8	11.4	7.3
2000	11.4	40.4	21.0	28.5	16.1	19.8	13.5	7.9

Source: Barro and Lee (2000).

a whole. Despite the regional progress, gender inequality in education still remains large in Guatemala (Barro and Lee, 2000).

Indicators of the quality and quantity of education inputs

In this section we analyze widely used measures of inputs into the education system and the efficiency with which they are used, including government resources devoted to education, their allocation among levels of education, measures of teacher quality and preparation, teacher–student ratios and time devoted to schooling. However, caution should be taken when making country and regional comparisons, as definitions and coverage may vary.

Improvement in many of the indicators will improve educational outcomes. What is not known, however, is what the trade-offs are and how these trade-offs vary among countries. These are the difficult policy choices that will require much more – and country specific – data to evaluate.

Taken as a whole, the available indicators of input quality and quantity in Central America do not present a promising picture. Lack of resources and inefficiency are reflected in large dropout and repeater rates. For instance, in 1990, repeater rates in primary education in Central America were 11.6 per cent, above the Latin American average of 10.5 per cent. In fact, Central America has the largest repeater rate in primary education after sub-Saharan Africa (Barro and Lee, 1996).

Dropout rates in primary school in Central America are also large, over 55 per cent, well above the Latin American average of 37 per cent. Dropout rates have even increased since the 1980s (Table 3.6).

Government spending on education

As a share of GDP, government spending on education in Central America is slightly below the rest of Latin America. From 1990 to 1996, spending in Central America averaged less than 3 per cent of GDP; for Latin America as a whole, spending averaged slightly more than 3 per cent of GDP. Within Central America, spending ranged from 1.6 per cent of GDP in Guatemala to 5.2 per cent in Panamá in 1996 (Table 3.7). In the mid-1990s, all countries allocated over 90 per cent of total education expenditures to current spending, with the exception of Nicaragua that allocated over 80 per cent (World Development Indicators, 2002).

Based on simple calculations, the efficiency of public education spending in Central America appears to be somewhat lower than the average for developing countries. Figure 3.1 plots the illiteracy rate against primary school spending per student, controlling for GDP per capita.[19] The objective is to analyze the extent to which additional spending per student will lead to higher achievement, over and above the effect of higher income and all the other socioeconomic variables correlated with it. Regression results for a selected group of developing countries suggest that primary school spending per student and GDP per capita explains almost 70 per cent of the variation in illiteracy, and both independent variables are statistically significant. This is promising, since illiteracy is a true output indicator – enrollment only places the student in school, it does not guarantee educational attainment. The regression estimates that a 1 per cent increase in spending reduces illiteracy by almost 1 per cent. Again this is promising, although it is impossible to assess cost efficiency without knowing the other effects of increases in education spending.

While this regression is indicative at best, it does imply that efficiency is lower in Central America than in the other developing countries in the sample, because illiteracy is higher than would be predicted by the regression in Costa Rica, the Dominican Republic, El Salvador, Guatemala, and Nicaragua (the other two Central

Table 3.6 Drop-out and repetition rates in primary education

Year	Costa Rica	Dominican Republic	El Salvador	Guatemala	Honduras	Nicaragua	Panamá	Central America	Latin America
				Repetition rate in primary education					
1970	10.0	22.0	16.0	16.0	—	13.0	15.0	15.3	14.7
1980	8.0	18.0	9.0	15.0	16.0	17.0	13.0	13.7	12.3
1990	11.0	—	8.0	—	12.0	17.0	10.0	11.6	10.5
				Drop-out rate in primary education					
1970	29.2	65.0	76.1	69.2	63.3	70.0	14.5	55.3	37.9
1980	25.1	65.0	40.3	58.7	63.3	62.5	27.2	48.9	34.6
1990	21.0	86.0	76.0	64.0	66.0	59.0	21.0	56.1	37.0

Source: Barro and Lee (1996).

Table 3.7 Government education spending (as a per cent of GDP)

Year	Costa Rica	Dominican Republic	El Salvador	Guatemala	Honduras	Nicaragua	Panamá	Central America	Latin America
1985	4.1	1.5	—	1.5	4.0	—	4.4	—	3.1
1986	4.5	1.3	—	1.6	4.5	—	4.3	—	3.2
1987	4.2	—	—	1.8	4.5	—	4.9	—	3.2
1988	4.1	—	—	1.8	—	—	5.1	—	3.0
1989	4.1	—	2.0	1.8	4.0	—	5.1	—	2.8
1990	4.4	—	1.9	1.4	—	3.4	4.7	—	2.8
1991	3.4	—	1.8	1.3	3.8	3.4	4.6	3.1	3.0
1992	3.3	1.3	1.9	1.4	—	3.1	5.0	3.0	3.1
1993	3.5	1.6	1.8	1.5	—	2.8	4.7	2.7	2.9
1994	3.5	1.9	2.0	1.5	3.4	2.8	4.5	2.8	3.3
1995	3.5	1.9	2.2	1.7	3.6	3.1	5.0	3.0	3.3
1996	4.1	1.9	2.3	1.6	—	3.2	5.2	3.0	3.3
1997	—	2.2	2.5	—	—	3.7	5.0	—	—
1998	6.0	—	—	2.0	4.0	4.2	—	—	—

Source: World Development Indicators (2002).

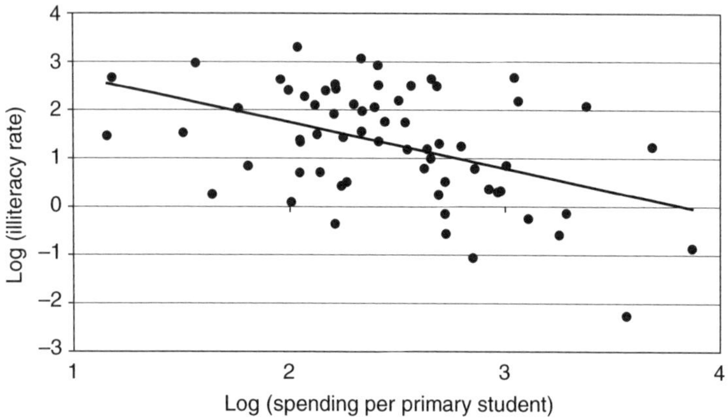

Figure 3.1 Relationship between illiteracy rate and spending on education

American countries were not in the regression sample). These findings are in line with those of Gupta *et al.* (1997). They find that government education spending is relatively efficient in Latin America but that performance of Latin America compared to Asia declined in the 1990s. Within the Latin American region, Guatemala, Honduras, and Nicaragua are found to be relatively inefficient. When looking at the sub-sample of higher-income countries, Costa Rica appears as relatively inefficient, compared to Argentina, Colombia, and México.

Data on the allocation of expenditures between levels of education is scarce. The existing data for the mid-1990s suggests that there is a strong bias towards higher education, particularly in Guatemala and Honduras. For example, in the mid-1990s, public spending per student in Honduras was eight times higher in tertiary education than in primary education, and nearly six times higher in Guatemala (Table 3.8).

Studies have found that increased spending on primary and secondary education promotes schooling enrollment. Gupta *et al.* (2002) find that a 5 percentage points increase in the share of education spending devoted to primary and secondary education increases gross secondary enrollment by over 1 percentage point. However, the authors stress that increasing attainment through reallocations alone can be difficult, as it is also necessary to improve other key determinants of educational outcomes.

Table 3.8 Current government education spending per student by level (as a ratio of spending in pre-primary and primary education)

	1970	1975	1980	1985	1991	1995	1996
Costa Rica							
Secondary	2.2	2.0	2.1	2.2	2.1	1.9	1.9
Tertiary	4.7	—	6.2	7.4	5.9	—	—
Dominican Republic							
Secondary	2.7	—	—	1.2	—	—	1.2
Tertiary	16.8	—	—	4.6	—	—	2.3
El Salvador							
Secondary	1.2	1.8	1.2	—	—	0.8	—
Tertiary	20.8	11.7	12.0	—	—	1.2	—
Guatemala							
Secondary	2.0	—	2.2	—	1.7	0.9	0.9
Tertiary	7.7	—	—	—	—	5.5	—
Honduras							
Secondary	2.4	—	1.4	1.5	1.8	—	—
Tertiary	—	—	7.7	9.6	8.1	8.1	—
Nicaragua							
Secondary	—	—	1.2	1.7	—	0.7	—
Tertiary	—	—	4.8	10.8	—	—	—
Panamá							
Secondary	2.2	1.6	1.0	1.3	1.2	1.2	1.2
Tertiary	8.1	4.3	2.6	3.5	3.7	4.1	4.2

Sources: UNESCO statistics (2002), available via the Internet: http://www.unesco.org; World Development Indicators (2002); and IMF staff estimates.

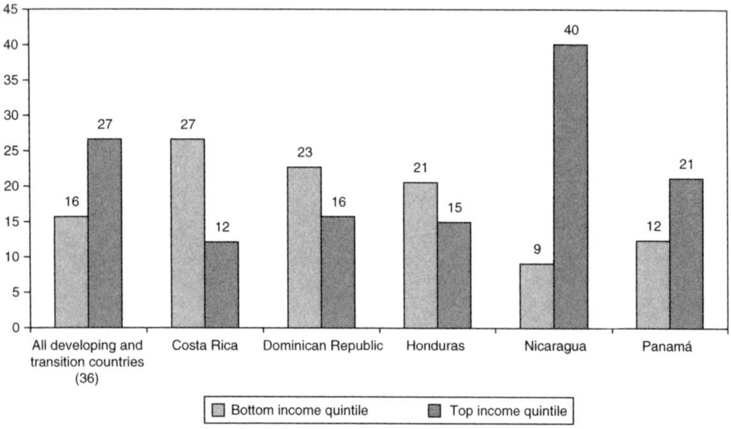

Figure 3.2 Benefit incidence of public spending on education, 1990s (in per cent of total spending)

Available evidence shows that education spending is well targeted towards the poor in only three countries. The limited studies of benefit incidence of education spending show that the poorest 20 per cent of income distribution in Costa Rica, the Dominican Republic, and Honduras benefit more than the richest 20 per cent, while in Nicaragua and Panamá the rich capture more of the benefits than the poor (Figure 3.2). Nicaragua's situation is rather extreme whereby 40 per cent of benefits are captured by the top 20 per cent as compared with 9 per cent by the bottom 20 per cent. In general, tertiary education seems to benefit primarily the well-to-do (Chu *et al.*, 2000), which is consistent with trends in educational attainment for higher education in the region.

Teacher salaries and teacher quality

Teacher quality has been identified as a key input in student learning. For instance, studies for the United States show that 40 per cent of the variance in test scores in reading and mathematics in schools in Texas was explained by the qualification of teachers. Similar results have been found in Alabama, New York City, Michigan, Georgia, and Virginia. For the case of Honduras, Bedi, and Marshall (1999) find that improvements in teacher quality have a significant effect on student achievement tests.

Teacher wages in Central America are high by regional standards. For instance in 1990, the average real salary of primary school teachers was four times GDP per capita in Central America, compared to 2.6 times GDP per capita in Latin America (Table 3.9). The average ratio in Central America is also higher than the average of 3.6 for all developing countries (Barro and Lee, 1996), and has increased consistently since the 1960s. Within the Central American region, Nicaragua and Honduras exhibit the largest ratio of primary school teacher wages to GDP per capita.

Higher wages need not guarantee higher quality. Evaluating the relationship among pay, quality, and performance is problematic at best. Hanushek, Kain, and Rivkin (1999), using data from the UTD Texas School Project, find that salaries are only weakly related to performance on teacher certification tests, but teacher certification tests are not related to student achievement. The study does find a relationship between teacher salaries and students' math and reading performance, but only for existing experienced teachers. For northeast Brazil, Harbison and Hanushek (1992) conclude that teacher wages are not significantly related to education outputs. Gupta *et al.* (1997) find a negative significant relationship between efficiency of education spending and relative government wages. Consequently, countries with relatively higher teacher wages incur larger costs, but may not achieve significantly higher educational attainment than countries with relatively lower teacher wages.

Compensation of school teachers in the region is higher than compensation for workers with similar characteristics in other professions. This is the finding of a recent study of 12 Latin American countries (including Costa Rica, El Salvador, Honduras, and Panamá. Using household survey data, Liang (1999) finds that teachers are paid less than nonteachers when not controlling for work time. However, teachers work significantly less than others, about 15 hours per week.[20] When controlling for work and vacation time, wages for teachers are actually higher than for workers with similar characteristics in 11 out of the 12 cases under study. Also, disparities in teacher pay are lower than in other professions and rural teachers are paid on average 10 to 30 per cent less than urban teachers. Within Central America, teachers in Honduras earn 44 per cent more per hour worked than nonteachers.

Table 3.9 Trends in quality indicators in the education sector

Year	Costa Rica	Dominican Republic	El Salvador	Guatemala	Honduras	Nicaragua	Panamá	Central America	Latin America
				Student–teacher ratio in primary education					
1960	25.9	57.7	37.0	30.5	31.8	35.3	28.5	35.2	37.0
1970	29.8	55.4	37.4	36.0	35.3	37.3	27.1	36.9	36.0
1980	27.7	50.0	48.0	33.8	36.7	35.3	27.3	37.0	31.0
1990	31.9	47.1	42.2	34.0	38.1	33.3	23.0	35.7	28.0
				Student–teacher ratio in secondary education					
1960	21.5	16.3	14.9	6.8	9.7	12.6	22.9	15.0	17.0
1970	16.5	25.6	25.0	13.8	14.2	26.0	20.7	20.3	19.0
1980	19.0	—	23.7	17.9	28.4	33.1	21.0	23.8	21.0
1990	19.0	—	28.2	14.2	22.8	34.7	20.1	23.2	19.0
				Ratio of real salary of primary education teachers over real GDP per capita					
1960	2.6	2.5	—	3.0	3.4	2.5	3.5	2.9	2.6
1970	3.8	3.0	4.4	3.3	4.2	3.7	2.5	3.6	2.9
1980	2.1	1.2	—	1.5	2.9	2.6	2.5	2.1	2.1
1990	3.7	—	—	—	4.0	5.7	2.6	4.0	2.6

Source: Barro and Lee (1996).

This premium is 38 per cent in Costa Rica, 37 per cent in El Salvador, and 33 per cent in Panamá. In addition, public school teachers are paid more than private ones in El Salvador, Honduras, and Panamá (the opposite occurs in South America). The disparities in pay are 46 per cent, 20 per cent, and 28 per cent, respectively (Liang, 1999).

The level of training for teachers varies significantly among the countries in Central America. Teachers in Costa Rica, El Salvador, and Panamá all receive tertiary education. On the other hand, teachers in Guatemala, Honduras, and Nicaragua are trained in normal schools, which are similar to secondary schools. Close to one third of teachers in Nicaragua are uncertified. The percentage of uncertified teachers in the other countries is less significant (Alvarez and Majmudar, 2001).

Student–teacher ratios and schooling time

Student–teacher ratios in primary and secondary education in Central America are above Latin American averages. These ratios have increased since the 1960s (Table 3.9). It is not surprising that Panamá and Costa Rica have the lowest student–teacher ratios. On the other hand, the historically low student–teacher ratios in secondary schools in Guatemala and Honduras warrant additional analysis. The important question, however, is whether reductions in the generally high student–teacher ratios would put to best use the resources in Central America.

In the majority of Latin American countries, schooling time in primary education is low, both in terms of days and hours per year. Additionally, a large share of the already low schooling time is spent on administrative duties and disciplinary actions and less to curriculum teaching per se. This affects low-income children in particular, who cannot compensate these shortages with family inputs (Martinic, 1998).

Scheduled schooling time in Central America, however, is higher than in Latin America as a whole. However, teacher union conflicts and strikes severely diminish the effective number of school days students have. For instance in 2001, teachers were on strike for two months in Honduras, in response to a dispute over wages with the central government.

Provision of health services

This section describes the current status and recent trends in the provision of health services in Central America. First, it summarizes some studies that quantify the impact of investments in health on economic performance, second, it describes trends in health status in Central America and compares them with trends in other regions of the world, and finally analyzes health quality indicators, including the effectiveness of public health spending.

Returns to investment in health

Aside from their – arguably more important – effect on general quality of life, investments in health care can increase human capital and enhance productivity. Studies have found that health has a positive impact on earnings, although the magnitude of the effect depends on the health measure, the particular sample and the estimation method used in the analysis.[21] These studies show that public health services and community characteristics, as well as private health inputs and reduced exposure to disease, are associated positively with the health of adults and with greater income-generating capacity (Savedoff and Schultz, 2000). Although case-studies are scarce for Central America, Espinosa and Hernández (2000) conclude that better housing conditions and the availability of community and health services have a significant effect on health status in Nicaragua. Furthermore, better health status is associated with higher hourly income, on average. The point estimates in this study are much larger than in studies of higher-income countries (Savedoff and Schultz, 2000), suggesting that investments in health may be even more valuable in developing countries.

Trends in health status

Using health as a measure of progress suggests Central America has developed quite fast. Life expectancy at birth in the region has increased from an average of 54 years in the 1960s to nearly 70 years in the 1990s (Table 3.10). Reductions in infant and child mortality rates have played an important role in this increase. Improvements in health status in Central America have even been faster than for Latin America as a whole. Part of the explanation may reside in that investment in girls' education has been relatively large compared to other developing regions, and women's educational attainment has been shown to be an important contributing factor to improved health status (Savedoff and Schultz, 2000). Fast progress in health status is not surprising, given the relative ease of adopting advances from developed countries.

Table 3.10 Trends in health status[1]

Year	Costa Rica	Dominican Republic	El Salvador	Guatemala	Honduras	Nicaragua	Panamá	Central America	Latin America
				Infant mortality rate (in per cent)					
1960	67.5	113.7	119.2	122.9	130.5	126.2	59.8	105.7	97.5
1970	39.8	91.1	101.5	98.9	96.3	96.4	40.7	80.7	75.8
1980	17.4	65.9	69.6	74.2	62.5	75.0	29.7	56.3	53.5
1990	13.3	42.6	36.5	46.7	41.6	42.0	23.0	35.1	34.8
1999	12.4	38.9	30.1	40.2	34.4	34.3	20.2	30.1	30.0
				Child mortality rate (in per cent)					
1960	112.0	149.0	210.0	202.0	204.0	209.0	104.0	170.0	154.1
1970	77.0	111.5	160.0	168.0	170.0	168.0	71.0	132.2	123.5
1980	29.0	77.7	120.0	109.7	103.0	143.0	36.0	88.3	79.9
1990	14.9	50.9	43.0	59.0	54.4	52.3	25.4	42.8	42.8
1999	14.0	46.8	36.0	52.0	46.0	43.0	25.0	37.5	38.0
				Life expectancy at birth (in years)					
1960	63.8	54.5	53.4	48.0	48.9	49.6	62.6	54.4	57.9
1970	69.0	60.4	57.6	54.2	55.2	55.8	67.3	59.9	62.1
1980	73.9	63.6	59.6	58.6	62.7	60.4	71.0	64.3	66.0
1990	76.1	67.2	68.0	63.3	68.5	66.9	73.4	69.1	69.0
1999	76.8	67.3	69.5	64.9	69.8	68.6	73.9	70.1	69.8

Notes: [1] Average for the available years in each decade.

Sources: World Development Indicators (2002); and Fund staff estimates.

For instance, life expectancies were much higher in Central America in 1990 than in the developed world just 20 to 30 years earlier.

There are still marked disparities in health status across Central America. Costa Rica has health status indicators that are comparable or better than some developed countries. Panamá also has very good health indicators. On the other hand, health development in other countries is still lagging, particularly in the cases of Guatemala, Nicaragua, and Honduras. It should be noted, however, that even the lagging countries have made important progress in improving health outcomes over time.

There are important differences in the health status of the poor versus the nonpoor in the region. For example in Nicaragua and the Dominican Republic, infant mortality rates have been reported to be over 20 percentage points higher among poor households versus rich households. In Guatemala, mortality rates for the poor are over 10 percentage points above the rates for the nonpoor (Table 3.11). In Nicaragua, there is evidence that poor children exhibit larger malnourishment rates than the nonpoor and report illness with 50 per cent greater frequency (Nicaragua's PRSP). These discrepancies are lower than the Latin American average and highlight the importance of improved health infrastructure – for example, sanitation and clean water – and nutrition on health. It is relatively easy to immunize poor children against, say, measles, and diphtheria. It is much more difficult to ensure that they have adequate nutrition or access to clean water. Moreover, spending on improvements in these areas, which may have

Table 3.11 Infant mortality rates by income quintile

	Guatemala	**Nicaragua**	**Dominican Republic**	**Latin America**[1]
Poorest	56.9	50.7	66.7	68.9
Second	79.7	53.7	54.5	59.4
Middle	55.7	45.7	52.3	50.6
Fourth	46.7	40.2	33.5	40.7
Richest	35.0	25.8	23.4	29.3

Note: [1]Includes statistics for Bolivia, Brazil, Colombia, Haiti, Paraguay, Peru, Guatemala, Nicaragua, and Dominican Republic.

Sources: D. R. Gwatin, S. Rustein, K. Johnson, R. P. Pande, and A. Wagstaff for the Health, Nutrition, and Poverty/Poverty Thematic Group of the World Bank.

the highest return in terms of health improvement, does not show up as health spending in national accounts.

Health status in rural areas is worse than in urban areas. For instance in Guatemala, infant mortality per 1000 live births is only 18 in urban areas but rises to 29 in rural areas and 32 among indigenous populations. Similar trends have been documented for other Latin American countries (Savedoff and Schultz, 2000). In Honduras, in addition to poorer infrastructure and lower income, there are evident deficiencies in medical attention in rural areas, due to lack of both medical supplies and doctors, as there are no incentives to work in the more remote areas (Honduras' PRSP). Wang (2001), in a study including the Dominican Republic, El Salvador, Guatemala, and Nicaragua, concludes that factors affecting child mortality rates differ between urban and rural areas. In urban areas, access to electricity has been singled out as a key determinant of health outcomes for children and infants. In rural areas, expanding vaccination is found to significantly reduce mortality rates.

Health quality indicators

Organization of health systems

Organization of health systems vary across the region. The first and most prevalent type of organization can be characterized as 'fragmented'. Formal sector workers and their families are covered by social security subsystems; health ministries provide services for the low income and middle classes; and the private sector provides services for the rich. Almost half of the population in the region is covered under this type of system, including Haiti, Suriname, Guyana, Paraguay, the Andean countries, and all Central American countries with the exception of Costa Rica. The second category is composed of 'integrated public systems', where the public system predominates. This category includes the English-speaking Caribbean countries and Costa Rica. The third category would be 'subcontractor systems', where the public sector plays a role in mobilizing resources but the private sector is mostly in charge of service delivery (Brazil). The fourth category is composed of 'intensive contracts use systems', characterized by the prominent role of the social security systems, including the systems in Uruguay and Argentina (Inter-American Development Bank, 1996).

Health systems in all Central American countries, with the exception of Costa Rica, are characterized by rigidity and fragmentation. The organization of the financing scheme makes resource allocation complicated, with detrimental effects on quality. The staff of medical facilities usually has limited capacity to decide the allocation of expenditures within the hospital and consequently there are important mismatches between needs and resources and an emphasis on curative over preventive health care.

Public facilities are of generally poor quality. For example in Nicaragua, studies by the Inter-American Development Bank and the World Bank found that health facilities were in generally bad conditions due to lack of maintenance, with over 70 per cent of health posts requiring rehabilitation. In El Salvador, users consistently complained about the low quality of public health posts and units, especially relative to higher levels of services from health centers and hospitals (Filmer *et al.*, 1997). In the Dominican Republic, the Inter-American Development Bank estimated that over 30 per cent of hospitals are underutilized (Inter-American Development Bank, 1996). Finally, there are large discrepancies between expenditures on personnel and the actual staff costs of treating patients and no accountability for performance or effective management (Filmer *et al.*, 1997). Contrary to these characteristics, the health system in Costa Rica is considered equitable and efficient (Inter-American Development Bank, 1996).

Medical staff is generally in excess supply in Central America. In the Dominican Republic, the workload has been reduced to three hours per day. In Nicaragua, doctors are required to serve very few hours. In Costa Rica, nearly 40 per cent of nurses of the public system can be on leave at the same time. Finally, the absenteeism rate among doctors is high in Panamá (Inter-American Development Bank, 1996).

Government spending on health

Health resource allocation involves complex trade-offs. The first trade-off is between the public provision of health services and other public or private uses of funds to maximize welfare. The second set of trade-offs involves allocating those resources dedicated to health care in a manner that improves the health of the population, protects people from financial catastrophe, and distributes health care and risk protection equitably. These are not simple trade-offs. Moreover,

Table 3.12 Government and private health expenditures

	Public Spending		Private Spending		Total
	Social security	Other	Insurance	Other	
Costa Rica	4.7	0.8	0.0	1.5	6.8
Dominican Republic	0.5	1.4	1.1	3.6	6.5
El Salvador	1.7	1.5	0.2	4.6	8.3
Guatamala	1.3	0.7	0.2	2.2	4.4
Honduras	0.6	3.0	0.2	2.3	6.4
Nicaragua	1.2	2.2	—	2.1	5.7
Panamá	3.2	2.0	0.5	1.8	7.5
Central America	1.9	1.7	0.3	2.6	6.5
Latin America	1.8	1.6	0.7	2.3	6.6

Source: World Health Organization (2001).

market imperfections, including information asymmetry, agency problems, moral hazard and entry barriers, make the allocation decisions even more difficult and may call for additional government intervention (Hsiao, 2000).

Central America as a region invests a relatively large share of GDP in health. In 1998, total expenditures on health averaged 6.5 per cent of GDP, roughly the same as Latin America as a whole. Of this, 3.6 per cent of GDP came from public resources – again similar to Latin America as a whole – and the remainder was financed privately (Table 3.12). Only Guatemala and the Dominican Republic allocated less than 3.2 per cent of GDP to public health spending.

The relationship between public health spending and health indicators is weaker than might be expected. Figure 3.3 plots infant and child mortality rates against government health spending per capita, again controlling for GDP per capita.[22] The regressions on which the figure is based explain more than 80 per cent of the variation in mortality rates. They indicate that a 1 per cent increase in government spending will decrease mortality by slightly more than one-tenth of a percent. More important – since it is impossible to assess without more information whether the effect on mortality along with other effects of higher spending would be cost effective – the coefficient on public spending is only roughly one-and-a-half times its standard error in each of the regressions.

Public health spending matters as health status of the poor is more sensitive to public spending than that of the rich. A study by Gupta *et al.*

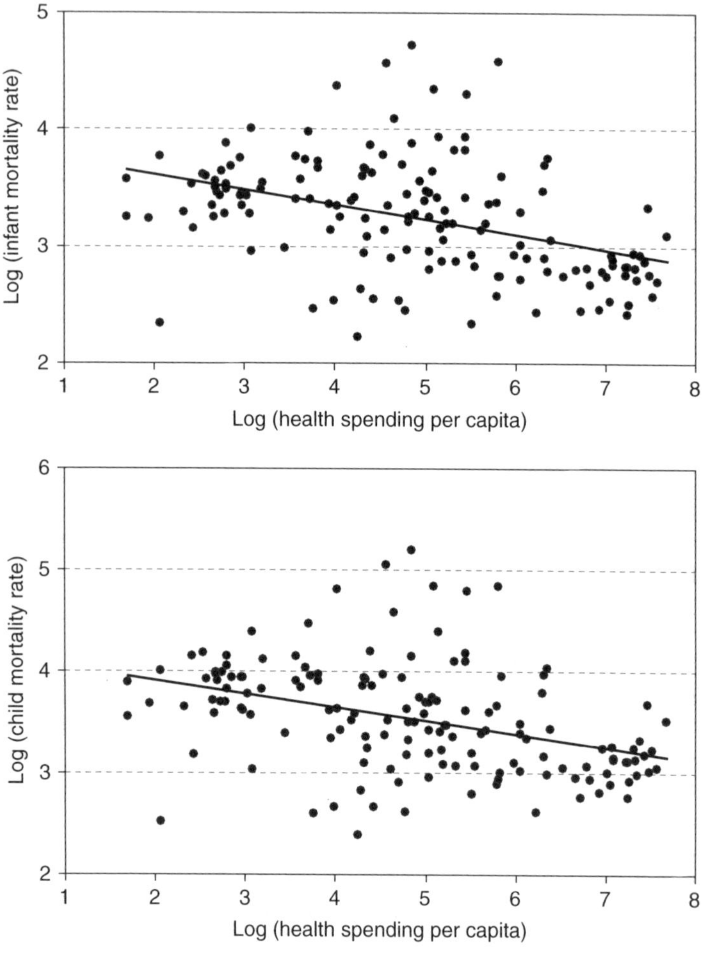

Figure 3.3 Relationship between mortality rates and government health spending

(2001), that includes all countries under the present analysis, finds that the poor have significantly worse health status than the nonpoor and that the poor are more strongly affected by public spending on health than the nonpoor. For child mortality rates, the authors find that a 1 per cent increase in public spending on health reduces child mortality by twice as many deaths among the poor.

Similar results were found for infant mortality rates. In addition, they find some evidence that the returns to public spending on health are higher among the poor regardless of the benefit incidence. Also, the relationship between public spending in health care and the health status of the poor is stronger among low-income countries.

Other quality characteristics

While quality indicators for health have generally improved in the region, marked differences still remain across countries. For example, the percentage of births attended by health staff is 97 per cent in Costa Rica, but only 35 per cent in Guatemala, and 51 per cent in Honduras. There has been a considerable improvement in immunization rates. For example, in the case of immunization against measles, all countries have reached rates over 90 per cent during the 1990s (Table 3.13). Immunization against illness, in turn, has been shown to be very effective for poverty reduction.

There is also evidence that the poor have less access to good quality health care. For example, in Nicaragua, the extremely poor must travel three times the distance to reach health facilities compared to nonpoor households. Poor children in Nicaragua, besides reporting greater frequency of illness, have half the access to doctors when sick compared to the nonpoor. Also, extremely poor women are half as likely as nonpoor women to be attended by doctors when giving birth (Nicaragua's PRSP).

Health spending is well targeted in three out of the four countries for which data are available. The limited studies of benefit incidence of health spending show that the poorest 20 per cent of income distribution in Costa Rica, Dominican Republic, and Honduras benefit more than the richest 20 per cent, while in Nicaragua the richest 20 per cent benefit more from health spending as was the case in the education sector (Figure 3.4). Much like the incidence of education spending, Nicaragua's incidence of health spending is rather extreme vis-à-vis other countries; 25 per cent of benefits are captured by the richest 20 per cent as compared with 10 per cent by the poorest 20 per cent.

Social safety nets

Economic downturns – and especially those that lead to financial crises – can result in increased poverty and unemployment and their attendant social problems. It is therefore crucial that countries design and

Table 3.13 Quality indicators in the health sector

Year	Costa Rica	Dominican Republic	El Salvador	Guatemala	Honduras	Nicaragua	Panamá	Central America	Latin America
			Percentage of births attended by health staff[1]						
1970	83.0	—	49.0	16.0	34.0	—	73.5	51.1	—
1980	97.0	81.0	69.0	40.3	46.0	41.0	84.0	65.5	—
1990	97.0	94.0	88.5	35.0	51.0	63.0	—	71.4	—
1998	—	—	90.0	—	—	65.0	—	—	—
			Immunization against measles (percentage of children under 12 months)						
1980	60.0	29.0	45.0	23.0	35.0	15.0	47.0	36.3	32.9
1985	81.0	54.0	71.0	23.0	53.0	49.0	83.0	59.1	56.0
1990	90.0	96.0	98.0	68.0	90.0	82.0	99.0	89.0	88.9
1995	94.0	96.0	93.0	83.0	89.0	81.0	84.0	88.6	87.8
1999	92.0	96.0	75.0	93.0	98.0	97.0	90.0	91.6	91.5

Note: [1] Average for the available years in each decade.

Sources: World Development Indicators (2002); and Fund staff estimates.

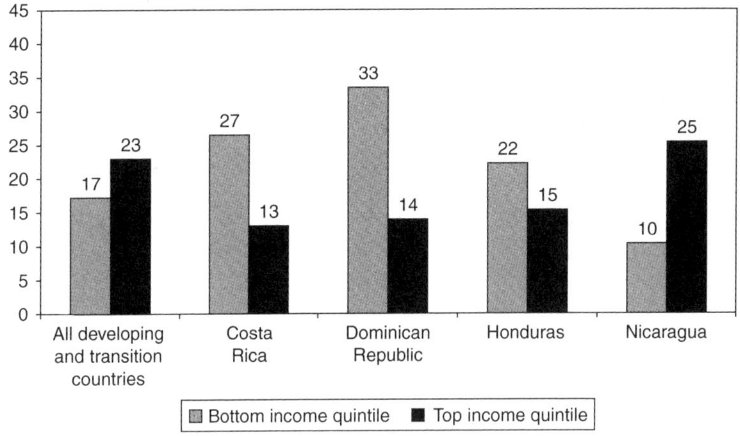

Figure 3.4 Benefit incidence of public spending on health, 1990s[1] (in per cent of total spending)

Note: [1] Data are for the 1990s except for the Dominican Republic (1989).

implement social safety nets to respond to economic crises. Social safety nets should address the needs of the most vulnerable groups and be flexible enough to adapt to specific characteristics of adverse economic shocks. In this sense, pre-crisis planning and evaluation are essential to provide reliable and timely information on vulnerable groups and on the relative effectiveness of alternative social programs in reaching the poor.

A wide range of available instruments can be used to assist the poor in the event of an economic crisis. Instruments for managing adverse shocks can be classified in three categories (Inter-American Development Bank, 2000). First, there are market-based arrangements such as financial intermediaries and insurance companies, allowing households to smooth income and consumption over time. Second, the government provides public insurance to protect against unemployment and illness and safety nets to focus on the special needs of the poor. Finally, there are informal self-insurance mechanisms arranged through extended families and social networks. Although informal safety nets play an important role in providing social protection for the poor, their effectiveness is limited and they are imperfect substitutes for formal safety nets. Major social safety nets may include: cash or in-kind transfers, price subsidies, public works, fee waivers for social services, feeding and nutrition programs, targeted human development, and microfinance programs, as well as social insurance targeted to the poor.

Effective social safety nets should provide appropriate protection for the poor, promote efficient targeting, and avoid counterproductive incentives. They should also be well managed, transparent, and operate within a sound fiscal and macroeconomic framework. The key objectives of a social protection program should be to: (1) guarantee a minimum consumption level and access to basic services, to prevent temporary poverty from becoming permanent; (2) strengthen the asset base of the poor to reduce their vulnerability to shocks and prevent the intergenerational transfer of poverty; (3) ensure continued investment in human capital; and (4) reduce the risk exposure of the poor (Inter-American Development Bank, 2000).

The design of safety nets should reflect the characteristics and location of poor populations and the administrative and implementation capacity of the government. Ideally, safety net instruments should be in place before a crisis occurs. When this is not possible, social safety nets should focus on those existing programs that can be easily targeted to the poor and adapted for increased utilization during adverse economic shocks. To improve the effectiveness of social safety nets, efforts should be coordinated among different ministries and levels of government, to reduce overlap and waste. In this sense, transparency and accountability are essential. Governments should make every effort to protect and even increase social spending and allocations for social safety nets in the event of a crisis.

Latin America does not have adequate prevention and compensation systems to reduce the effects of shocks on the poor (Inter-American Development Bank, 2000). In the absence of reforms that address the needs of the most vulnerable groups, macroeconomic shocks will continue to exacerbate poverty and inequality, and curtail growth.

Central American countries have a number of social safety net mechanisms in place. These can be grouped in three main categories: food and cash transfers, targeted human development programs and employment and infrastructure programs. Costa Rica, El Salvador, Honduras, Nicaragua and Panamá have at least one program in each category. Social safety nets in Dominican Republic, on the other hand, focus exclusively on food and cash transfers. Guatemala has a school feeding program and several infrastructure programs but no targeted human development programs (Table 3.14). Some existing programs are described in Box 3.1.

The high levels of poverty and inequality suggest that governments could do more in reaching and protecting the most vulnerable groups of society. In this sense, it is crucial that the existing programs have good evaluation mechanisms, so that governments identify and support those programs that are effective for poverty reduction and discontinue those that are ineffective. Clearly, better targeting of social safety nets and preventing leakage to nonpoor populations is crucial in this matter. The urban rural differences in access to basic infrastructure and the large size of the informal labor market present difficult challenges,[23] and governments should therefore put particular emphasis in reaching the rural poor. Also, social safety nets in Central America should not only aim at providing protection against adverse economic shocks, but also against natural disasters that occur in the region. As mentioned before, pre-crisis planning is essential.

Governance

Governance is an all-encompassing term with wide ranging implications for improving the performance of the public sector. Governance typically refers to 'traditions and institutions by which authority is exercised which tend to include (1) the process by which governments are selected, monitored and replaced; (2) the capacity of the government to effectively formulate and implement policies; and (3) the respect of citizens and the state for the institutions that govern economic and social interactions among them,' (Kaufmann *et al.*, 2002). This definition applies mostly to the public sector and has been used widely in the literature on governance. But the East Asian crisis of late 1990s and the collapse of large corporations (e.g. Enron in 2001) demonstrate that corporate governance does matter as well, and that part of promoting governance in the public sector is to provide appropriate regulation and oversight of the private sector.

Corruption is an obvious aspect of poor governance. Corruption is often defined as abuse of public office for private gains. Good governance requires not only that institutions exist to identify corruption, but also prosecute corrupt practices effectively.

Table 3.14 Social safety nets in Central America

Country	Food and cash transfers	Targeted human capital development programs and early childhood interventions	Employment and Infrastructure Programs
Costa Rica	*Cash Transfers*	*Targeted Human Development Programs*	*Employment Programs*
	Fondo de Desarrollo Social y de Asignaciones Familiares (FODESAP)	Programa Nacional de Lucha Contra la Pobreza (PNCP)	Programa Nacional de Generacion de Empleo
	Plan de Compensacion Social (PCS)		Pro Trabajo
			Incentivos para la Reinsercion Laboral y el Empleo Temporal (IRLET)
	Instituto Mixto de Ayuda Social (IMASI)	*Early Childhood Interventions* Childhood National Society (PANI)	Ideas Productivas
			Llave en Mano
			Intermediacion en el Mercado de Trabajo
			Training Programs
			Becas de Capacitacion para el Empleo
			Formacion Integral para Mujeres Jefas de Hogar
			Formacion y Reconversion para los Movilizados
			Talleres Publicos
			Formacion Profesional para el Desarrollo Socio Laboral de Personas con Discapacidad

Dominican Republic	*Cash Transfers* Transfer Program to Low Income Countries *School Feeding Programs* Operation Youth Quake		
El Salvador	*Cash Transfers* Family Gardens Program SNF *School Feeding Programs* School Lunch Program	*Early Childhood Interventions* Salud Materno-Infantil (SMI) Salud y Nutricion Materno-Infantil	*Employment Programs* CONARA/SRN, FEPADES *Social Investment Funds and Public Works* MOP, CONADES, DIGCO, MOA, MOL, BFA Fondo de Inversion Social (FIS) *Training Programs* INSAFORP
Guatemala	*School Feeding Programs* Programa Nacional de Alimento Escolar		*Social Investment Funds and Public Works* Fondo de Inversion Social (FIS) Fondo de Solidaridad para el Desarrollo Comunitario (FSDC)

Table 3.14 Continued

Country	Food and cash transfers	Targeted human capital development programs and early childhood interventions	Employment and Infrastructure Programs
			Fondo Nacional para la Paz (FONAPAZ) Programa de Asentamientos Urbanos y Vivienda Fondo del Desarrollo Indigena Guatemalteco (FODIGUA)
Honduras	*Cash Transfers* Junta Nacional de Bienestar Social (JNBS) *Food Subsidies* Suplidora Nacional de Productos Basicos	*Targeted Human Development Programs* Programa de Asignaciones Familiares (PRAF)	*Employment Programs* Programa de Apoyo al Sector Informal *Social Investment Funds and Public Works* Fondo Hondureňo de Inversion Social (FHIS) *Training Programs* Occupational Training Project (PFO)
Nicaragua	*Cash Transfers* Integrated Rural Development Projects Programas para el Desarrollo de la Poblacion	*Early Childhood Interventions* Fondo Nicaraguense de la Niňez y la Familia	*Employment Programs* Actividades Productivas PRONORTE

	Desplazada, Refugiada y Repatriada		PRODERE
	Food Subsidies		
	Basic Grains Program		*Social Investment Funds and Public Works*
			Proyectos de Impacto Rapido
	School Feeding Programs		PEC
	Early Morning Snack		Fondo de Inversion Social (FISE)
	School Lunch Program (FES)		
Panamá	*Food Subsidies*	*Early Childhood Interventions*	*Social Investment Funds and Public Works*
		Programa de Alimentacion Complementaria Materno Infantil	
	Programa Nacional de Alimento y Nutricion		Fondo de Emergencia Social (FES)
	School Feeding Programs		
	Meriendas Escolares		
	Almuerzos del Fondo de Emergencia Social		
	Nuevo Programa de Almuerzos Escolares		

Source: Inter-American Development Bank (2000).

Box 3.1 Safety net programs in Central America

Costa Rica: The program *Triángulo de Solidaridad* constitutes an innovative initiative that redefines the design and administration of social programs in the country. This initiative encourages investments in human development through the cooperation of communities, local governments, and state institutions. The specific objectives are to strengthen citizen participation in decision making for social development, protect programs that focus on human rights and gender equity, and promote governance. Projects are expected to solve urgent problems in health, education, and the productive sectors.

Honduras: The PRSP outlines the main objectives and strategy for the protection of the most vulnerable groups. Two large programs include the Honduras Family Allowance Program (PRAF) and the *Fondo Hondureño de Inversión Social* (FHIS). PRAF was introduced in 1990 as a cash transfer mechanism to protect incomes of the poor after the adjustment program initiated a year earlier. The program promotes human capital development. In order for families to receive the benefits, their children are required to attend schools and pregnant women must participate in pre- and post-natal care. The program also covers nutrition needs, and its coverage is fairly extensive. FHIS was put in place in response to the devastating effects of Hurricane Mitch. This fund proved to be highly valuable in directing emergency assistance to local villages (Wodon, 2000). Currently, FHIS is involved in the construction and improvement of schools and health centers, water and sanitation projects, and road and flood-control infrastructure development. Social funds should be flexible to modify its operations during a crisis, for instance by putting more emphasis on labor intensive projects and by having the fund involved in hard hit areas. In this sense, it is important that these labor-intensive projects are identified before a crisis hits.

El Salvador: El Salvador has several programs in place, including two programs on pre- and post-natal health care, several employment and training programs, social investment funds and public works and a school-feeding program. Coverage of the nutrition program was found to be deficient. The school-feeding program reaches only 9.6 per cent of poor children in urban areas and 32 per cent in rural areas (Wodon, 2000).

Nicaragua: The PRSP sets as a long-run goal ensuring that the most vulnerable groups have the same or favored access to social and development programs as the rest of the population. The PRSP recognizes that full social protection for the poor will take time, and in the meantime, some new programs have been designed to immediately provide

(*Continued*)

assistance to the poorest. These immediate efforts will assist young children and extremely poor households by enhancing their demand and access to basic social services. These programs attempt to provide incentives for school attendance and health care. The government is also strengthening the capacity of public institutions responsible for social safety nets and the targeting of specific programs. There will also be increased public support for informal safety nets through enhancement of local capacities.

Improving health and education levels requires improved governance. Corruption can have a large impact on the provision of public services, particularly on education services and health care. Reducing corruption improves the efficiency with which public resources are transformed in public services, thereby resulting in higher school enrollment rates and lower mortality rates (Gupta *et al.*, 2001). It can also improve the targeting of existing spending on education and health care (Gupta *et al.*, 2000). For these reasons, it is crucial that governments institute transparent procurement procedures and enhance financial accountability of public spending. In addition, the capacity to formulate and execute the budget should be strengthened, with a larger share of resources allocated to primary education and basic health care, and reducing out-of-pocket expenses borne by the poor.

Transparency in operation of the public sector can improve governance. Transparency should reduce arbitrary discretion and minimize conflict of interest. In addition, it should also require that public officials adhere to an ethical code. Adherence to IMF's code of Fiscal Transparency and quality of fiscal data is one way to promote transparency. Countries voluntarily collaborate with the IMF in drafting a Report on the Observance of Standards and Codes (ROSC) for public administration. The report assesses performance against a slate of best practices in fiscal management. These reports are then posted on the IMF web site, and progress can be assessed periodically when updating the ROSC.

As of June 2002, Nicaragua and Honduras were the only countries in Central America that have a completed fiscal ROSC posted on the IMF web site, but ROSCs for other countries are underway. Both countries have made good progress in improving fiscal transparency and provide more comprehensive information on budget execution. However, there is room for improvement. For example, the dissemination of budget execution can be improved; internal and external controls can be strengthened; the budget can be cast in a medium-term framework; and the macroeconomic underpinning of the budget can be made transparent (Nicaragua).

Corruption, transparency, and poor governance are closely related. Corruption can be defined as monopoly plus discretion minus accountability. Other reformulations are possible. Therefore, corruption varies directly with the degree of monopoly power (government or otherwise) and the level of discretion, and inversely with the degree of accountability. Appropriate reforms along these dimensions will tend to decrease corruption.

The World Bank has developed new indicators of governance. Recently, measures of governance have been created by three World Bank Economists that score performance on six dimensions that underlie the definition of governance given earlier. These are: (1) voice and accountability; (2) political stability and lack of violence; (3) government effectiveness; (4) rule of law; (5) control of corruption; and (6) regulatory quality (Kaufmann *et al.*, 2002). These indicators are subjective, but provide a potentially valuable starting point for assessing governance. Governance scores have been recently compiled by these economists for some 170 countries for two points in time: 1997/98 and 2000/01.

Based on the above data set, Central America does better than Latin America on three out of six governance indicators. These are: voice and accountability, political stability, and regulatory quality (Table 3.15). For example, in 2000/01, 62 per cent of countries had a lower score on voice and accountability than the average score in Central America, compared with 59 per cent for Latin America as a whole. By contrast, Central America had lower scores than Latin America as a whole on corruption, rule of law, and effectiveness of government. For example, only 43 per cent of countries had lower levels of corruption than Central America, whereas the corresponding number for Latin America is 90 per cent. Within Central America, Costa Rica performs the best across all six with at least 70 per cent of countries having a lower score on all six dimensions. In fact, Costa Rica's score is close to the OECD average. According to these data, Guatemala has the worst rating within Central America on voice and accountability and on political stability; and Honduras on government effectiveness, regulatory quality, rule of law and corruption. On average,

Table 3.15 Indicators of governance

	Voice and accountability		Political stability		Government effectiveness		Regulatory quality		Rule of law		Control of corruption	
	1997/98	2000/01	1997/98	2000/01	1997/98	2000/01	1997/98	2000/01	1997/98	2000/01	1997/98	2000/01
Costa Rica	88	91	82	86	74	78	92	85	71	71	77	81
El Salvador	50	62	48	71	45	46	99	87	30	31	43	47
Guatemala	34	40	22	20	46	31	67	53	11	14	20	29
Honduras	52	52	37	57	36	33	44	39	17	10	12	32
Nicaragua	58	51	39	61	30	28	38	39	26	21	19	24
Panamá	71	72	56	70	43	49	94	86	40	53	38	42
Dominican Republic	51	65	55	65	17	46	71	76	65	57	24	50
Regional averages												
Central America	58	62	48	61	42	44	72	66	37	37	33	43
Latin America and the Caribbean	60	60	46	54	49	49	67	59	44	46	47	51
Latin America	60	59	44	52	50	46	71	60	41	42	42	46
OECD	92	92	88	90	91	90	87	88	90	90	91	90
Sub-Saharan Africa	38	36	30	28	35	32	34	36	33	33	37	34
Eastern Europe	61	67	56	55	49	51	54	54	53	57	50	54
Former Soviet Union	32	32	37	31	19	21	17	15	29	27	18	22
East Asia	42	42	62	58	59	57	48	49	54	54	55	49
South Asia	37	32	28	26	30	30	43	35	35	32	43	34
Middle East and North Africa	32	33	48	50	50	54	41	49	58	56	47	52

Notes: Each entry in the table indicates per cent of countries worldwide that rate below selected country or a region for each governance indicator. Higher score for any indicator, shows better governance outcome. All indicators are subjective or based on individuals' perceptions. Each average is the sample.

Sources: Kaufmann, Kraay, and Zoido-Lobaton (2002).

Central America made significant strides between 1997/98 and 2000/01 in political stability and control of corruption.

Countries in the region have taken on various measures to address governance and corruption. Panamá's original anti-money laundering law has been broadened to include drug-related offenses, proceeds from fraud, extortion, embezzlement, corruption of public officials, kidnapping and acts of terrorism. In Nicaragua, the comptroller's office is being strengthened; a new procurement law has been adopted, along with establishment of mediation courts and approval of a law on dispute settlements. In the Dominican Republic, the treasury system is being strengthened through an integrated financial management program, with assistance from the Inter-American Development Bank. In Guatemala, the existing integrated financial management system is being extended to agencies outside the central government; and laws on probity and procurement are under consideration.

Summary and policy conclusions

The basic lessons of this chapter are straightforward. The potential returns to investments in education and health are high – in fact, these investments are essential if Central American countries are to reach their full potential. In addition, investments in social safety nets are necessary to protect the poor and achieve growth with equity. The key, however, is to make these investments efficiently. To do so requires careful and comprehensive analysis of the particular conditions in each country, as well as the cost of alternative reforms. Unfortunately, existing evidence provides no simple blueprint, a task made more difficult by the observed diversity among the countries in the region. The evidence does, however, provide many paradigms that can be assessed within the particular context of each country to develop and implement reforms in these areas.

Poverty and inequality are higher in Central America than in Latin America. Latin America, in turn, is the most unequal region of the world. While poverty has declined modestly in the 1990s, inequality in Central America has risen and continues to be high and persistent. This high and rising level of inequality is an impediment for pro-poor growth and calls for reforms in several areas studied in this paper, including composition and level of spending, quality of education and health, the design and implementation of social safety nets, and reforms in the areas of governance and transparency. The quality of the fiscal adjustment of the 1990s does not seem to have contributed much to easing of poverty and inequality in the region.

Improvements in the quality of education and health, particularly for the poor, have been identified as an effective channel to promote pro-poor growth. However, despite the large returns identified, quality of human capital in Central America is generally low, and there are important differences in accessing basic social services between rural and urban areas and poor and nonpoor populations.

Government spending on education has increased only modestly in Central America and remains well below Latin American averages. Studies for developing countries, including Central America, stress that increased public spending on education is associated with better indicators of educational attainment, although improvements in initial conditions and governance are also necessary to increase targeting and efficiency of public spending. Moreover, a reallocation of resources towards basic education could lead to important gains, especially for the poor. Within educational expenditures, teachers' wages are large, especially in Guatemala and Honduras. Teachers' wages in Central America are found to be high by regional standards, and most Central American teachers earn comparatively more than workers in other professions with similar characteristics and education. However, the evidence linking teacher wages to improved educational achievement is meager at best.

Allocations of public resources for health have increased in most countries since the mid-1980s. Central America as a region invests relatively large amounts of public resources in health. Studies have found that increased public resources for health care have been associated with better health status of the population, although the effectiveness of public health care spending in promoting health is weaker than that found in the case of public education spending. However, stronger effects have been found when looking at the health status of the poor and in low-income countries, suggesting that better targeting of health care spending would be a powerful tool for poverty reduction. Similarly, improving the efficiency of spending may be as important as increasing the amount of resources.

As the first generation of reforms in the 1990s are being consolidated in the region, further progress on such reforms would require mainstreaming the complementary second-generation reforms.

Progress on second-generation reforms invariably involves increasing transparency of public sector operations, improving governance, solidifying incentives for better performance of the public sector, institutional reform and strengthening the rule of law to reduce discretion and opportunities for corruption and poor governance.

Recent trends in indicators of governance in Central America are encouraging. There has been progress in voice and accountability and in political stability. However, regulatory quality seems to have deteriorated significantly. Governments should concentrate on improving several aspects of governance and reducing corruption, as this is critical for increasing the effectiveness of public spending and social safety nets, and can lead to improvements in quality and distribution of human capital, promoting higher levels of pro-poor growth.

Notes

1. Other definitions of the region may contain a different country composition.
2. See Cardemil, Di Tata, and Frantischek (2000) for some details.
3. PPP exchange rates reflect international differences in the prices of goods and services. Market exchange rates measure the relative values of currencies, which are affected by more than variations in the prices of goods and services and can vary significantly from PPP exchange rates.
4. The classification is based on the values of 1999 per capita GNI using World Bank Atlas method which relies on average of the exchange rate in 1999 and previous two years and inflation rate differential between each country and the G5 countries. Based on this methodology, the World Bank adopts the following income classification: low income, $755 or less; lower-middle income, $756–2995; upper-middle income, $2996–9265; and high income, $9266 or more.
5. The current cutoff for eligibility is a 1999 per capita GDP level of US$885. The PRGF was introduced in September 1999.
6. A PRSP describes the macroeconomic, structural, and social policies that a country will implement to foster growth and reduce poverty under a three-year economic adjustment program supported by PRGF resources.
7. Poverty is measured using the headcount index, which is the percentage of the population with a consumption or income less than the poverty line. International poverty lines make it possible to compare poverty rates across countries by making adjustments for cross-country differences in prices using a common metric, the purchasing power equivalent of US$2 per day. (Poverty rates based on US$1 per day tell the same qualitative story, but would naturally result in lower poverty rates.) Measures of poverty for the Central American countries are based on consumption, which is judged to be a better measure of cost of living.

8. This finding is likely to hold for early 1990s as well. A stronger claim cannot be made due to lack of international poverty rates for two countries (The Dominican Republic and Guatemala) in early 1990s.
9. There are many measures of inequality. The Gini coefficient is the most widely used measure, ranging from 0 (perfect equality) to 100 (perfect inequality). However, it has the undesirable attribute, assuming we are most interested in eliminating poverty, that the impact of the very rich has the same effect on the measure as that of the poor.
10. Using US$1 a day definition, poverty in Latin America and the Caribbean was unchanged during the 1990s at about 15 per cent (World Development Indicators, 2002, p. 4). Therefore, by this definition, the very poor have continued to be poor by the end of the decade.
11. These are Costa Rica, El Salvador, Honduras, Nicaragua, Panamá.
12. The correlation coefficient for the sample of seven countries is lower at 0.74, but is still statistically significant (with a *t*-statistic of 2.9). Persistence of inequality is also a feature of larger cross-country data (see Li *et al.*, 1998).
13. Section IV explores this issue in more detail. For the seven countries in the region, the correlation coefficient between growth in the 1990s and the Gini coefficient in early 1990s is −0.33 with a *t*-ratio of −1.3. Knowles (2001) provides a stronger correlation using a larger sample of countries.
14. This is the Gini-adjusted growth elasticity derived as (1- initial Gini)* – 3 in which part of growth elasticity varies with initial inequality. See Ravallion (1997, 2001) for details. Initial inequality is inequality at the start of the 1990s.
15. Sources of spending and revenue are IMF's World Economic Outlook database. Magnitude of Nicaragua's deficit may be overstated as GDP is likely to be understated.
16. Nicaragua's wage bill is higher than Guatemala (as per cent of GDP) perhaps reflecting understatement of its GDP alluded earlier. Guatemala has lower wage bill when expressed as fraction of total spending.
17. Note that these comparisons ignore cross-country differences in the size of government arising from differences in the size of subnational levels of government and extrabudgetary accounts.
18. For the year 2002, Honduras' PRSP projects that nearly 40 per cent of the total cost of new programs and projects envisaged for poverty reduction will be allocated to investing in human capital. For the same year, Nicaragua's PRSP projects that 35 per cent of the total cost of the strategy will be devoted to education and health for the poor.
19. The data are from World Development Indicators (2002). Spending and income are measured on a PPP basis. Logarithmic transformations were applied to all variables. The regression should either adjust for enrollment rates or include them as another independent variable. This was not done, because too many observations would be lost. Enrollment rates in Central America all fall within a 10 percentage point range, however.
20. Given the low average workload, it is common for teachers to hold other positions. It is estimated that 90 per cent of teachers in El Salvador and

more than half of teachers in Guatemala have other jobs (Alvarez and Majmudar, 2001).

21. There are several challenges in the estimation of the effect of investments in health on earnings, for instance finding a good proxy for health investments, measurement error, and endogeneity problems.
22. The mortality and income variables are from World Development Indicators. The health spending data were compiled by the World Health Organization. Spending and income data are measured on a PPP basis. Logarithmic transformations were applied to all variables.
23. Corbacho (2000) finds that the size of the informal sector in Central America is very large, exceeding 40 per cent of total employment and has grown in most countries during the 1990s.

References

Alvarez, Benjamin and J. Majmudar (2001) 'Teachers in Latin America: Who is Preparing Our Children for the Knowledge Century?' *LCHSD Paper Series No. 67*, Washington, DC: World Bank.

Baldacci, Emanuele, Maria Teresa Guin-Siu, and Luiz de Mello (2002) 'More on the Effectiveness of Public Spending on Health Care and Education: A Covariance Structure Model', *IMF Working Paper 02/90*, Washington, DC: International Monetary Fund.

Barro, Robert, and Xavier Sala-I-Martin (1995) *Economic Growth*, London: McGraw-Hill.

Barro, Robert J. and J. W. Lee (2000) 'International Data on Educational Attainment: Updates and Implications', *CID Working Paper No. 42*, Cambridge, MA.: Center for International Development at Harvard University.

—— (1996) 'International Measures of Schooling Years and Schooling Quality', *The American Economic Review*, Vol. 86, No. 2, pp. 218–23.

Bedi, Arjun S. and J. H. Y. Edwards (1997) 'The Impact of School Quality on the Level and Distribution of Earnings – Evidence from Honduras', *LASHD Paper Series No. 13*, Washington, DC: World Bank.

Bedi, Arjun S. and J. H. Marshall (1999) 'School Attendance and Student Achievement: Evidence from Rural Honduras', *Economic Development and Cultural Change*, pp. 657–82.

Behrman, Jere R. and N. Birdsall (1983) 'The Quality of Schooling: Quantity Alone is Misleading', *The American Economic Review*, Vol. 73 (December), No. 5, pp. 928–46.

Birdsall, Nancy and J. L. Londoño (1997) 'Asset Inequality Matters: An Assessment of the World Bank's Approach to Poverty Reduction', *American Economic Review, Papers and Proceedings*, Vol. 87, No. 2, pp. 32–7.

Bourguignon, F., Pereira, L., and N. Stern (2002) 'Evaluating the Poverty Impact of Economic Policies: Some Analytical Challenges', paper presented at the IMF Conference on Macroeconomic Policies and Poverty Reduction, Washington, DC.

Card, David, and A. Krueger (1996a) 'Labor Market Effects of School Quality: Theory and Evidence', in G. Burtless (ed.), *Does Money Matter? The Link Between Schools, Student Achievement and Adult Success*, Washington, DC: Brookings Institute.

—— (1996b) 'School Resources and Student Outcomes: An Overview of the Literature and New Evidence from North and South Carolina', *Journal of Economic Perspectives*, Vol. 10 (Fall), pp. 31–50.

Cardemil, Leonardo, Juan Carlos Di Tata, and Florencia Frantischek (2000) 'Central America: Adjustment and Reforms in the 1990s', *Finance and Development*, Vol. 37 (March) No. 1.

Case, Anne and M. Yogo (1999) 'Does School Quality Matter? Returns to Education and the Characteristics of Schools in South Africa', *NBER Working Paper No. 7399*, Cambridge, MA.: National Bureau of Economic Research.

Chen, Shaohua and Martin Ravallion (2001) 'How Did the World's Poorest Fare in the 1990s'? *Review of Income and Wealth*, (September) No. 3, pp. 283–300.

Chu, Ke-young, H. Davoodi, and S. Gupta (2000) 'Income Distribution and Tax and Government Social Spending Policies in Developing Countries', *IMF Working Paper 00/62*, Washington, DC: International Monetary Fund.

Corbacho, Ana (2000) 'Labor Markets in Central America: Informal Versus Formal Sectors', *Development Discussion Paper No. 747*, Harvard Institute for International Development, Cambridge, MA: Harvard University.

Corbacho, Ana (2001) 'Education, Income Distribution and Growth', *Ph.D. Dissertation in Economics*, New York: Columbia University.

Deininger, Klaus, and Lyn Squire (1996) 'A New Data Set for Measuring Income Inequality' *The World Bank Economic Review*, Vol. 10, No. 3, pp. 565–91.

Li, Hongyi, Lyn Squire, and Heng-fu Zou (1998) 'Explaining International and Intertemporal Variations in Income Inequality', *Economic Journal*, Vol. 108, No. 446, pp. 26–43.

Dollar, David, and A. Kraay (2000) 'Growth is Good for the Poor', *World Bank Discussion Paper No. 2587*, Washington, DC: World Bank.

Duryea, Suzanne, and C. Pagés (2002) 'Human Capital Policies: What They Can and Cannot Do for Productivity and Poverty Reduction in Latin America', *IADB Working Paper No. 468*, Washington, DC: Inter-American Development Bank.

Espinosa Ferrando, Jaime and C. Hernandez Alvarez (2000) 'Productivity and Health Status in Nicaragua', in W. Savedoff and P. Schultz (eds), *Wealth from Health: Linking Social Investments to Earnings in Latin America*, Washington, DC: Inter-American Development Bank.

Filmer, D., J. Hammer, and L. Pritchett (1997) 'Health Policies in Poor Countries: Weak Links in the Chain', *World Bank Discussion Paper No. 1874*, Washington, DC.: World Bank.

Government of Nicaragua (2001) 'A Strengthened Growth and Poverty Reduction Strategy', available via the Internet <http://www.imf.org>

Gupta, Sanjeev, B. Clements, E. Baldacci, and C. Mulas-Granados (2002) 'Expenditure Composition, Fiscal Adjustment and Growth in Low-Income Countries', *IMF Working Paper 02/77*, Washington, DC: International Monetary Fund.

Gupta, Sanjeev, H. Davoodi, and E. Tiongson (2001) 'Corruption and the Provision of Health Care and Education Services', in A. K. Jain (ed.), *The Political Economy of Corruption*, London: Routledge.
Gupta, Sanjeev, L. Dicks-Mireaux, R. Khemani, C. McDonald, and M. Verhoeven (2000) 'Social Issues in IMF-Supported Programs', *IMF Occasional Paper No. 191*, Washington, DC: International Monetary Fund.
Gupta, Sanjeev, K. Honjo, and M. Verhoeven (1997) 'The Efficiency of Government Expenditure: Experiences from Africa', *IMF Working Paper 97/153*, Washington, DC: International Monetary Fund.
Gupta, Sanjeev, M. Verhoeven, and E. Tiongson (2001) 'Public Spending on Health Care and the Poor', *IMF Working Paper 01/127*, Washington, DC: International Monetary Fund.
—— (2002) 'The Effectiveness of Government Spending on Education and Health Care in Developing and Transition Economies', *European Journal of Political Economy*, Vol. 18 (November), pp. 717–37.
Hanushek, Eric A. and D. Kim (1995) 'Schooling, Labor Force Quality and Economic Growth', *NBER Working Paper No. 5399*, Cambridge, MA: National Bureau of Economic Research.
Hanushek, Eric A. and J. A. Luque (2002) 'Efficiency and Equity in Schools Around the World', *NBER Working Paper No. 8949*, Cambridge, MA: National Bureau of Economic Research.
Hanushek, Eric A. J. F. Kain, and S. G. Rivkin (1998) 'Teachers, School and Academic Achievement', *NBER Working Paper No. 6691*, Cambridge, MA: National Bureau of Economic Research.
—— (1999) 'Do Higher Salaries Buy Better Teachers'? *NBER Working Paper No. 7082*, Cambridge, MA.: National Bureau of Economic Research.
Harbison, Ralph W., and E. A. Hanushek (1992) 'Educational Performance of the Poor: Lessons from Rural Northeast Brazil', Oxford: Oxford University Press.
Hsiao, William (2000) 'What Should Macroeconomists Know About Health Care Policy? A Primer', *IMF Working Paper 00/136*, Washington, DC: International Monetary Fund.
Inter-American Development Bank (1996) *Como organizar con exito los servicios sociales, Progreso Economico y Social en America Latina, Informe 1996*, Washington, DC: Inter-American Development Bank.
Inter-American Development Bank (1998) *Facing Up to Inequality in Latin America, Economic and Social Progress in Latin America, 1998–99 Report*, Washington, DC.
Inter-American Development Bank (2000) *Social Protection for Equity and Growth*, Washington, DC.
International Monetary Fund, *World Economic Outlook*, <http://www.imf. org>
Kaufmann, Daniel, Aart Kraay, and Pablo Zoido-Lobaton (2002) 'Governance Matters II: Updated Indicators for 2000/01', *World Bank Policy Discussion Paper Series No. 2772*, Washington, DC: World Bank.
Knowles S., 2001, 'Inequality and Economic Growth: The Empirical Relationship Reconsidered in Light of Comparable Data', *WIDER Discussion Paper Series No. 128*, Helsinki: United Nations.

Krueger, Alan, and D. M. Whitmore (2000) 'The Effect of Attending a Small Class in the Early Grades on College-Test Taking and Middle School Test Results: Evidence from Project Star', *NBER Working Paper No. 7656*, Cambridge, MA.: National Bureau of Economic Research.

Krueger, Alan (2002) 'Economic Considerations and Class Size', *NBER Working Paper No. 8875*, Cambridge, MA.: National Bureau of Economic Research.

Li, Hongyi, Lyn Squire, and Heng-fu Zou (1998) 'Explaining International and Intertemporal Variations in Income Inequality', *Economic Journal*, Vol. 108 (January), pp. 26–43.

Liang, Xiaoyan (1999) 'Teacher Pay in 12 Latin American Countries: How Does Teacher Pay Compare to Other Professions, What Determines Teacher Pay, and Who are the Teachers'? *LCHSD Working Paper No. 49,* Washington, DC: World Bank.

Martinic, Sergio (1998) 'Tiempo y Aprendizaje', *LCSHD Paper Series No. 26*, Washington, DC: World Bank.

Ravallion, M, and Gurave Datt (2001) 'Why Has Economic Growth Been More Pro-Poor in Some States of India Than in Others'? *Journal of Development Economics,* Vol. 68 (August), pp. 381–400.

Ravallion, M. (1997) 'Can High Inequality Developing Countries Escape Absolute Poverty'? *Economics Letters*, Vol. 56, pp. 51–7.

Ravallion, Martin, and Shaohua Chen (1997) 'What Can New Survey Data Tell us About Recent Changes in Distribution and Poverty'? *World Bank Economic Review*, Vol. 11, No. 2, pp. 357–82.

Ravallion, Martin (2001) 'Growth, Inequality and Poverty: Looking Beyond Averages' *World Development*, Vol. 29, No. 11, pp. 1803–15.

Republic of Honduras (2001) 'Poverty Reduction Strategy Paper', (August) <http://www.imf.org/external/np/prsp/201/hud>

Savedoff, William D. and P. Schultz (2000) (eds), *Wealth from Health: Linking Social Investments to Earnings in Latin America*, Washington, DC.: Inter-American Development Bank.

Székely, Miguel (2001) 'The 1990s in Latin America, Another Decade of Persistent Inequality, But With Somewhat Lower Poverty', *IADB, Working Paper No. 454*, Washington, DC: Inter-American Development Bank.

Wang, Limin (2001) 'Health Outcomes in Low-Income Countries and Policy Implications: Empirical Findings from Demographic and Health Surveys', unpublished; Washington, DC: World Bank.

Wodon, Quentin T. (2000) 'Poverty and Policy in Latin America and the Caribbean', *World Bank Technical Paper No. 467*, Washington, DC: World Bank.

World Bank (2002) *World Development Indicators*, Washington, DC.

World Health Organization (2001) Macroeconomics and Health: Investing in Health for Economic Development, Report of the Commission on Macroeconomics and Health, Geneva.

Young, Phillip *et al.* (2001) The Dominican Republic: Stabilization, Reform and Growth, *IMF Occasional Paper No. 206* Washington, DC: International Monetary Fund.

4

Trade Structure and Policy

Guillermo Perry, Daniel Lederman, and Rodrigo Suescún

Introduction

Historically there has been a close trading relationship between the United States and the Central American region. In the last few years this relationship has flourished, mainly as a result of unilateral efforts on both sides. Since 1983, the United States has granted unilateral preferential trade treatment to countries in the region through the Caribbean Basin Initiative (CBI) while Central American countries have achieved significant advances in unilateral trade liberalization through deep trade reforms undertaken during the 1990s. What policy options do these developments offer to the region?

This chapter begins by reviewing the main trends in the trade structure of Central American countries over the last two decades, the growing role of the United States as the major trading partner, the effect of domestic trade policies as well the effects of NAFTA and recent developments in U.S. agricultural and trade policies (the 2002 Farm Bill). This analysis is aimed at understanding a set of trade-related issues that should be taken into account both in the upcoming trade negotiations with the United States and multilaterally under the current round of WTO negotiations (the Doha round) which strives for freer trade, particularly with regard to agricultural trade.

The importance of the trade link between the United States and Central America naturally raises the question of deeper forms of integration. Our discussion is organized around the criteria set by the Optimum Currency Area (OCA) literature in order to evaluate the likelihood of a successful monetary union. Standard OCA criteria are then supplemented with other arguments relevant for the choice of a monetary regime worth discussing in the case of Central America, such as *de facto* dollarization and the possibility of importing monetary credibility through monetary integration. The chapter ends with a discussion of the implications of trade policies and the choice of exchange rate regime for fiscal policies and institutions, as well as the conditions required for successful hard pegs or unilateral dollarization.

Trade structure

The Central American region is open to trade, its export base is relatively diversified and trade is carried out with a small number of trading partners, primarily the United States. Although international trade encompasses a higher share of national production than in earlier decades, the region has historically exhibited strong linkages with world commodity markets. Figure 4.1 shows that trade openness (measured as exports plus imports relative to GDP) in the region has exhibited an upward trend;[1] increasing from slightly below 50 per cent for the majority of countries to around 100 per cent for Costa Rica, 70 per cent for Panamá, El Salvador (and the Dominican Republic) and 50 per cent for Guatemala by the late 1990s. The two HIPC countries also show a high degree of openness: 120 per cent for Nicaragua and 100 per cent for Honduras by the late 1990s (lower panel of Figure 4.1). The increase in international trade was caused by deliberate policies implemented during the 1990s, especially in Costa Rica, El Salvador, Honduras, and Nicaragua.

Figure 4.2 depicts an indicator of export diversification – the Herfindahl index of export-revenues concentration,[2] indicating a clear trend across the region towards export diversification since the mid-1980s. An interesting case is that of El Salvador, which went from having the most concentrated export structure in 1986 to having the most diversified by the late 1990s. In contrast, Costa Rica's trend toward diversification was partially reversed in 1999 by foreign investments in the electronic equipment producing sector.

Figure 4.3 depicts the geographic distribution of regional exports. The main destination of Central American exports is the US marketplace. Again, there is a historical regularity in the trade pattern of these countries. Costa Rica has traditionally placed 40 per cent of its

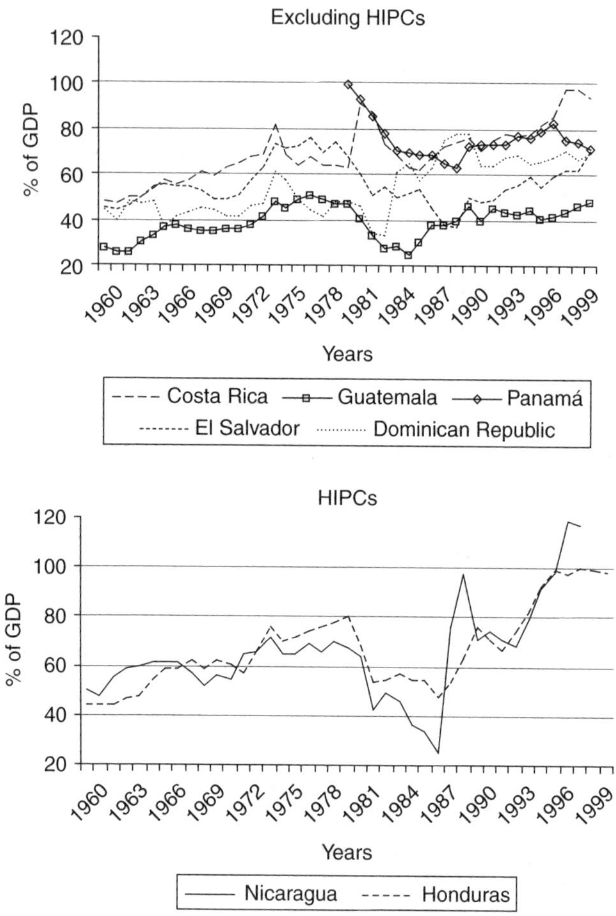

Figure 4.1 Central America: trade indicators

exports in the US market. This figure used to represent around 10 per cent of its GDP, but now, given the advances in trade liberalization, exports of this magnitude represent almost 25 per cent of its GDP.

Honduras and Panamá conduct 40–60 per cent of their export trade with the United States, Guatemala 40 per cent, El Salvador and Nicaragua 20–40 per cent, and the Dominican Republic 90 per cent in the recent past. Measured as a fraction of GDP (not shown in

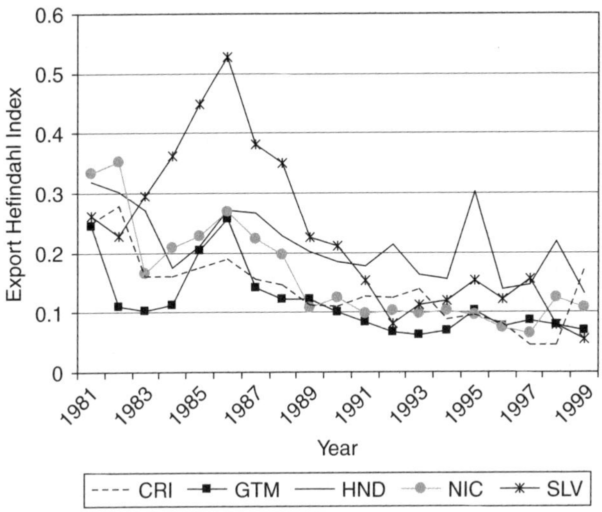

Figure 4.2 Central America: concentration of merchandise exports, 1981–99

Figure 4.3), exports to the United States have surged in Costa Rica, Guatemala, Honduras, Nicaragua, and the Dominican Republic during the 1990s.

Intraregional trade is relatively small in general terms. It is negligible for the Dominican Republic, and small and shrinking for Costa Rica and Honduras. El Salvador is the only case where intraregional trade seems to be gaining importance, but not at the expense of the US market. Also, México has traditionally absorbed only a tiny fraction of Central America's exports. In sum, regional trade flows are not very big: on average, no more than 18 per cent of the region's exports have gone to the region itself and México.

Figure 4.4 shows the geographical origin of imports. Like exports, import trade is conducted with a small set of partners, predominantly with the United States. On average 40 per cent of all imports come from the United States. México and other subregional neighbors do not represent an important source of import trade. Like exports, Central America's imports from the US market surged during the 1990s, with the notable exceptions of Panamá and El Salvador.

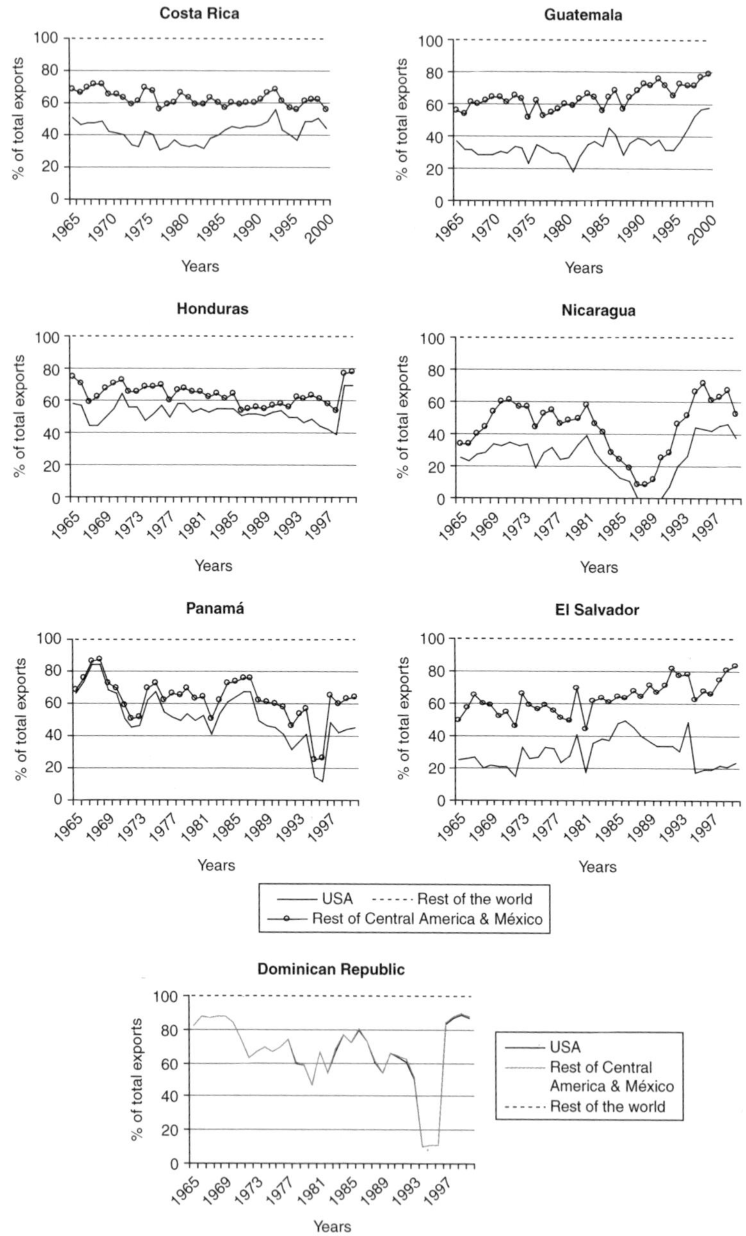

Figure 4.3 Central America: direction of exports

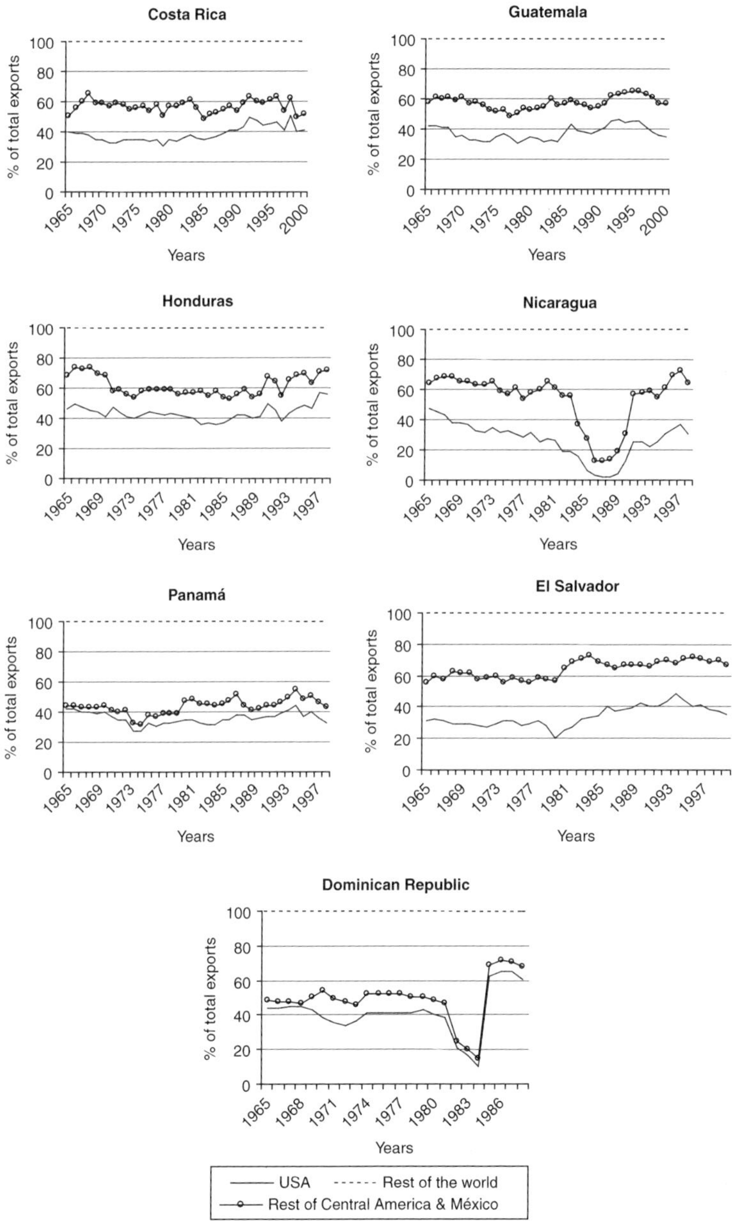

Figure 4.4 Central America: direction of imports

Trade policies

The descriptive analysis of the preceding section has put into perspective long-run trade developments and identified the profound changes that took place during the 1990s. Most of these changes were a direct consequence of structural reforms undertaken over the last decade. This section focuses more specifically on trade reforms, discussing the evolution of tariff and nontariff restrictions to trade as well as the policy response induced by the signing of NAFTA. In turn, we discuss the relation between trade reforms and observed outcomes in terms of trade structure and growth.

Tariff and nontariff barriers

Table 4.1 shows the evolution of average (most-favored nation) tariffs for a number of countries in the Latin American and Caribbean region. Costa Rica stands out as a determined reformer. From an average tariff of 53 per cent in 1985 this country passed to the lowest level in the region: 3.3 per cent in 1999. Guatemala followed suit from a level of 50 per cent to 7.6 per cent in the same time period. El Salvador, Honduras, Nicaragua and even the Dominican Republic, with a relatively high current level of 14.5 per cent, were all also involved in a remarkable overhaul of their tariff structure.

The overhaul of the tariff structure included the reduction of the average rate as well as the reduction in its dispersion. Table 4.2 presents some figures on tariff dispersion for the region. Though the gains along this dimension are not very notable throughout the nineties, there is a significant reduction relative to the levels observed during the second half of the eighties. Relative to the Chilean structure – which is almost flat – there is still some room to reduce Central America's tariff dispersion.[3]

Table 4.1 underscores the difference between Central and South American efforts to dismantle trade barriers. In general, tariff restrictions are on average higher in South America. The use of nontariff restrictions to hamper imports used to be very popular in the Latin American Countries (LAC) region as well. Figure 4.5 shows that this type of protectionist barrier has also tended to disappear, more so in Central America than in the rest of Latin America.

Table 4.1 Central America: average tariffs (in per cent)

	1985	1986	1987	1988	1989	1990	1991	1992	1993	1994	1995	1996	1997	1998	1999
Central America and the Caribbean															
Costa Rica	53.0	21.1	16.4	16.4	16.4	16.4	16.4	15.0	11.7	11.2	11.2	11.2	9.9	8.0	3.3
Dominican Republic					88.0	21.1	21.1	21.1	21.1	17.8	17.8	17.8	14.5	14.5	14.5
El Salvador		23.0	21.1	21.1	16.0	16.0	16.0	16.0	13.1	10.1	10.2	10.2	10.2	5.7	5.7
Guatemala	50.0	50.0	25.0	25.0	16.0	16.0	16.0	16.0	16.0	10.8	12.0	11.4	11.4	8.4	7.6
Honduras					41.9						9.7	9.7	9.7	9.7	8.1
Jamaica		42.5	19.3	19.3	20.0	20.0	20.3	20.3	19.3	19.3	19.3	21.3	21.3	21.3	17.9
Nicaragua	54.0		21.0			8.0				17.4	10.7	9.5	6.9	5.9	10.9
Trinidad & Tobago				83.0	17.0	17.0	19.9	18.7	18.7	18.7	18.7	18.7	18.7	18.7	18.4
Rest of Latin America															
Argentina	28.0	39.5	39.5	43.7	43.7	21.0	12.2	11.8	10.9	10.9	10.5	11.2	11.3	13.5	11.0
Bolivia	20.0	21.9	20.0	18.6	17.0	13.4	10.0	9.8	9.8	10.0	9.7	9.7	9.7	9.7	9.0
Brazil	80.0	74.1	51.0	50.6	42.2	31.8	25.1	20.7	14.2	11.9	12.0	12.2	11.9	14.6	13.3
Chile	36.0	20.2	20.2	15.1	15.1	14.9	11.0	11.0	11.0	11.0	11.0	11.0	11.0	11.0	10.0
Colombia	83.0	46.4	46.4	47.6	47.6	23.2	6.7	11.7	11.7	11.8	13.3	11.7	11.7	11.7	11.8
Ecuador	50.0	41.4	41.4	39.9	39.9	33.0	33.0	11.3	9.3	11.8	12.3	11.4	11.4	11.3	12.9
Mexico	34.0	27.8	11.3	10.6	10.6	13.1	13.1	13.1	13.0	13.0	12.6	13.1	13.1	13.3	10.1
Paraguay	71.3	19.3		19.3		16.0	15.7	9.2	9.2	8.0	9.3	9.4	9.6	9.5	9.0
Peru	64.0	63.0	63.0	67.8	68.1	26.0	17.6	17.4	17.6	16.3	16.3	16.3	13.3	13.2	13.0
Uruguay	32.0	35.7	29.7	27.0	27.0	23.0	21.5	18.2	17.0	14.7	9.3	9.7	10.0	12.2	4.6
Venezuela	30.0	30.6	32.9	33.8	30.6	19.0	16.0	15.7	15.7	11.8	13.4	13.4	11.9	12.0	12.6

Source: IDB.

Table 4.2 Central America: tariff dispersion (standard deviation)

	1985	1986	1987	1988	1989	1990	1991	1992	1993	1994	1995	1996	1997	1998	1999
Central America and the Caribbean															
Costa Rica	27.4	11.2	8.8	8.8	8.8	8.8	8.8	8.1	6.4	6.2	8.5	6.2	5.5	4.6	7.8
Dominican Republic						11.2	11.2	11.2	11.2	9.5	9.5	9.5	7.9	9.2	7.9
El Salvador		12.2	11.2	11.2	8.6	8.6	8.6	8.6	7.2	5.6	7.6	5.7	5.7	3.4	3.4
Guatemala	25.9	25.9	13.2	13.2	8.6	8.6	8.6	8.6	8.6	6.0	7.5	6.3	6.3	9.5	4.4
Honduras					21.8						7.5	5.4	5.4	5.4	7.8
Jamaica		22.1	10.3	10.3	10.6	10.6	10.8	10.8	10.3	10.3	10.3	8.8	11.3	11.3	8.4
Nicaragua	27.9		11.2			4.6				9.3	7.4	5.3	4.0	7.3	7.3
Trinidad & Tobago					6.7	6.7	14.9	15.3	11.9	11.9	11.9	11.9	11.9	11.9	8.3
Rest of Latin America															
Argentina	14.5	20.5	20.5	21.5	21.5	8.6	8.6	7.4	5.0	6.7	7.6	7.0	6.8	6.9	8.3
Bolivia	3.5	4.5	4.5	1.9	1.9	2.7	1.1	1.0	0.2	1.1	1.3	1.3	1.2	2.0	1.1
Brazil	36.7	30.0	30.0	26.2	17.2	19.8	17.3	14.2	9.5	8.2	6.9	8.5	7.7	7.3	7.8
Chile	3.2	1.7	1.7	1.0	1.0	0.9	0.9	0.7	0.7	0.7	0.7	0.7	0.7	0.7	0.7
Colombia	28.2	16.8	16.8	17.6	17.6	14.2	8.3	6.3	6.3	6.3	4.9	6.3	6.3	6.2	6.2
Ecuador		39.0	39.0	38.6	38.6	20.4	20.4	6.0	6.0	6.3	5.6	6.4	6.4	6.4	6.3
México	15.4	14.3	14.3	7.0	7.0	4.5	4.5	4.5	4.4	4.4	5.4	10.6	10.6	13.5	9.4
Paraguay		15.2	15.2	15.2	15.2	13.0	1.4	7.8	6.8	7.7	6.9	7.1	6.7	6.5	7.4
Peru	26.8	25.9	25.9	27.4	27.4	22.6	22.6	4.4	4.4	4.4	4.4	4.4	4.4	2.9	2.6
Uruguay	16.2	18.8	18.8	14.4	14.4	9.7	9.7	5.9	5.9	5.9	7.1	7.3	6.9	7.9	4.3
Venezuela	28.6	30.2	30.2	31.4	31.4	17.1	17.1	11.3	11.3	11.3	4.8	4.8	6.1	6.1	5.9

Source: IDB.

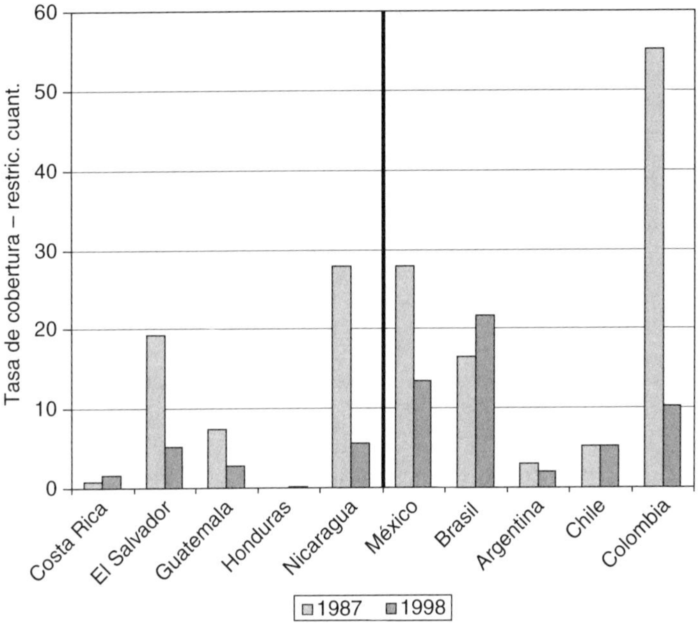

Figure 4.5 Incidence of nontariff measures

The impact of NAFTA in Central America

The emergence of the North American Free Trade Agreement (NAFTA) in 1994 could have been a source of disruption in the pattern of trade flows in the region. However, as discussed in the section entitled trade structure, that a number of Central American countries (Costa Rica, Guatemala, Honduras, Nicaragua, and the Dominican Republic) witnessed, throughout the 1990s, an unprecedented increase in trade, both in import and export trade, with the United States. This implies that NAFTA preferential treatment, with its potential trade diversion effect, was to some extent counterbalanced. As an example, Table 4.3 shows the share of apparel imports of NAFTA-countries captured by Central American countries and México in the 1990s. It is notable that only Costa Rica experienced a decline in its market share, but this was probably due to export growth in other sectors of the Costa Rican economy.

Table 4.3 NAFTA markets shares in apparel (in per cent of total apparel imports)

	1991–94	1995–2001
México	3.74	10.76
Costa Rica	1.79	1.5
Guatemala	1.48	2.04
Honduras	1.27	3.28
Nicaragua	0.03	0.41
El Salvador	0.67	2.06
Central America	**5.24**	**9.29**

This section reviews the main policies that helped minimize the potentially harmful effects of NAFTA on Central America. Three factors are important: (1) The Caribbean Basin Initiative (CBI, established prior to NAFTA) through which the United States unilaterally granted trade preferences to goods produced by countries in the region. By 2000 the CBI also provided preferential access to the United States for apparel exports from the beneficiary countries.[4] (2) NAFTA's rules of origin in apparel did not allow México to exploit the preferential access in these goods. In fact, in the year 2000, only about 65 per cent of Mexican exports of textiles and apparel entered qualified for NAFTA preferences (Cadot *et al.*, 2002). If the rules of origin were more flexible, it is likely that México's apparel market share would have risen even more. (3) The unilateral liberalization efforts by Central American countries probably helped to spur exports by reducing the anti-export bias of import protection.

Thus, the combination of the CBI and Central American trade liberalization reforms appear to have offset most of the possible adverse effects of NAFTA on the Central American region. This conclusion is supported by recent empirical evidence based on the estimation of a gravity model for the 1980–2000 sample period (Montenegro and Soloaga, 2002).

Moreover, Central American countries introduced important reforms regarding foreign direct investment (FDI). FDI is another important variable that might have turned out distorted with the treatment provided by NAFTA to México. FDI flows are key determinants of this region's export performance because they have been closely linked to export activities. For example, *maquiladora* programs provide tax exemptions to foreign investment when production is entirely shipped to markets abroad. Monge-Naranjo (2002) argues that, in response to NAFTA, the Central American countries provided fiscal and regulatory incentives to attract foreign investors, like direct fiscal subsidies, the development of Export Processing Zones (EPZs), and the reform of FDI regimes. Most of the countries of the region offer the same tax treatment to intermediate inputs, exports, remittances and profits as well as similar procedures for clearing customs.

What happened to foreign investment flows? Figure 4.6 shows that during the 1970–90 period foreign direct investment flows did not surpass a 3 per cent of GDP ceiling for the majority of countries in the area (the only exception was the Dominican Republic at the beginning of the 1970s). During the 1990s there was a remarkable change: a surge in investment flows, not only in Costa Rica, but also in the Dominican Republic, El Salvador, Nicaragua, and Panamá.

Policy reforms and economic growth

The relation between commercial openness and economic growth is a topic of active research and debate. Many comparative, large, cross-country studies find a significant positive relation between trade liberalization and economic development.[5]

Figure 4.7 shows the result of a recent study that decomposes observed growth rates into four types of factors: cyclical, convergence, exogenous, and policies (including both trade reforms and other structural reforms).[6] This empirical study supports the conclusion that the type of reforms carried out in the region has had a statistically significant effect on enhancing growth. This effect has been positive for all the Central American countries included in our sample (Costa Rica, El Salvador, Honduras, Nicaragua, and Panamá). Keeping constant any other determinant, policy reforms have contributed 3 percentage points annually to the observed sample-period growth in Nicaragua, 2 percentage points in El Salvador, and 1 percentage point each in Costa Rica and Panamá.

This experiment does not separate the effect of trade policies from other types of structural reforms. However, Lora and Panizza (2002) argue it is precisely in the trade area that LAC countries have achieved the greatest reform advances. According to these authors, all countries

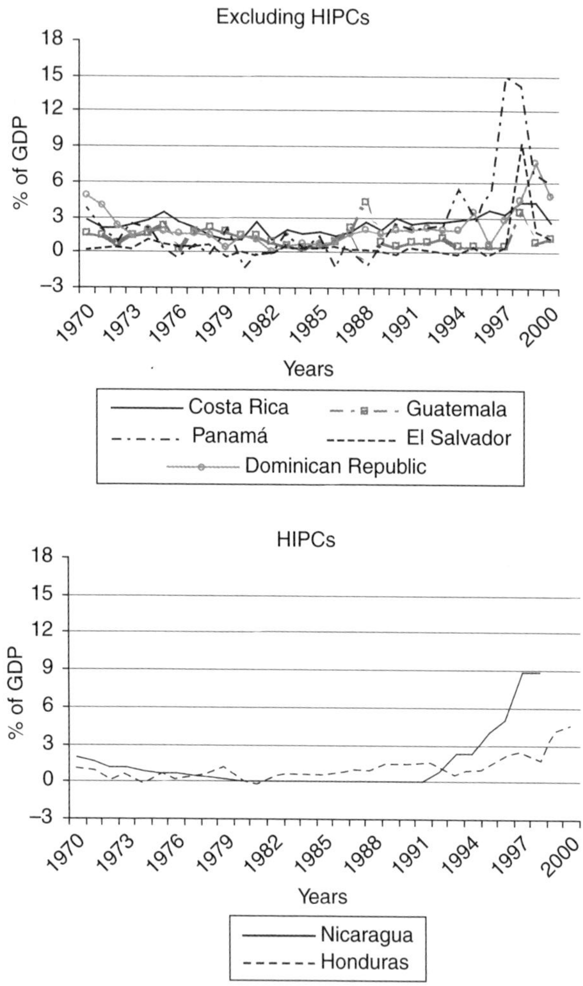

Figure 4.6 Central America: foreign direct investment

in the region have attained a reform index of at least 0.8 (on a scale from 0 to 1), on account of the reduction of average tariffs from a level of 40 per cent to a level close to 10 per cent. Advances in other reform areas are much less impressive.

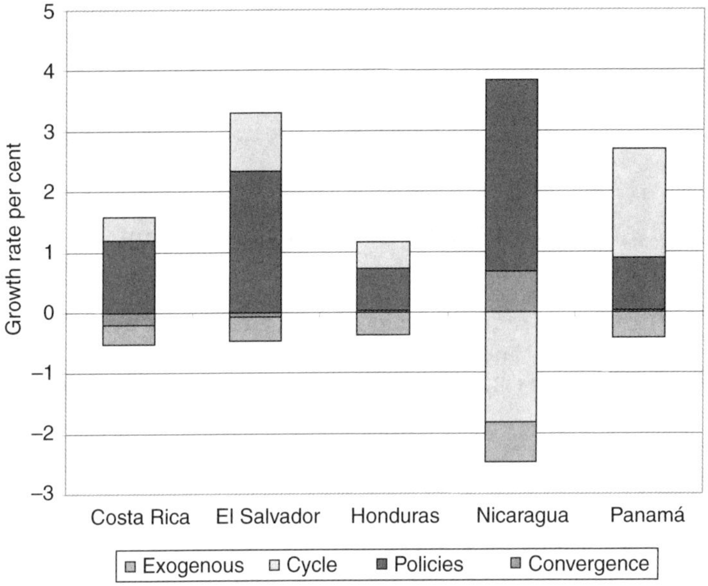

Figure 4.7 Central America: decomposition of growth rates

A possible additional source of growth related to trade is the observed diversification of the export base, as shown in recent empirical studies. Lederman and Maloney (2002) show that concentration of export revenue and growth are negatively correlated. According to De Ferranti *et al.* (2002) there are many possible factors that explain this result: (i) high concentration can be associated with high macroeconomic volatility which in turn hampers growth; (ii) concentration may also hamper productivity affecting intra-industry trade; or (iii) high export concentration may be related to civil conflicts or other institutional failures.

The United States and Central America trade relation: further trade integration

The boom in the United States–Central America trade is the reflection of historical ties and recent deliberate efforts on both parts to renew and strengthen them. A natural step forward in this process is a regional initiative toward the construction of a deeper preferential trade agreement with the United States. This instrument may enhance further growth and development through incentives created by expanded markets and greater competition and foreign investment flows. But it may also spur economic transformation and structural reforms.

A trade agreement between Central America and the United States

In particular, a NAFTA-like trade agreement, which would replace unilateral, partial, and short-lived privileges granted by the United States through the CBI may have the capacity to 'lock in' reforms and market access, crucial determinants of today's investment flows. Such an agreement may thus result in important institutional improvements with possible effects on domestic investment and on the attraction of foreign investment flows to the region.

However, further trade integration may also carry important short-term costs in terms of resource reallocation between sectors. For Central America, the impact of freer trade on agriculture may be particularly important. The case of México with NAFTA is an instructive experience. Seven years of evidence shows that the agricultural provisions negotiated within NAFTA effectively ensured more open trade than before the treaty, despite the inclusion of safeguard clauses, special treatment for some commodities and the phasing out of the structure of protection. Thus, México producers of importable commodities (barley, beans, maize, sorghum, soybeans, wheat) have felt the pressure of tariff-free imports coming from Canada and the United States. On the other hand, Méxican exportables (fruit and vegetables) have entered (or will enter, after a transition period) duty-free to the United States and Canada.

Yuñez-Naude (2002) studies the effect of NAFTA on Méxican production and relative prices. The author finds that the relative price of all basic crops (importables) has fallen since the introduction of NAFTA while imports increased. The domestic production of importables remained relatively unchanged with some productivity gains registered in commercial crops. Agricultural exports to the United States, on the other hand, increased since NAFTA came into force and productivity gains are observed in competitive crops as well. No evidence of significant rural out-migration has been reported probably because low-productivity production in rain-fed land was not displaced but continued in order to provide for household's own consumption.

In Central America, sensitive commodity imports correspond to food necessities like rice, beans, wheat, and so on. Free trade of sensitive staples could bring positive welfare effects for the poor whereas domestic producers of importables, a generally powerful interest group across the region, would be negatively affected. To smooth the transition of small producers to a more competitive regime, government intervention could be required as long as the domestic support is consistent with WTO agreements.

The 2002 US farm bill

A recent issue in agricultural trade is the US Farm Security and Rural Investment Act (FSRI) or 'Farm Bill', signed into law in May 2002.[7] The new US agricultural policy initiative increases the legislated level of government subsidies for agricultural producers.

What could be the likely effect of the Farm Bill on Central America? In principle, developing countries could be affected. Unable to compete with low-cost, subsidized US imports, local farmers in less developed countries could be displaced, turning the production structure more dependent upon imports and increasing trade deficits. However, recent empirical evidence does not support this argument. Hoekman *et al.* (2002) find that domestic support programs generally exert little impact on world prices and on welfare in developing countries. In contrast, import restrictions, such as onerous tariffs on agricultural imports, are much more damaging for developing countries than subsidies because they tend to have larger impacts on world prices of agricultural products. Figure 4.8 shows the Hoekman *et al.* (2002, Appendix Table 2) estimates of the impact of either a 50 per cent cut in import tariffs or a 50 per cent cut in direct support payments by all countries in the world, not just the United States. For the Central American countries, the increase in per capita income of the tariff cut is 10–12 per cent higher than the impact of a cut in subsidies. Thus, the focus should be on reducing import barriers in the United States, rather than on subsidies. Moreover, the estimates of the impact of the subsidies estimated by these authors are likely to

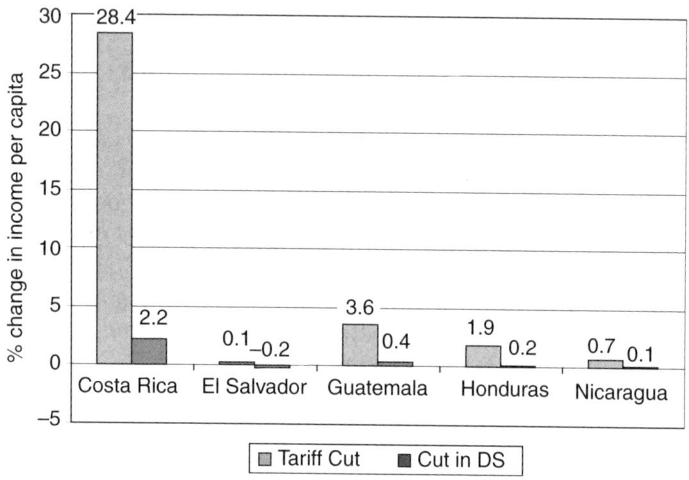

Figure 4.8 Estimated impacts of 50 per cent cuts in agricultural import tariffs and domestic support subsidies around the world (partial equilibrium estimates based on econometric estimates of world price elasticities)

Source: Hoekman, Ng, Olarreaga (2002, Appendix Table 2).

be higher than the impacts from US subsidies only, primarily because the European Union, Japan, and other high-income countries have support programs that are directly linked to contemporaneous production decisions.

Nevertheless, the US farm policy might have important political repercussions. The US initiative could affect the reform of agricultural world trade since it is opposed to the objectives of the current round of WTO negotiations. In the Doha Ministerial Declaration (November 2001) there is an agreement to reform agricultural trade on the basis of three pillars: 'substantial improvements in market access'; reductions of, with a view to phasing out, all forms of export subsidies. Although the US government has declared its intentions of pursuing the Doha objective of 'substantial reductions in trade-distorting domestic support', the Farm Bill could discourage the developing world from pursuing freer agricultural trade. In the Central American countries, rural poverty is already rising due to the prolonged coffee crisis, and policymakers are feeling strong pressures to provide additional special treatment to agricultural activities.

We believe that policymakers should consider relief programs that focus on providing temporary relief to poor farm workers, while not providing incentives for continued production of commodities that are not profitable in the long run. While a detailed discussion of such programs goes beyond the scope of this paper, the general principles for the design of efficient social safety nets and insurance schemes should be considered. Finally, it cannot be over-emphasized that any such program would need to consider fiscal constraints.

Central America and the United States: beyond trade

So far, we have highlighted the close trade relations between Central America and the United States. This section shows that the economic relation between these economic blocks is even deeper, which naturally brings us to the possibility of monetary integration, and in general, to assess the choice of an appropriate exchange rate regime for the region.

The theory of optimum currency areas (OCA) is the right place to start. This theory spells out a set of criteria that, if met, increases the likelihood of a successful monetary integration. Some of these criteria are trade openness, high degree of trade interdependence among the countries involved in the monetary union, high capital and labor mobility, and a prevalence of symmetric shocks to the economies. As discussed above, the Central American countries fulfill the first two criteria.

Though Central American labor markets are not very flexible and there are no deliberate efforts at facilitating labor circulation, significant migration flows do take place. An indirect approach to gauge the level of migratory flows is given by the size of remittances from migrants residing in the United States to Central America. Funkhouser (2002) argues that remittances are a development phenomenon for all countries in Central America with the exception of Costa Rica. Table 4.4, taken from Funkhouser (2002), indicates that US remittances to Dominican Republic amount to 34 per cent of export revenue in 1999, 63 per cent in El Salvador and Nicaragua, 21 per cent in Honduras and 19 per cent in Guatemala. If remittance levels are related to migration these data indicate that the degree of labor mobility has been also significant.

The degree of cross-border capital mobility is more difficult to assess, because in principle it is possible to introduce different types

Table 4.4 Estimates of remittance levels (in millions of US dollars, and in per cent)

	IMF 2000	IDB				Orozco (2001)	
		1999	% of Exports	% of FDI	% of Tourism	2001	% of Exports
Central America and the Caribbean							
Cuba						930	40
Dominican Republic	1,689	1,747	34	129	69	1,807	27
El Salvador	1,751	1,580	63	684	749	1,920	60
Guatemala	563	535	19	364	94	584	16
Haiti		720	220	2,400	1,241	810	150
Honduras	410	368	21	160	189	460	17
Jamaica	789	781	52	150	63	959	30
Nicaragua	320	345	63	115	352	610	80
Rest of Latin America							
Bolivia	101					103	7
Brazil	1,113	1,898	4	6	48	2,600	4
Colombia	1,118	612	5	44	60	670	2
Ecuador	1,084	1,247	28	196	363	1,400	20
Mexico	6,573	6,795	5	60	94	9,273	7
Paraguay	152						
Peru	718	819	13	40	81	905	11
Venezuela	195						

Source: Funkhouser (2002).

of controls on different types of assets. According to an IMF (2001) measure of financial openness (gross stocks of foreign assets and liabilities as a ratio of GDP), Costa Rica, Dominican Republic, El Salvador, and Guatemala can be considered as open economies. FDI flows, in particular, are highly liberalized as a result of structural reforms to FDI regimes undertaken during the 1990s across the region. And most countries have large off-shore financial systems, partially due to previous financial repression at home.

The criteria of symmetric shocks is far from being satisfied, given the nature of the economies potentially involved in the monetary union. However, the US economy already exerts a strong and swift effect on the region. To the extent that commercial and financial ties are reinforced with a monetary integration, the importance of

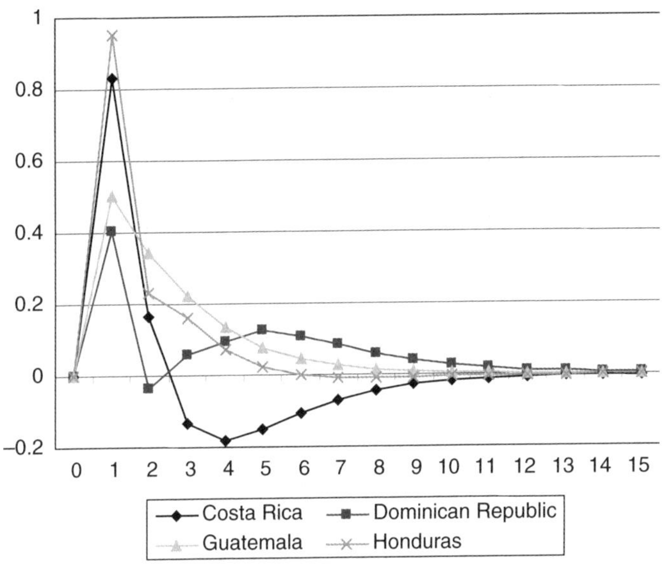

Figure 4.9 Central America response to US growth rate innovation

asymmetric shocks would be reduced. The quantitative effect of US growth changes on growth in the region can be explored by a simple VAR analysis. This allows the study of the response of individual country's endogenous variables to an impulse in the form of an instantaneous change in the US growth rate.

Figure 4.9 depicts the responses of four Central American countries – Costa Rica, Guatemala, Honduras, and Dominican Republic – obtained from individual VARs. An increase in the US growth rate of 1 percentage point is transmitted most strongly and almost instantaneously to Costa Rica and Honduras. Their growth rates will be at least 0.8 percentage points higher. The impact on the Dominican Republic and Guatemala is not as potent, but still substantial, since their growth rates increase by 0.4 percentage points. VARs (not included in Figure 4.9) also show that higher growth in the US economy is generally associated with an improvement in the terms of trade, an appreciation of the RER, but with an ambiguous effect on the trade balance of individual countries.

Some other features of Central American countries

Factors other than those discussed above may also play into the consideration of a possible monetary integration. The literature mentions two additional factors worth taking into account in the Central American case: the degree of dollarization and credibility problems. In theory, dollarization or any other type of hard peg, is supposed to bring about gains in credibility in the form of lower spreads on sovereign bonds and domestic interest rates, mainly as a result of the elimination of currency risk. Dollarization should also significantly reduce transaction costs for trade. Sometimes it is also argued that this type of exchange rate arrangement induces fiscal discipline because there is no monetary financing of the deficit nor seigniorage revenue. However, these benefits are not easily substantiated; hard pegs have tended to be plagued with speculative attacks and collapses of exchange arrangements, and the dollarized economy of Panamá has tended to show higher fiscal deficits than other countries in the region (Goldfajn *et al.*, 2001).

On the other hand, *de facto* 'asset dollarization' weakens the ability to pursue an independent (not included in Figure 4.9) monetary policy and the advantages of having a flexible exchange rate regime. Many economies in the region show high degrees of de facto dollarization. The degree of dollarization is very high for Nicaragua (70 per cent) and relatively high for two other countries in the sample, Costa Rica and Honduras (30–40 per cent). These three countries exhibit an upward trend, indicating that this process may continue in the near future. It is important to notice that these figures do not take into account the large off-shore banking transactions carried out in dollars all over the region. To complete the picture, since May 2001 Guatemalan authorities allowed residents to hold in their domestic banking system assets and liabilities denominated in foreign currency.

In addition, 'liability dollarization' is an important and pervasive phenomenon in these countries. This dollarization implies balance sheet vulnerability to a devaluation, since agents (households, banks, firms in the nontradable sector, government) have a large fraction of their liabilities denominated in dollars, and there are often no matching assets denominated in dollars. Balance sheet vulnerabilities also reduce the attractiveness of a flexible exchange rate regime. Countries with high asset dollarization usually have high levels of liability dollarization, as most domestic credit is by necessity in dollars. In contrast, in countries with low levels of asset dollarization and where domestic credit is mostly in local currency, liability dollarization is restricted to governments and large firms in the nontradable sector with access to foreign credit markets and even then it is less pervasive. In addition, hard pegs tend to stimulate liability dollarization as it represents a form of implicit exchange rate guarantee. They also inhibit the development of instruments for currency hedging.

Implications for monetary arrangements

Standard OCA criteria, the degree of financial integration and de facto dollarization and, to a lesser extent, the possibility of importing monetary credibility, conform all to a framework within which monetary integration – that is, a dollar-based monetary integration – is a potentially useful arrangement for the region. Full dollarization of Central American economies could be a reasonable choice as both the trade structure and the financial monetary structure are closely tied to the dollar.

Successful unilateral dollarization requires, however, a level of foreign reserves sufficient to: (i) withdraw monetary liabilities in local currency and exchange these dollars; and (ii) maintain a limited lender of last resort facility for the central bank. For the latter, the central bank has to impose high reserve requirements and ensure a sound financial system or build up its own precautionary fund, as El Salvador has done.

Obviously, a full monetary integration with the United States would be superior, as it would provide lender of last resort facilities and likely improvements in banking regulation and supervision. It would also bring more significant credibility gains (and thus lower interest rates and longer term credit) as the exit costs would be much higher than under unilateral dollarization. However, such a development is unlikely in the short term. It would probably be possible only after trade agreements have been in place for some time and there has been higher macroeconomic and financial sector regulatory convergence. Not even NAFTA is yet considering such a step.

Fiscal policy will also play a specially important role under hard pegs or fully dollarized economies. When giving up monetary policy and exchange rate flexibility, output stabilization will be assigned to fiscal policy. But, countercyclical fiscal policy is easier said than done. Most of the developing world and many developed countries pursue procyclical policies. The capacity to pursue countercyclical fiscal policies depends on appropriate institutional arrangements and rules that allow governments to save in times of plenty, in spite of the strong political pressures to spend out visible surpluses (see Perry, 2002).

Moreover, trade reforms in the region have hit public revenues by reducing trade taxes. Negotiation of a new trade agreement with the United States would further reduce revenues. Preliminary calculations indicate (Figure 4.10) that losses would amount from 3 per cent to 8 per cent of current revenues. Full dollarization would also imply the loss of seigniorage revenue. These developments call for substantial fiscal consolidation, before countries are able to use fiscal policy as a business cycle stabilizer.

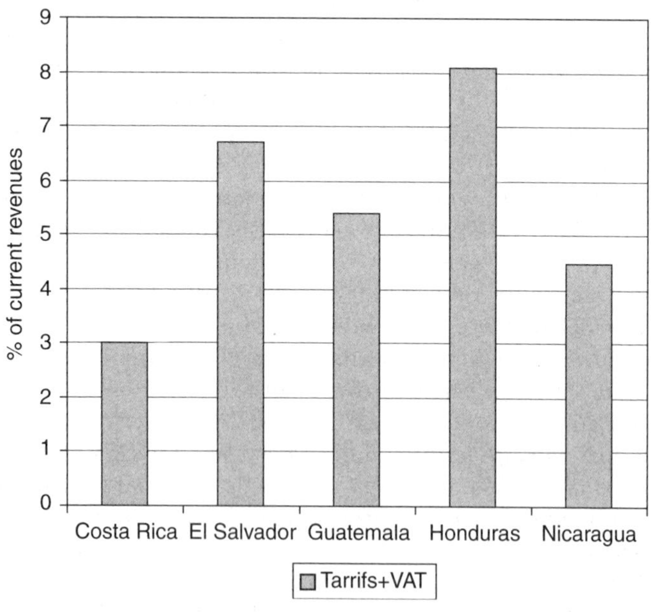

Figure 4.10 Estimated fiscal effect of a FTA with the United States

Conclusions

Trade liberalization has been an effective means to bring growth and development to the Central American region. During the last decade the process of integration with the US economy has witnessed an unprecedented intensification of trade and possibly foreign investment. But it also brought further financial dollarization. This chapter has assessed a set of policy options that emerge as a natural step forward in the development of this integration process.

The building of a deeper preferential trade agreement with the United States is a very important initiative that can bring benefits, but the magnitude of such benefits will certainly depend on complementary policies, including macroeconomic policies. A long-term trade agreement, in lieu of the existing temporary unilateral preferences granted by the United States, would guarantee access to the US market and preference margins, thus attracting more foreign direct investment and providing a further boost to exports as long as quality of domestic institutions does not deteriorate and as long as macroeconomic stability is maintained.[9] Liberalization of agricultural trade could bring positive welfare effects for the poor through cheaper staples, but might require some temporary support for low income farmers that may be forced to reconvert. The fiscal and structural implications of such programs need to be assessed carefully.

In the medium and long term, full dollarization, preferably under a monetary arrangement with the United States, is an initiative to be considered seriously, as both the trade structure and the financial monetary structure are already closely tied to the dollar and such links would be furthered by a bilateral trade agreement. Full unilateral dollarization, however, requires enough reserves not just to withdraw present domestic currency liabilities of the Central Bank, but also to retain limited lender of last resort capacity in the case of eventual bank runs. It also requires strengthening of banking sectors and stricter prudential regulation and supervision. Fiscal policy under this setup would represent the only instrument available to stabilize the business cycle and to cope with adverse shocks. The design of an appropriate institutional framework and significant fiscal consolidation would be required to allow governments to effectively pursue credible countercyclical fiscal policies.

Notes

1. This may not be true for Panamá. Panamá's sample period only starts by the end of the 1970s.
2. The Herfindahl index is defined as follows:

$$H = \sum_{i=1}^{n} \left(\frac{x_i}{\sum_{i=1}^{n} x_i} \right)^2$$

where n is the number of export products and x_i is the dollar amount of good i exports. If $H = 1$, only one export commodity accounts for all export revenue, signalling extremely high concentration. If $H = 0$, each of the n goods contributes with the same share $\frac{1}{n}$ to total export revenue.
3. Tables 4.1 and 4.2 include information up to year 1999. Updated data, but from other sources, up to year 2001 tells the same story.
4. The CBI rule of origin is more restrictive than the NAFTA rules of origin for apparel. In the CBI, apparel exports to the United States must be made with textiles and yarns produced in the United States. In the NAFTA, the textiles and yarns can originate in any of the beneficiary countries.
5. See for example, Dollar (1992), Ben-David (1993), Sachs and Warner (1995), Edwards (1998), Frankel and Romer (1999), Dollar and Kraay (2000), and World Bank (2001).
6. Loayza *et al.* (2002).
7. The core of the Farm Bill is a price and income support program composed of: (1) Loan Deficiency Payments, (2) Countercyclical Payments, and (3) Direct Payments.

   The Loan Deficiency Payment provision creates a price floor, thus limiting the downside price risk, with a loan instrument in which the loan rate per unit of production is determined in advance. The loan can be repaid at the set loan rate plus interest costs but, if the market price is lower than the loan rate, the loan can be repaid at market prices with no interest charges. Producers have the right to receive the difference between the loan rate and the market price – the so-called Loan Deficiency Payment – even if they do not take out loans.

   The Direct Payment provision corresponds to a fixed annual direct payment to a producer based on the farm's historical production and acreage. On the other hand, the Countercyclical Payment provision is intended to stabilize farm income when commodity prices are lower than target prices. The implied transfers are based on historical production as well. Given the historical references taken into consideration to calculate the amount of Direct and Countercyclical payments, it is generally thought that these provisions do not distort production decisions. These programs decouple production and support and satisfy WTO definition for not being included in a country's Aggregate Measurement of Support (AMS).

   However, current planting decisions may be distorted if producers expect that current production will become the basis for historical production and, thus payments, in the future. On the other hand, Loan Deficiency payments are expected to have a direct distorting effect on production decisions.

8. The VAR consists of two subsystems. The first includes the US growth rate and nominal interest rate. The identification of the structural innovation to the US growth rate is based on the Choleski decomposition. The second subsystem includes in addition to the two preceding US variables, which are treated as exogenous, four endogenous variables: the individual country's growth rate, the trade balance to output ratio, the bilateral real exchange rate (log change) and terms of trade. Individual VARs are estimated using annual data for the 1965–2000 sample periods.
9. Although this paper has not addressed the factors that explain FDI flows, it is worth mentioning that FDI is driven by fundamentals, such as the quality of public institutions, education of the labor force, economic growth, and macroeconomic stability (see, for example, Chapter 4 in De Ferranti *et al.*, 2002; and Calderón *et al.*, 2002).

References

Ben-David, D. (1993) 'Equalizing Exchange: Trade Liberalization and Income Convergence', *Quarterly Journal of Economics*, 108, pp. 653–79.

Burki, S. and G. Perry (1997) 'Towards Open Regionalism', Annual World Bank Conference on Development in Latin America and the Caribbean, Washington, DC: pp. 3–9.

Cadot, O., J. de Melo, A. Estevadeordal, A. Suwa-Eisenman, and B. Tumurchurur (2002) 'Assessing the Effects of NAFTA's Rules of Origin', *mimeo*, Office of the Chief Economist, LCR, The World Bank.

Calderón, C., N. Loayza, and L. Servén (2002) 'Greenfield FDI vs. Mergers and Acquisitions: Does the Distinction Matter?' *mimeo*, Office of the Chief Economist for LCR, The World Bank.

De Ferranti, D., G. Perry, D. Lederman, and W. Maloney (2002) *From Natural Resources to the Knowledge Economy*, World Bank, Washington, DC: World Bank.

Dollar, D. (1992) 'Outward Oriented Developing Economies Really Do Growth More Rapidly: Evidence from 95 LDCs 1976–1985', *Economic Development and Cultural Change*, 40, pp. 523–44.

Dollar, D. and A. Kraay (2000) 'Trade, Growth and Poverty', *mimeo*, Washington, DC: The World Bank Development Research Group.

Edwards, S. (1998) 'Openness, Productivity and Growth: What Do We Really Know?' *Economic Journal*, 108, pp. 383–98.

Frankel, J. and D. Romer (1999) 'Does Trade Cause Growth?' *American Economic Review*, 89, pp. 379–99.

Funkhouser, E. (2002) 'Remittances to Latin America: What Do We Know?', in Q. Wodon (ed.), *Internal and International Migration: Poverty, Remittances, and Brain Drain*, Washington, DC: World Bank, forthcoming.

Goldfajn, I. and G. Olivares (2001) 'Full Dollarization: The Case of Panamá', *Economía*, Vol. 1, No. 2, pp. 101–55.

Hoekman, B., F. Ng, and M. Olarreaga (2002) 'Reducing Agricultural Tariffs versus Domestic Support: What's More Important for Developing Countries?' *mimeo*, Trade Unite, The World Bank.

Honahan, P. and A. Shi (2002) 'Deposit Dollarization and the Financial Sector in Emerging Economies', *mimeo*, World Bank.

IMF (2001) *World Economic Outlook*, October, Washington, DC: IMF.

Lederman, D. and W. Maloney (2002) 'Trade Structure and Growth', *mimeo*, Office of the Chief Economist, LCR, The World Bank.

Loayza, N., P. Fajnzylber, and C. Calderón (2002) 'Economic Growth in Latin America and the Caribbean. Stylized Facts, Explanations, and Forecasts', *mimeo*, Office of the Chief Economist, LCR, The World Bank.

Lora, E. and U. Panizza (2002) 'Un Escrutinio a las Reformas Estructurales en America Latina', *IADB Working Paper # 471*.

Monge-Naranjo, A. (2002) 'The Impact of NAFTA on Foreign Direct Investment Flows in México and the Excluded Countries', *mimeo*, Office of the Chief Economist, LCR, The World Bank.

Montenegro, C. and I. Soloaga (2002) 'NAFTA's Impact on Third Countries: Recent Evidence with a Gravity Model Approach', *mimeo*, Office of the Chief Economist, LCR, The World Bank.

Perry, G. (2002) 'Can Fiscal Rules Help Reduce Macroeconomic Volatility in LAC?' *mimeo*, Office of the Chief Economist, LCR, The World Bank.

Sachs, J. and A. Warner (1995) 'Economic Reforms and the Process of Global Integration', *Brookings Papers on Economic Activity*, 1, pp. 1–118.

World Bank (2001) 'Globalization, Growth, and Poverty: Building an Inclusive World Economy', *mimeo*, Washington, DC.

Yuñez-Naude, A. (2002) 'Lessons from NAFTA: The Case of México's Agricultural Sector', *mimeo*, World Bank.

5
Choice of Exchange Rate Regimes

Robert Rennhack, Erik Offerdal, and Valerie Mercer-Blackman

Introduction

The 20 economies in the Central America and Caribbean region (CAC)[1] share a number of common structural features. Compared with other developing countries, they tend to be small, open to trade and financial flows, and often have domestic financial markets at an earlier stage of development. At the same time, these economies employ a wide range of exchange rate regimes: full dollarization in El Salvador and Panamá, a fixed peg in the six countries of the Eastern Caribbean Currency Union and Bahamas, Barbados and Belize, crawling pegs or bands in Costa Rica, Honduras, and Nicaragua, and various degrees of managed floats in the nine other countries.

This chapter addresses the question of whether this range of exchange regimes makes sense based on the structural characteristics of these countries. First we review the theoretical considerations behind the choice of an exchange rate regime and present the data on the structural features of a group of 70 countries, including the CAC region. Then we estimate ordered probit regressions for this sample of countries that seek to explain their choice of exchange rate regime in terms of several structural characteristics. Because the results of the probit regressions need to be interpreted with caution, we also constructed an index of the structural features of a sample of developing countries to assess the choice of exchange rate regime by the CAC countries.

The results suggest that the diversity of exchange rate regimes among the CAC countries is similar to the choices made by other developing countries. The smaller Caribbean countries generally have GDP of less than US$1 billion, often with trade equivalent to GDP, and like other very small and open economies, these countries have adopted exchange rate pegs. Of course, these countries need to back the exchange rate pegs with the correct macroeconomic policies, especially a sustainable fiscal position. For the Central American countries and the larger Caribbean economies, the results suggest that most of these countries have chosen an exchange regime that is consistent with their structural characteristics. However, there are some questions about the advisability of crawling pegs.

Theoretical considerations in the choice of exchange regime

Mussa *et al.* (2000), Poirson (2001), and Juhn and Mauro (2002) identify the range of structural, long-term factors that can influence the choice of exchange rate regimes:

- *Size and openness of the economy*: Small, highly open economies tend to opt for an exchange rate peg to help anchor inflationary expectations. Because these economies typically have very small nontraded goods sectors, the nominal exchange rate exerts little influence over the relative price of traded and nontraded goods but is a key determinant of overall inflation. Also these types of countries tend to have financial markets that may be too small and illiquid to allow for an adequately functioning market for foreign exchange.
- *Inflation*: Countries with a history of high inflation tend to adopt flexible regimes to insulate the real exchange rate from the effects of inflation. Moreover, an exchange rate peg would probably lack credibility if inflationary expectations were to remain high.
- *The extent of capital mobility*: Countries with a high degree of capital mobility tend to encounter difficulties in sustaining a so-called soft exchange rate peg. As a result they face two options: opt for a hard exchange rate peg (dollarization or a currency board) and give up an independent monetary policy; or adopt a flexible exchange regime and gain some degree of monetary independence.
- *Stance of fiscal policy*: Countries with a history of high fiscal deficits tend to adopt flexible regimes, because concerns about fiscal sustainability tend to undermine confidence in an exchange rate peg.

- *The degree of currency substitution*: A high degree of currency substitution pushes a country in the direction of adopting an exchange rate peg. In these kinds of countries, the effectiveness of monetary policy is limited and unhedged foreign currency-denominated debt may be sizable.
- *Volatility in the terms of trade*: Countries with volatile terms of trade, especially those that depend on a few export products, tend to rely on a flexible exchange rate regime to help absorb the effects of those shocks.
- *Diversification of the economy*: Diversified countries would tend to opt for flexible regimes to help ensure that the exchange rate helps protect the competitiveness of exports, on average.
- *Per capita GDP*: Larger developed countries tend to have deeper financial markets and stronger institutions and are better able to support a flexible exchange rate.

It is important to add that historical factors can also play a role in the choice of exchange rate regime. A country that has maintained an exchange rate regime for many years faces a cost in making the transition to a new regime, which must be factored into the decision. Institutional weaknesses also play a role and may work in opposite directions: some countries with weak monetary institutions or political instability have opted for flexible arrangements, because they are unable to sustain a peg, whereas others have tried a currency board or dollarization as a way to enforce policy discipline.

Overview of the economic structure of the CAC countries

Before the debt crisis of the 1980s, all of the CAC countries had exchange rate pegs. However, as part of their adjustment strategy to external difficulties, three of these countries (Costa Rica, Honduras, and Nicaragua) moved to crawling peg exchange rate regimes, while another five countries (Dominican Republic, Guatemala, Guyana, Haiti, Jamaica, and Trinidad and Tobago) adopted floating exchange rates with varying degrees of foreign exchange intervention.[2] (Table 5.1). The smaller Caribbean countries have been able to maintain exchange rate pegs for at least the past 25 years. Panamá,

Table 5.1 Exchange rate regimes and trade structure of the 20 CAC countries

	Current exchange rate regime in place since	Largest export partner[1]		Principal export in percent of total exports	Principal export
		Share	Country		
Fixed peg		39.0		44.2	
Antigua and Barbuda	1976	54.5	Germany	62.2	Tourism
Bahamas	1949	28.8	United States	75.0	Tourism
Barbados	1975	15.5	United States	58.5	Tourism
Belize	1976	28.9	United States	30.0	Tourism
Dominica	1976	22.5	United Kingdom	33.3	Tourism
El Salvador[2]	2001	59.7	United States	7.0	Coffee
Grenada	1976	30.0	United States	45.0	Tourism
Panama[2]	1904	45.9	United States	17.9	Canal tolls
St. Kitts and Nevis	1976	60.3	United States	39.4	Tourism
St. Lucia	1976	51.9	United States	72.6	Tourism
St. Vincent and the Grenadines	1976	31.3	United Kingdom	45.0	Tourism
Trinidad and Tobago[3]	1991	46.8	United States	80.0	Petroleum
Crawling peg		57.1		14.3	
Costa Rica	1988	43.7	United States	17.0	Bananas
Honduras	1996	69.9	United States	8.0	Bananas
Nicaragua	1993	57.7	United States	18.0	Coffee

Floating[4]		58.8		36.0	
Dominican Republic	1995	87.3	United States	31.0	Bananas
Guatemala	1994	58.6	United States	9.0	Coffee
Guyana	1991	22.4	United States	19.2	Gold
Haiti	1994	86.7	United States	83.0	n.a.
Jamaica	1991	39.2	United States	38.0	Tourism
Memorandum items					
Eastern Caribbean Region[5]		36.0		51.2	
Rest of the Caribbean and Central America		57.1		24.8	

Notes

[1] All data are for 2000, except Belize, Grenada, St. Kitts and Nevis, St. Lucia, and St. Vincent and the Grenadines, for which the data is from 1998.

[2] For the purposes of this discussion, we made no formal distinction between the official dollarization in El Salvador and Panama, and the fiscal peg in the other countries in this group.

[3] The country reports a managed float, but according to the IMF classification it is included with the countries that peg.

[4] All countries in this group have a managed float, although the degree of intervention varies both between countries and over time.

[5] Includes Antigua and Barbuda, the Bahamas, Barbados, Belize, Dominica, Grenada, St. Kitts and Nevis, St. Lucia, and St. Vincent.

Sources: International Monetary Fund, world Economic Outook and *Direction of Trade*, and Fund staff estimates.

of course, has been fully dollarized for the past century, and El Salvador adopted full dollarization in 2001.[3]

The countries with exchange rate pegs or full dollarization tend to depend less on a single trading partner than the countries with some type of flexible regime. On average the fixed peg countries sell about 40 per cent of their exports to their principal trading partner, compared with 60 per cent of the exports of the other countries. However, the flexible regime countries have much more diversified export bases, with a single product accounting for about 15 to 30 per cent of exports, compared with an average of 45 per cent for the countries with pegs.[4]

Moreover all of the CAC countries seem to have limited de facto exchange rate flexibility. An index of exchange rate flexibility shows that the CAC countries with flexible regimes actually have very little exchange rate flexibility compared with several industrialized countries with floating exchange rates (Table 5.2).[5] The CAC countries with de jure flexible regimes appear to actively use policy instruments to limit exchange rate flexibility, as suggested by the relatively high volatility of central bank interest rates and net international reserves, compared with industrial countries. The only exception is Haiti, which has a relatively high degree of exchange rate flexibility.

We also compared the CAC countries to a sample of 77 countries according to a range of structural characteristics for the period 1995–2000 (Table 5.3). These characteristics include the size of the economy, inflation, the degree of openness to international trade, the degree of economic diversification, the variability of the terms of trade and the degree of capital mobility. The CAC countries are relatively small, with nominal GDP (in PPP terms) of about US$11 billion on average, compared with US$320 billion on average for the whole sample. This reflects in large part the smaller population of each of the CAC countries. Nominal GDP per capita in the CAC countries averaged US$6,000 versus US$9,000 for the group of 77 countries. In general, the CAC countries have significantly lower inflation (4.7 per cent versus 10 per cent for the sample). They also tend to be more open to international trade, have a somewhat more variable terms of trade and have much less diversified economies. These conclusions remain valid when we compare the CAC countries to a smaller sample of 57 developing countries.

Table 5.2 Selected countries with differing exchange rate regimes: volatility of exchange rate, interest rate, and international reserves, January 1996–December 2001

	Indices of exchange rate flexibility[1]			Volatility of[2]			Ratio of exchange rate volatility to		International reserves	
	EXR	PEG	FLT	exchange rate[3]	interest rate	international reserves	interest rate volatility	international reserve volatility	in months of imports	in per cent of GDP
Caribbean and Central American countries				1.1	0.6	18.9	1.9	0.1	3.4	12.2
Costa Rica	1	5	0.13	0.2	0.6	8.6	0.3	0.0	2.0	8.0
Dominican Republic	2	7	0.09	0.8	0.8	8.9	0.9	0.1	1.2	5.3
Guatemala	2	7	0.13	1.9	0.3	47.3	6.4	0.0	5.2	12.2
Guyana	2	7	0.06	1.0	0.2	3.6	4.4	0.3	4.1	45.5
Haiti	2	7	1.67	2.4	1.1	7.6	2.3	0.3	1.9	4.6
Honduras	1	6	0.10	0.9	0.8	8.8	1.2	0.1	5.2	23.1
Jamaica	2	7	0.03	1.8	0.9	6.9	2.0	0.3	5.2	19.3
Nicaragua	1	5	0.12	0.6	0.3	10.5	1.9	0.1	2.9	20.4
Trinidad and Tobago				0.4	0.4	7.0	1.0	0.1	5.9	22.9
Industrialized countries				1.7	0.1	14.8	12.0	0.1	2.6	3.2
Japan	2	7	5.61	2.9	0.0	7.9	216.5	0.4	10.3	9.5
United States	2	7	4.94	1.3	0.2	2.7	6.6	0.5	0.5	0.6
Australia	2	7	0.97	2.5	0.2	5.9	15.0	0.4	2.5	5.0
Canada	2	7	0.23	1.1	0.2	5.7	4.7	0.2	1.4	4.9
Israel	1	6	1.03	1.7	0.5	4.8	3.2	0.3	6.0	21.2
New Zealand	2	7	0.27	2.6	0.3	6.9	8.6	0.4	10.3	6.1
United Kingdom	2	7	1.03	1.7	0.1	141.8	14.5	0.0	1.1	2.6

Notes

[1] Defined in Appendix 1and in text. EXR and PEG are as of March 2001, and FLT is for the year 2000.

[2] Volatility is defined as the standard deviation of the monthly growth rate of the series for the exchange rate and for international reserves and as the standard deviation of the difference for the interest rate.

[3] Bilateral versus the US dollar for all countries except the United States; nominal effective exchange rate for the United States.

Sources: IMF, International Financial Statistics, and World Economic Outlook.

Table 5.3 Mean of regression variables by selected groups and for 20 CAC countries (annual averages 1995–2000; in per cent unless otherwise indicated)

Variable as defined for regressions[1]	Number of observations	Per capita GDP[2]	Inflation	Sectoral diversification	Openness	Variability of terms of trade	Capital controls index[3]	Nominal GDP[4]
All countries	77	9070	10.0	25	80	7.5	8.0	321.4
Fixed (EXR = 0)	37	10722	5	23	93	6.6	7.5	165
Intermediate regime (EXR = 1)	7	6729	16	25	67	9.7	8.9	48
Floating regime (EXR = 2)	33	9759	10	28	76	6.2	7.4	751
Developed economies	20	22234	2	50	85	2.7	9.6	939
Fixed (EXR = 0)	11	20600	2	45	84	2.0	9.8	415
Intermediate regime (EXR = 1)								
Floating regime (EXR = 2)	9	24230	2	56	85	3.5	9.4	1580
Developing countries	57	5635	10	17	83	8.1	6.9	218
Fixed (EXR = 0)[5]	26	6542	6	13	96	8.6	6.5	60
Intermediate regime (EXR = 1)	7	6729	16	25	67	9.7	8.9	48
Floating regime (EXR = 2)	24	4332	13	18	73	7.2	6.7	440
Developing countries excluding countries with annual average inflation above 40 percent[6]								
Total	54	5661	7	17	85	8.0	6.8	220
Fixed (EXR = 0)	25	6676	4	13	98	8.8	6.4	61
Intermediate regime (EXR = 1)	6	6863	11	26	71	7.0	9.0	34
Floating regime (EXR = 2)	23	4244	10	18	74	7.3	6.7	442
Africa	10	3348	12	14	79	9.8	6.7	60
Asia	8	3884	8	24	83	5.7	4.6	944
Europe and Middle East	8	8169	13	22	84	7.6	7.5	134
Latin America and Carribean	31	6170	9	14	84	8.4	7.4	104

All countries without controls	26			19	73	12.2		
variable Fixed (EXR = 0)	11			13	79	13.4		
Intermediate regime (EXR = 1)	1			24	100	2.4		
Floating regime (EXR = 2)	14			23	67	12.0		
Central American and Carribean	20	6054	4.66	12	105	8.2	7.4	10.62
countries Fixed								
(EXR = 0)	12	7664	1.84	10	112	9.2	6.3	5.12
Antigua and Barbuda		9495	1	2	165	54.5	8.5	1
Bahamas		15112	1	9	110	2.0	4.5	4
Barbados		13447	2	10	113	2.3	6.5	4
Belize		4839	1	16	111	0.0	4.0	1
Dominica		5158	1	8	118	3.7	2.5	0
El Salvador		4153	3	22	58	5.4	9.0	25
Grenada		5961	1	7	118	5.0	5.0	1
Panamá		5489	1	8	77	3.2	10.0	15
St. Kitts and Nevis		10575	3	10	124	8.2	6.5	0
St. Lucia		5402	2	6	134	9.2	4.0	1
St. Vincent and Grenadines		4824	1	7	119	4.9	5.5	1
Trinidad and Tobago		7516	3	8	100	12.1	9.0	10
Intermediate regime								
(EXR = 1)	3	4032	10.98	10	89	8.8	9.7	16.92
Costa Rica		7430	10	24	53	6.9	9.5	26
Honduras		2426	13	19	99	5.4	9.5	15
Nicaragua		2239	9	16	115	14.1	10.0	10
Floating regime								
(EXR = 2)	5	3402	7.63	15	96	5.3	8.9	20.01

Table 5.3 Continued

Variable as defined for regressions[1]	Number of observations	Per capita GDP[2]	Inflation	Sectoral diversification	Openness	Variability of terms of trade	Capital controls index[3]	Nominal GDP[4]
Dominican Republic		4 881	5	17	84	3.6	7.5	40
Guatemala		3 540	6	14	44	6.8	9.0	37
Guyana		3 501	5	11	211	5.5	9.5	3
Haiti		1 449	12	7	39	6.4	8.5	11
Jamaica		3 642	10	14	101	4.3	10.0	9

Notes
[1] For definitions, see Appendix 1. EXR is the index of the regime as of March 2001. All other variables are averages for the period 1995–2000, except for CONTROLS, where values for non-CAC developing countries are for 1991–95 as in Poirsson
[2] In current international dollars.
[3] Index number from 1 to 10. See Gastanaga *et al.* (1998) for construction. Available only for 2000.
[4] In billions of current international dollars.
[5] Consists of 9 ECU-member countries and Denmark.
[6] These were Ecuador (41.75 per cent), Turkey (77.16 per cent), and Venezuela (45.15 per cent).

Table 5.4 Results for ordered probit regressions on expected choice of exchange rate regime

	(1)	(2)	(3)
Constant	−6.465	−0.13	−7.23
	−1.759	*−0.06*	*−1.82*
GDPC	−0.445	−0.13	−0.44
	−1.499	*−0.56*	*−1.50*
INFL	0.300	0.38	0.30
	1.693	*2.26*	*1.69*
SECTDIV	0.411	0.95	0.41
	0.661	*1.55*	*0.67*
OPEN	0.474		
	1.232		
TTGVAR	−0.305	−0.66	−0.11
	−0.089	*−0.23*	*−0.03*
CONTROLS	0.027	0.01	0.03
	0.365	*0.10*	*0.34*
GDP	0.375		0.40
	2.348		*2.39*
CAPMOB			
IMPGDP			1.15
			1.36
AGSIZE		0.41	
		2.24	
Likelihood ratio (pseudo-R2)	0.18	0.12	0.18
P-value of joint significance	0.0007	0.0066	0.0005
No. of observations	77	77	77

Large sample, including developed countries.
Dependant variable: EXR (flexibility of exchange rate regime applied by country in March 2001).
(*z statistics in italics*).

There are also significant differences among the CAC countries. The Caribbean countries with exchange rate pegs have small economies (GDP of about US$1–2 billion), virtually no inflation (about 1 per cent a year), a very high degree of openness to international trade, and a relatively volative terms of trade. The two dollarized countries – El Salvador and Panamá – have relatively large economies, a much lower degree of openness to international trade and low inflation. The CAC countries with flexible exchange regimes have much larger economies, relatively high inflation and are fairly open to international trade.

An econometric approach to assessing exchange regimes

The recent empirical studies of the choice of exchange rate regime have relied on probit regressions, which allow for a discrete dependent variable, to assess whether the choice of exchange rate regime by the CAC countries was related to their long-run structural characteristics.[6] Regressions were first estimated for the choice of exchange rate regime in 2001 for a full set of countries and independent variables, averaged over the period 1995–2000. The dependent variable is a simple measure of exchange regime flexibility, assigning a value of 0 to an exchange rate peg, 1 to an intermediate regime, and 2 to a flexible regime. The independent variables are GDP measured in US dollars, per capita GDP, inflation, the degree of economic diversification, the degree of openness, the variability in the terms of trade, and the extent of capital controls.[7]

We estimated the equations for two samples: a group of 77 countries, including 20 developed countries[8] and a smaller sample of the 57 developing countries. For the larger sample, the independent variables are jointly significant at the 95 per cent confidence level, but only two variables – the size of economy and the history of inflation – are statistically significant on an individual basis (Table 5.4). The fit of the equations improves for the group of 57 developing countries, and size of the economy and inflation history are still the two statistically significant explanatory variables (Table 5.5). Reinhardt and Rogoff (2002) suggest that including high inflation countries could bias the results. When we excluded from the smaller sample the three economies with historical inflation above 40 per cent, the history of inflation remained statistically significant and the fit of the equation improved.

We also tested whether different specifications of the measures of openness and capital mobility would improve the results. Optimal currency theory suggests that it is not sufficient to just be small or to be open, but both conditions must hold for a peg to be optimal. A variable (*AGSIZE*) was constructed to capture both size and openness jointly – the value of this variable will be small for a small open economy and vice versa.[9] The coefficient for this variable had the expected sign and was statistically significant in the larger sample but not in the smaller sample. We replaced the measure of capital

Table 5.5 Results for ordered probit regressions on expected choice of exchange rate regime

	(4)	(5)	(6)	(7)	excl. INFL > 40 (8)	(9)
Constant	**−6.962**	**−7.100**	**−10.153**	**1.736**	**−8.921**	**−8.296**
	−1.318	*−1.400*	*−2.000*	*0.591*	*−1.529*	*−1.477*
GDPC	**−0.463**	**−0.429**		**−0.393**	**−0.367**	**−0.450**
	−1.119	*−1.060*		*−1.102*	*−0.836*	*−1.083*
INFL	**0.513**	**0.498**	**0.605**	**0.595**	**0.803**	**0.526**
	2.322	*2.364*	*2.760*	*3.061*	*2.773*	*2.296*
SECTDIV	**0.615**	**0.986**	**−0.585**	**2.517**	**0.750**	**0.456**
	0.138	*0.263*	*−0.146*	*0.951*	*0.201*	*0.101*
OPEN	**0.613**	**0.602**	**0.512**		**0.608**	
	1.129	*1.118*	*1.008*		*1.014*	
TTGVAR	**−2.174**		**−1.819**	**−1.542**	**−1.341**	**−1.978**
	−0.487		*−0.499*	*−0.426*	*−0.225*	*−0.423*
CONTROLS	**0.053**	**0.052**	**0.052**		**0.099**	**0.052**
	0.665	*0.652*	*0.636*		*1.084*	*0.645*
GDP	**0.381**	**0.367**	**0.357**		**0.393**	**0.423**
	1.796	*1.763*	*1.837*		*1.732*	*1.936*
CAPMOB						
IMPGDP						**1.591**
						1.397
AGSIZE				**0.245**		
				0.803		
Likelihood Ratio (pseudo-R^2)	0.27	0.26	0.25	0.21	0.32	0.28
P-value of joint significance	0.0001	0.0001	0.0001	0.0002	0.0000	0.0001
No. of observations	57	57	57	57	54	57

Excluding advanced economies, and predictions for 20 CAC countries.
Dependant variable: EXR (flexibility of exchange rate regime applied by country in March 2001).
(*z statistics in italics*).

[1] All other countries were countries whose exchange rate regime was correctly predicted. Codes are: CRI = Costa Rica, DR = Dominican Republic, GUA = Guatemala, GUY = Guyana, HAI = Haiti, HND = Honduras, JAM = Jamaica, NIC = Nicaragua. Countries in bold are countries that have flexible regimes and are predicted to fix.

restrictions with a variable that measures *de facto* capital mobility (the sum of capital inflows and outflows to GDP), but the coefficient of this measure of the effect of capital mobility was also statistically insignificant.

We preferred the results of the smaller sample, because the large disparity between the size of the developed and the developing countries tended to distort the results. The small sample results suggest that large economies with high inflation on average tend to opt for a flexible exchange rate, while small economies with low inflation tend to adopt exchange rate pegs. The impact of capital flows on the choice of exchange regime appears to be indeterminate. Moreover, per capita GDP, external vulnerability and diversification of the economy do not appear to be individually relevant in the choice of exchange rate regime.

In most cases, each country's actual exchange rate regime is consistent with the regime predicted by the probit regression. We analyzed the residuals from equation 8, which provided the best overall fit for the smaller sample (Figure 5.1). In all but four countries, the actual and predicted regimes are the same, suggesting that these countries are choosing exchange rate regimes that are consistent with the structural variables in the equation. In the case of Honduras, Nicaragua, and Costa Rica, each of these countries has a crawling peg exchange rate regime, and the regression suggests that a flexible regime would be more consistent with the structural characteristics used in this analysis. The residuals also suggest that Guyana might benefit from less exchange rate flexibility, probably reflecting the relatively small size of its economy. Nonetheless, Guyana may be opting for a managed float for other reasons.

An index approach

While the probit regressions yield interesting results, Juhn and Mauro (2002) show that the econometric work on the choice of exchange rate regimes needs to be interpreted with caution. In general the results are sensitive to sample size, with few statistically significant coefficients on an individual basis.

For this reason, we developed an index approach that sought to rank countries according to their suitability for an exchange rate peg, based on certain structural characteristics (Annex 3). Specifically, we constructed two indices – one that ranked countries by the size of their economies and their inflation history and the other that ranked countries by a wide range of structural features including size, inflation history, public debt, capital mobility, and terms of trade

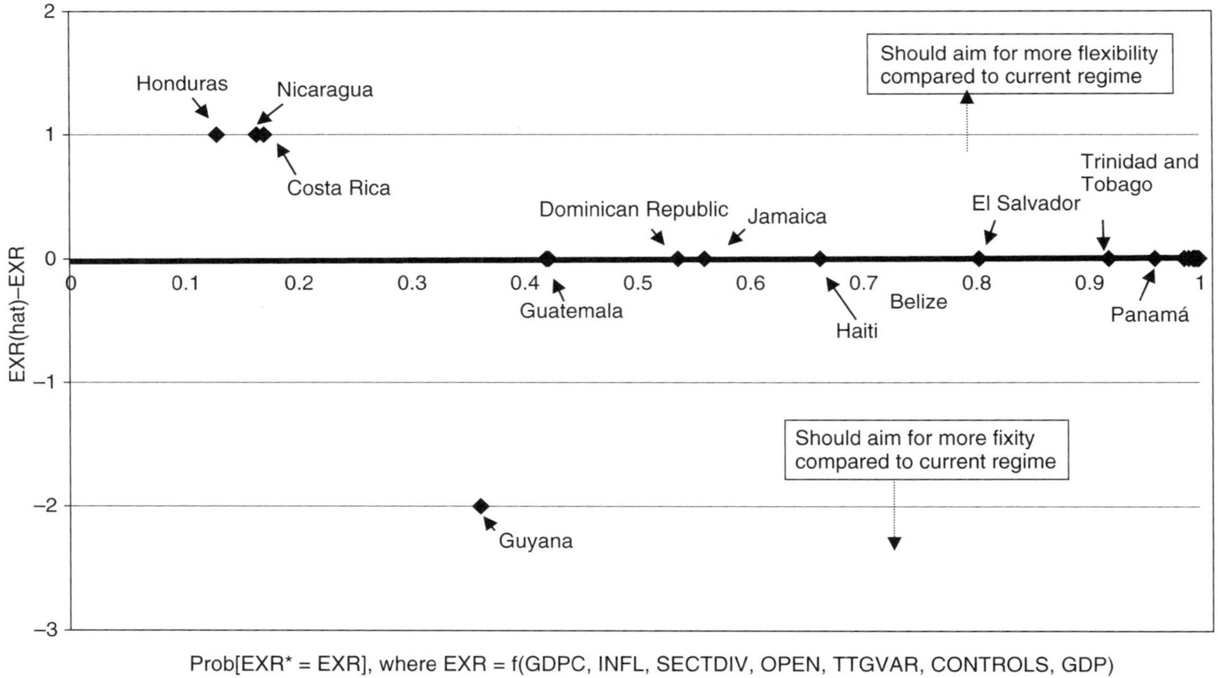

Figure 5.1 Discrete errors of Central America and Carribbean countries' EXR. Ordered probit results using a sample of 54 developing countries with moderate inflation (equation 8)

volatility. The results of both indices suggest that the ECCU, Belize, the Bahamas, Barbados, and Panamá are well suited for an exchange rate peg, based on their small size and history of low inflation compared to the other developing countries in the sample (Table 5.6). Clearly these countries need to maintain fiscal and other policies to this exchange rate regime sustainable. However, the results are less clear cut for the other countries. For example, Guyana and Trinidad and Tobago appear to have features that would support an exchange rate peg, yet both of these countries have flexible exchange rate regimes, most likely to address other concerns.

Table 5.6 Index approach to suitability of exchange rate regime

	Index 1	PEG		Index 2	PEG
1. Belize	18.91	3.00	1. Dominica	1.78	1.00
2. Dominica	19.03	1.00	2. Belize	2.01	3.00
3. St. Lucia	19.34	1.00	3. St. Vincent and Grenadines	2.20	1.00
4. Grenada	20.69	1.00	4. Grenada	2.51	1.00
5. St. Vincent and Grens.	20.77	1.00	5. Bahamas	2.58	1.00
6. Gabon	24.59	1.00	6. Bahrain	2.72	3.00
7. Antigua and Barbuda	24.95	1.00	7. Antigua and barbuda	2.93	1.00
8. Barbados	25.31	3.00	8. Barbados	3.01	3.00
9. Mauritius	25.38	7.00	9. St. Lucia	3.17	1.00
10. Guyana	25.62	7.00	10. St. Kitts and Nevis	3.74	1.00
11. Trinidad and Tobago	25.85	3.00	11. Panamá	4.27	1.00
12. Malaysia	26.04	3.00	12. Jordan	6.48	3.00
13. Elsalvador	26.46	1.00	13. Trinidad and Tobago	7.86	3.00
14. Srilanka	26.62	7.00	14. Senegal	8.35	1.00
15. St. Kitts and Nevis	26.96	1.00	15. Gabon	8.62	1.00
16. Cotedivoire	27.04	1.00	16. Guyana	9.27	7.00
17. Panamá	27.12	1.00	17. Mauritius	9.84	7.00
18. Jamaica	27.54	7.00	18. Cameroon	10.69	1.00
19. Kenya	28.48	7.00	19. Bolivia	11.12	5.00
20. Senegal	29.39	1.00	20. Cotedivoire	12.20	1.00
21. Jordan	29.40	3.00	21. Elsalvador	12.74	1.00
22. Morocco	29.51	3.00	22. Tunisia	14.37	7.00
23. Dominican Republic	29.73	7.00	23. Nicaragua	15.43	5.00
24. Guatemala	29.93	7.00	24. Dominican Republic	16.90	7.00

Table 5.6 Continued

	Index 1	PEG		Index 2	PEG
25. Cameroon	30.28	1.00	25. Guatemala	17.56	7.00
26. Bahamas	30.44	1.00	26. Paraguay	17.58	7.00
27. Honduras	30.48	6.00	27. Jamaica	18.70	7.00
28. Haiti	30.59	7.00	28. Kenya	19.11	7.00
29. Nigeria	30.96	7.00	29. Morocco	20.93	3.00
30. Tunisia	31.04	7.00	30. Costarica	21.18	5.00
31. Zimbabwe	31.10	5.00	31. Honduras	21.68	6.00
32. Chile	31.25	7.00	32. Srilanka	22.47	7.00
33. Paraguay	33.69	7.00	33. Haiti	24.07	7.00
34. Costarica	33.85	5.00	34. Israel	28.99	6.00
35. Saudi Arabia	34.07	3.00	35. Uruguay	31.63	6.00
36. Ecuador	34.46	1.00	36. Chile	31.82	7.00
37. Bolivia	36.26	5.00	37. Peru	35.43	7.00
38. Bahrain	36.39	3.00	38. Malaysia	36.87	3.00
39. Egypt	41.19	4.00	39. Saudi Arabia	39.52	3.00
40. Israel	41.27	6.00	40. Egypt	45.31	4.00
41. Pakistan	41.51	7.00	41. Zimbabwe	47.63	5.00
42. Philippines	42.27	7.00	42. Nigeria	50.81	7.00
43. Colombia	43.78	7.00	43. Zambia	51.33	7.00
44. Venezuela	44.22	6.00	44. Ecuador	53.02	1.00
45. Nicaragua	44.40	5.00	45. Pakistan	53.82	7.00
46. Peru	44.44	7.00	46. Philippines	58.44	7.00
47. Zambia	45.05	7.00	47. Colombia	64.41	7.00
48. Uruguay	47.88	6.00	48. Venezuela	72.61	6.00
Maximum	47.9		Maximum	72.6	
Minimum	18.9		Minimum	1.8	
Average	31.4		Average	22.1	
Median	30.1		Median	17.2	
Standard deviation	7.6		Standard deviation	19.2	
Correlation to PEG	0.20		Correlation to PEG	0.16	
Average − stdev	23.8		Average − stdev	2.9	
Average + stdev	38.9		Average + stdev	41.3	

Concluding remarks

This chapter looked at whether diversity of exchange rate regimes among the CAC countries – which at first glance appear very similar – was consistent with the structural characteristics of these countries. According to the results of the probit regressions and the index approach, the exchange rate regime choices made by the CAC countries are similar to the choices made by other developing countries. There are enough differences in structures of the CAC countries to explain the diversity in their choice of exchange rate regimes. Also, there is some evidence that crawling peg exchange regimes might present difficulties for some of these countries. However, the results of this study should be regarded as suggestive. As Juhn and Mauro (2002) point out, the results of econometric tests of the relationship between structural characteristics and exchange regime choice are sensitive to sample size and other factors. And the index approach also yields mixed results.

Appendix 5.1

Table 5.A1 Variables, definitions, data sources

Variable	Definitions	Source[1]
Variables used in Probit Regressions[2]		
EXR	Degree of exchange rate flexibility: 0 (peg), 1 (intermediate), 2 (independent float).	Based on IMF ARERA classification, as of 31 March, 2001.
GDPPC	Per capita GDP, PPP (current US$) average annual, 1995–2000.	World Bank, World Development Indicators (WB-WDI)
GDP	GDP at market prices, PPP (current US$), average annual 1995–2000.	WB-WDI
INFL	CPI inflation, average annual 1995–2000.	IFS
SECTDIV	Share of manufacturing in value added, average annual 1995–2000.	UN/DOTS[3] and WB-WDI
OPEN	Ratio of exports plus imports of goods and services to GDP, 1995–2000.	WB-WDI

Table 5.A1 Continued

Variable	Definitions	Source[1]
TTGVAR	Standard deviation of annual terms of trade growth, annual average 1995–2000.	WEO
IMPGDP	Share of imports of goods and services to GDP. Area, average 1995–2000.	WB-WDI
AGSIZE	Combined measure of openness and size. Variable equal to GDP/OPEN, where each variable is its average over the time period.	See above
CONTROLS	Index of (lack of) restrictions on capital account, 2000. Equal to the sum of five subindices each with a score between 0 and 2. The subindices grade the level of restrictions on: (i) inward direct investment, (ii) outward direct investment, (iii) right of nonresidents to own bank accounts, (iv) personal and commercial bank lending to non-residents; and (v) personal and commercial bank borrowing from non-residents. The composite index goes from 0 (high restrictions) to 10 (no restrictions).[4]	IMF *ARERA*[5]
CAPMOB	Absolute value of inward and outward flows of financial assets and liabilities (the sum of absolute values, if available, of IFS lines *78bdd, 78ebd, 78bfd, 78bgd, 78bhd* and *78bid* as a ratio to GDP). Annual averages 1995–2000 for all countries for which at least four of these lines are available.	IFS
Variables used in Index and Tables but not in Regressions		
PEG	1 (another currency as legal tender), 2 (currency union), 3 (single currency or SDR peg), 4 (basket peg), 5 (crawling peg, target zone or band,	Based on IMF *ARERA* classification, as of 31 March 2001.

Table 5.A1 Continued

Variable	Definitions	Source[1]
	crawling band), 6 (managed float without preannounced path), 7 (independent float).	
FLT	Exchange rate flexibility index, (0=perfect peg).	Authors' calculations (see Appendix 2)
FCDTD	(currency substitution): Ratio of foreign currency deposits to total deposits, 1998–2001.	IMF staff and national authorities
TRADEDEP	Share of trade with largest prime-currency trading partner to total trade (imports and exports of goods) multiplied by the variable OPEN. Prime-currency countries are: European Monetary Union, Japan, United Kingdom and United States.	DOTS
FISCAL	General government fiscal balance as a per cent of GDP, of GDP average 1998–2001.	WEO
MONEY	Growth in M2 as a share of GDP, average 1998–2001.	IFS

Notes

[1] IFS = IMF International Financial Statistics
IMF *ARERA* = IMF's Annual Report on Exchange Rate Arrangements
WB_WDI = World Bank World Development Indicators
UN = United Nations
DOTS = Direction of Trade Statistics, IMF
INS = IMF Information Services, IMF
WEO = World Economic Outlook, IMF

[2] In the Probit regressions, GDPC, GDP, and INFL are expressed in logs so as to reduce the possibility that large outliers are driving the relationships.

[3] Data for developed economies is taken from UN/DOTS and adjusted to the definition of WB-WDI. Data for developing countries is from WB-WDI.

[4] Selected restrictions related to national security (i.e. on defense industries, or vis-à-vis terrorist entities) were not considered as restrictions.

[5] Index from Gastanaga *et al.* (1998).

Appendix 5.2 Index of effective exchange rate flexibility (FLT)

Following the approach pioneered by Holden *et al.* (1997), and more recently followed by Poirson (2001), we measure the degree of *de facto* exchange rate flexibility of country *i* (*FLT*) by the ratio of the average absolute value of monthly nominal exchange rate depreciation (*ME*) to the average absolute value of the monthly change in reserves normalized by the monetary base in the previous month (*MR*), in order to proxy for the monetary impact of these changes. Both averages are calculated over 2000. For countries with any form of a fixed exchange rate system, *ME* is set to zero. For other countries with an officially fixed exchange rate, the bilateral nominal exchange rate used is the official one. For other countries, we use the bilateral exchange rate with the US dollar.

The rationale for using *FLT* as an indicator of *de facto* exchange rate flexibility is that if *MR* is high relative to *ME* (and therefore *FLT* is comparatively small) the monetary authorities are intervening relatively heavily on the foreign exchange market to offset market forces. *FLT* assumes values ranging from zero to infinity, with the limits being defined by a perfectly pegged policy at the one end ($ME = 0$) and a completely intervention-free policy at the other ($MR = 0$). A 12-month average is used to eliminate the effect of short-run fluctuations in either reserves or exchange rates, that do not accurately reflect longer run exchange rate policies. For country *k*:

$$FLT_k = \frac{ME}{MR} = \frac{\dfrac{\sum_{t=0}^{11} |E_{k,t} - E_{k,t-1}|}{E_{k,t-1}}}{\dfrac{\sum_{t=0}^{11} |R_{k,t} - R_{k,t-1}|}{H_{k,t-1}}}$$

where $E_{k,t}$ = nominal exchange rate in month *t* of country *k*, $R_{k,t}$ = net international reserves, minus gold, in month *t*, and H = monetary base in month *t*.

Appendix 5.3 The construction of the index of suitability for a peg

This index was constructed on the basis of the list of longer-term structural variables discussed in Appendix 5.2. Thirteen variables were considered[10]

1. Gross Domestic Product
2. GDP per Capita
3. Sectoral Diversification
4. Trade Dependence on the major trading partner
5. Trade Openness
6. Terms of Trade variability
7. Capital Controls
8. Actual Capital Mobility
9. Inflation
10. AGSIZE
11. Comovement of GDP growth between country and its major trading partner
12. Degree of Currency substitution; foreign currency deposits in banking system as share of total deposits
13. Public debt as share of GDP.

The calculation of the index is done in two steps: (i) a subindex is calculated for each of these variables, based on the *a priori* expectations of how they individually influence the choice of exchange rate regime; and (ii) several overall indices for each country are calculated as the average of the subindex values of those variables included in each index.

From step one, a variable where a high value would be expected to be conducive to a floating regime, for example, size – proxied here by GDP – the country in the sample with the highest GDP is designated as a numeraire for that variable and is assigned an index value of 100. The index values for the remaining countries are calculated as their GDP as percentage of the GDP in the numeraire country. This procedure is followed for variables 1, 2, 3, 6, 7, 8, 9, 10, 12, and 13. For the remaining three variables (4, 5, 11), the *a priori* expectation would be that a low value would be conducive to a floating regime. Thus, for the construction of the subindices for these three variables, the countries with the lowest value of each variable becomes the numeraire, and the remaining countries are assigned index values calculated as its variable as a percentage of the variable in the numeraire country.

Two overall indices are calculated:

Index 1 is, for each country, the average of the subindex values for all of the thirteen variables listed above.

Index 2 is the average of the subindices of only size (GDP), and inflation.

Notes

1. The focus of this chapter is on seven Central American countries (Costa Rica, Dominican Republic, El Salvador, Guatemala, Honduras, Nicaragua, Panamá); and 13 Caribbean countries (Antigua and Barbuda, Bahamas, Barbados, Belize, Dominica, Grenada, Guyana, Haiti, Jamaica, St. Kitts and Nevis, St. Lucia, St. Vincent and the Grenadines, and Trinidad and Tobago).
2. The IMF's classification of Trinidad and Tobago - which attempts to capture the *de facto* exchange rate regime - has varied over time, even though the *de jure* regime has been a managed float for some time. In March 2001 (the date used in the econometric analysis), Trinidad and Tobago was classified as a *de facto* exchange rate peg.
3. El Salvador temporarily floated its exchange rate during its civil war, but in 1993 the country returned to an exchange rate peg - the exchange regime it had followed from the mid-1930s to the mid-1980s.
4. These averages exclude Haiti, which depends on a single product for over 80 per cent of its exports.
5. We estimated the indicator of *de facto* flexibility pioneered by Holden *et al.* (1979) and developed in Levy-Yeyati and Sturzenegger (2003) (appendix table 2).
6. This methodology estimates the probability of adopting a particular exchange rate regime given a set of explanatory variables. The variable definitions, methodology and sample of non-CAC countries closely follow Poirson (2001) and are described in detail in Appendix 5.1.
7. Other recent studies (see Juhn and Mauro) have considered some short-term variables as regressors, and have generally found that: (i) measures of political instability are highly significant and associated with floating exchange rate regimes. Other variables such as: (ii) GNP growth and (iii) the coverage of reserves to imports have not been found to be statistically significant.
8. These countries are Australia, the Euro zone, Korea, Singapore, United States, and the United Kingdom.
9. As expected, all of the Caribbean countries have very small values of *AGSIZE*. Guyana follows closely behind Singapore as having the lowest value of *AGSIZE* in the full sample of 103 countries.
10. The first ten of these variables are defined in Appendix 5.1.

References

Alessina, A., Barro, R., and S. Tenreyno (2002) 'Optimal Currency Areas', *Paper presented at the March, 2002, NBER Conference in Washington, D.C.*

Bubula, A. and I. Ötker-Robe (2002) 'The Evolution of Exchange Rate Regimes Since 1990: Evidence from De Facto Policies', *IMF Working Paper No. 155.*

Calvo, G. (2000) 'The Case for Hard Pegs in the Brave New World of Global Finance', *Mimeo.*

Calvo, G. and Reinhart (2000) 'Fear of Floating', *NBER Working Paper No. 7993.*

Corbo, V. (2001) 'Is it time for a Common Currency for the Americas', *Journal of Policy Modeling*, Vol. 23, No. 3, pp. 241–8.

Corden, M. (2002) *'Too Sensational: On the Choice of Exchange Rate Regime'*, MIT Press, Boston, MA.

Department of Health and Human Services U.S.: *'Social Security Programs Throughout the World'*, various years.

Dornbusch, R. (2001) 'Fewer Monies, Better Monies', *American Economic Review*, Vol. 91, No. 2, pp. 238–42.

Eichengreen, B. and P. Masson (1998) 'Exit Strategies: Policy Options for Countries Seeking Greater Exchange Rate Flexibility', *Occasional Paper No. 168*, International Monetary Fund.

Fischer, S. (2001) 'Exchange Rate Regimes: Is the Bipolar View Correct?' *Journal of Economic Perspectives*, Vol. 15, No. 2, pp. 3–24.

Frankel, J. (1999) 'No Single Currency Regime is Right for all Countries or at all Times', *NBER Working Paper No. 7338.*

Greene, W. (2000) *'Econometric Analysis'*, 4th edition, McGraw Hill.

Heckman, J. and C. Pagés (2000) 'The Cost of Job Security Regulation: Evidence from Latin American Labor Markets', *NBER Working Paper No. 7773*, National Bureau of Economic Research, Cambridge, MA.

Holden, P., M. Holden, and E. Suss (1979) 'The Determinants of Exchange Rate Flexibility. An Emperical Investigation', *Review of Economics and statistics*, Vol. 61, pp. 327–33.

Juhn, G. and P. Mauro (2002) 'Long-Run Determinants of Exchange Rate Regimes: A Simple Sensitivity Analysis', *IMF Working Paper No. 104.*

Levy Yeyasi, E. and I. Sturzenegger, 'A de fact classification of Exchange Rate Regimes', *American Economic Review*, Vol. 93, No. 4, September, 2003.

Lora, E (2000) 'Las Reformas Estructurales en America Latina: Qué se ha reformado y cómo medirlo', *research department mimeo*, Inter-American Development Bank, Washington D.C.

McKinnon, R.I. (1963) 'Optimal Currency Areas', *American Economic Review*, Vol. 53 pp. 717–25.

Mussa, M. *et al.* (2000) 'Exchange Rate Regimes in an Increasingly Integrated World', *Occasional Paper No. 193*, International Monetary Fund.

Obstfeld, M. and K. Rogoff (1995) 'The Mirage of Fixed Exchange Rates', *Journal of Economic Perspectives*, Vol. 4, No. 9.
Poirson, H. (2001) 'How do Countries Choose their Exchange Rate Regime?' *IMF Working Paper No. 46.*
Reinhart, C. and K. Rogoff (2002) 'The Modern History of Exchange Rate Arrangements: A Reinterpretation', *NBER Working Paper No. 8963.*

6
Financial Dollarization: What to Do About It?

Alain Ize

Financial dollarization in Central America

Partial dollarization affects a wide set of countries across the world and has generally gained ground in recent years. The ratio of on-shore foreign currency deposits to total on-shore deposits increased sharply in Latin America, in transition economies, and in Central America over the period 1996–2001 (Table 6.1). It has also increased, albeit somewhat more moderately, in the Middle East, Africa, and Asia. It remained constant on average (and low) only in the Caribbean or developed countries. Yet, dollarization has declined in some developing countries, notably Egypt, some emerging

Table 6.1 Evolution of average foreign currency deposits to total deposits (in per cent, unless otherwise indicated)

Regions	Number of countries	1996	1997	1998	1999	2000	2001
South America	8	45.8	46.1	49.4	53.2	54.0	55.9
Transition Economies	26	37.3	38.9	43.5	44.3	46.9	47.7
Middle East	7	36.5	37.2	37.7	37.5	38.2	41.9
Africa	14	27.9	27.3	27.8	28.9	32.7	33.2
Asia	13	24.9	28.0	26.8	28.8	28.7	28.2
Central America and Mexico	7	20.6	20.8	22.0	22.1	22.5	24.7
Caribbean	10	6.3	7.6	6.8	6.7	6.1	6.2
Industrial Countries	14	7.4	7.5	7.5	6.7	7	6.6

Sources: IFS, EDSS, Central Banks' Statistical Publications.

Table 6.2 Central America: share of foreign exchange denominated deposits into total bank deposits, 1996–2001

	1996	1997	1998	1999	2000	2001
Nicaragua	62	64	68	68	70	71
Costa Rica	43	47	51	53	54	57
Honduras	33	30	31	32	32	36
El Salvador	6	7	8	9	9	100
Guatemala (on-shore)	0	0	0	0	0	5

Source: IFS, Central Banks' Statistical Publications.

economies, notably Israel and México, and some transition economies, notably Slovenia, Hungary, and Poland.

In Central America, the expansion of financial dollarization has been particularly high in Costa Rica and Nicaragua. In Guatemala, recorded financial dollarization is only starting to emerge, following the liberalization of domestic dollar-denominated accounts in May 2001. Prior to this liberalization, dollar deposits were mostly held in offshore accounts. Interestingly enough, El Salvador had the lowest unrepressed dollarization ratio in the region, prior to the full dollarization that took place at the beginning of 2001. It recently chose to follow the early example of Panamá and become the second fully dollarized country in the region.

Confronted with the switch to full dollarization of some of their immediate neighbors, the unrelenting increase in partial dollarization at home, and the recent currency and banking crises experienced by some of the highly dollarized Southern Cone countries, all remaining partially dollarized Central American countries face at this time the same three daunting questions: (i) should they seek to reverse the rise in dollarization or should they take it as a fact of life and accommodate it as well they can?; (ii) are highly dollarized (effectively 'dual-currency') regimes worth preserving (i.e. do they constitute a sound middle ground to accelerate financial development and yet maintain a minimum monetary independence) or is it time to call it quits and join the ranks of the fully dollarized?; and (iii) for countries who choose to maintain a dual-currency regime, what should they do to enhance the resiliency of their financial system and limit the risk of major crises?

The responses to the questions above are obviously complex and are only starting to be addressed in the academic literature. This chapter seeks to make a modest contribution to this debate by providing some pointers as to some of the relevant factors that may need to be considered. As a general background, the chapter starts by briefly reviewing dollarization types and their possible roots. It then surveys the prudential and monetary implications of dollarization. Based on this analysis, it suggests possible dynamic linkages between dollarization and monetary policy. The chapter concludes with a suggested (and at this stage quite tentative) reform agenda for countries that wish to reverse dollarization trends and a warning about some of the challenges that they are likely to face in this endeavor.

Dollarization: types and roots

Dollarization can take multiple forms. *Partial* dollarization occurs when the government maintains the status of the local currency as exclusive legal tender but allows financial or real transactions to be denominated in dollars, effectively allowing a bicurrency system to take hold. Partial dollarization can, in turn, take three forms: *payments* dollarization in residents' use, for transaction purposes, of foreign currency in cash, demand deposits, or central bank reserves; *financial* dollarization consists of residents' holding of financial assets or liabilities in foreign currency; *real* dollarization is the indexing, formally or de facto, of local prices and wages to the dollar. Financial dollarization can be also classified as *domestic* (e.g. the use of the dollar in claims by residents) or *external* (e.g. the use of the dollar in claims by nonresidents against residents). This last distinction is important because of home bias effects. As discussed in the classic international finance literature, the demand for financial instruments is a function of the consumption basket of the investor.[1] While a US resident is discouraged from buying a México peso bond if the peso exchange rate against the dollar is volatile, that same volatility induces a Méxican resident to prefer the peso bond to a dollar bond.

While payments dollarization reflects high inflation (that increases the cost of holding money), the primary explanation for financial dollarization must be based on second moments (volatilities). Domestic borrowers and lenders prefer to denominate contracts in foreign currency when its purchasing power in terms of domestic consumption is stable relative to that of the local currency, that is, when the expected volatility of the real exchange rate is low compared to that of inflation.[2] The persistence (or increase) of financial dollarization, notwithstanding a worldwide decline in inflation, can thus be explained by a parallel decline of inflation *and* real exchange rate volatilities, following stabilization.[3] In turn, the decline in the volatility of the exchange rate may reflect dollarization-induced 'fear of floating' (more on this follows).

Dollarization hysteresis may also reflect a lingering 'peso problem', as expected volatilities may deviate from recently observed volatilities, due to persistent fears of a return to high and unstable inflation. As the probability of such a regime collapse is likely to reflect many factors, including fiscal discipline and the political and institutional environment, financial dollarization can be explained by many other variables, besides observed volatilities. Moral hazard may also be an important additional factor in promoting financial dollarization and explaining its resilience, particularly in the context of tightly managed exchange rates. The risks associated with foreign currency loans are not fully internalized by borrowers, lenders or banks because they expect a government bail out in the event of an abrupt exchange rate depreciation. The maintenance of a stable exchange rate is perceived as an implicit commitment of the monetary authorities, and reneging on this commitment is a 'catastrophic' event which warrants government intervention to limit the resulting economic disruption.[4] Thus, pegs or quasi-pegs encourage dollarization by enhancing the value of the government guarantee.[5]

As for real dollarization, which may be proxied by the pass through of exchange rate changes on prices, it also reflects in part the desire of firms and workers to hedge against macroeconomic uncertainty.[6] Denominating prices and wages in local currency is preferable if, by increasing real price flexibility, it provides a more effective buffer against employment or output fluctuations. This should be the case when the monetary authority uses (or is expected to use) monetary policy countercyclically. A high financial dollarization and a low real dollarization can thus coexist. The possibility of an abrupt regime change, which provides a fertile ground for time inconsistency and moral hazard, is precisely what exacerbates financial dollarization. In contrast, *the rainy-day benefits of retaining the local currency* (the exchange rate is expected to depreciate under exceptionally large shocks that call for major real exchange rate realignments) is what maintains the attractiveness of the local currency for real contracts, that is, maintains real dollarization in check.

The evidence of a few countries for which detailed information is available suggest that payments dollarization is often more limited than financial dollarization. This seems largely to reflect the works of Gresham's Law, as the public keeps the better currency (the dollar) under the mattress and disposes of the freely and abundantly supplied local currency by using it for payments. While data limitations also prevent a direct measurement of real dollarization, measurements of the pass through of exchange rate changes into prices suggest that it rises with financial dollarization but remains generally limited.[7] Casual evidence in highly dollarized countries, such as Bolivia and Perú, indicates that the vast majority of wages continues to be paid in local currency, with only few exceptions (such as for some top executives). Nonetheless, dollar indexation appears to have made inroads over the years.[8] As to what may explain the outliers' relatively more successful experience in de-dollarizing, it appears that financial liberalization, that removed constraints on intermediation in local currency, was partly responsible for Egypt's and Israel's relative success. In addition, countries that have made a strong commitment to stabilize inflation, such as Israel, México, Poland, Hungary, and the Czech Republic (all of which have eventually adopted an inflation targeting framework) seem to have reaped benefits in terms of de-dollarization. While it is too early to derive definite conclusions, these experiences are nonetheless suggestive of the importance of credible and sustainable stabilization in promoting the use of the national currency.[9]

Risks and drawbacks of financial dollarization

High financial dollarization increases the vulnerability of financial systems in a variety of ways. First, the limited backing of banks' dollar liabilities by US dollars and their convertibility at par subjects the financial system to liquidity risk. This happens when the demand for local assets falls, due to a perceived increase in country risk, prompting depositors to convert their deposits into dollar cash or transfer them abroad. Because dollar liabilities need to be paid at par against foreign currency, equilibrating adjustments in the exchange rate of local dollars against US dollars cannot take place, unlike for domestic assets. Thus, unless liquid dollar liabilities are backed by sufficient liquid dollar assets abroad, banks may run out of dollar liquid reserves and fail to pay off dollar deposits or other dollar liabilities on demand, or as they fall due. Similarly, central banks may run out of international reserves to provide dollar lender of last resort support to distressed banks. When this happens, deposit contracts may need to be broken and disruptive or confiscatory measures taken, thereby validating creditors' fears and justifying the run. The 1982 'mex-dollar' induced banking and currency crisis in México provided an early warning of the vulnerabilities of dollarized systems when depositors look for the exit. The 2002 collapse of the Argentine currency board offers a more recent and vivid illustration.

Runs on banks' dollar liabilities can also be associated with expectations of large exchange rate depreciations that undermine the solvency of banks. While direct exposure to currency risk for banks is generally limited by tight regulatory limits on open foreign exchange positions, currency mismatches can affect banks indirectly by undermining the solvency of their borrowers. Banks with large domestic dollar liabilities must balance their foreign exchange positions by either extending dollar lending to local currency earners or holding dollar assets abroad. To maintain their profitability, banks generally end up on lending domestically a large share of their dollar deposits, effectively transferring the currency risk to their unhedged clients and retaining the resulting credit risk. The scope for borrowers' currency mismatch is enhanced by the disconnect between real and financial dollarization, that is, the fact that prices and wages continue to be set in local currency while financial dollarization is widespread.

Widening gaps between the multilateral real exchange rate (that defines the country's competitiveness) and the bilateral real exchange rate with respect to the US dollar (that governs the intensity of financial system stress) can thus give rise to difficult policy conflicts. The monetary authorities may feel compelled to depreciate the currency in response to an appreciation of the multilateral real exchange rate, caused for example by depreciations of the bilateral exchange rate against the dollar in neighboring countries. Yet doing so would increase financial system stress.

Banks' exposure is compounded by the macroeconomic ripple effects of large devaluations. Through balance sheet effects, large devaluations in highly dollarized economies are likely to be contractionary, thereby further undermining borrowers' capacity to service their debts. Heightened credit cycles constitute another key source of risk as credit booms are accentuated by the fact that incoming dollar flows feed domestic lending and, through the banking multiplier, boost dollar intermediation. The scope for intervention through a dollar-based monetary policy is of course extremely limited.

In turn, the interaction between prudential risks and the monetary regime instills *fear of floating*. Out of concern for the fragility of the financial system, the monetary authorities may seek to avoid at all costs large exchange rate fluctuations. Concerns about the potential inflationary impact of large exchange rate adjustments and the limited effectiveness of conventional interest rate-based monetary policy in highly dollarized economies can also exacerbate the monetary authorities' 'survival' instinct to cling to the exchange rate as a lifeline and main channel of conduction of monetary policy. This probably explains the generally intense intervention in the foreign exchange market and the use of the rate of crawl (rather than the interest rate) as the main instrument of monetary policy in many highly dollarized economies.

However, the less exchange rate volatility, the more dollarized an economy. Dollarization can thus become a 'trap', in which monetary policy ends up hostage of the need to protect the soundness of the financial system and keep inflationary expectations 'in the bottle'. The ever rising dollarization levels in most dollarized countries may thus reflect to a large extent these perverse dynamics in which rising dollarization and fear of floating feed back on each other.

Is there a way out?

A tightening of prudential regulations, that fully internalizes dollarization risks, is likely to be a key component of the required policy response to high and rising dollarization. In addition to eliminating moral hazard and leveling the playing field in favor of the local currency, internalizing dollarization risks should increase the capacity of dollarized financial systems to withstand liquidity or solvency shocks, thereby enhancing the scope for monetary and foreign exchange policy.

The existing regulatory response to dollarization risks appears to be generally uneven and often insufficient. At present, substantial flexibility is generally given to supervisors and banks as to how to address these risks. However, the close association between dollarization risks, the monetary and exchange rate regime, and moral hazard, seem to argue in favor of prudential activism. Because of expectations of a government bail out in the event of a catastrophic exchange rate devaluation, depositors do not have sufficient incentives to require higher risk premia on the deposits offered by the banks that lend primarily in dollars to local currency earners. In turn, because depositors will not reward them with lower risk premia, bank shareholders do not have sufficient incentives to adequately provision against such risks. Bail out expectations similarly induce dollar borrowers to discount the real cost and risks of dollar borrowing. Similar moral hazard failures affect banks' exposure to liquidity risk. As large international reserves held by central banks and abundant associated provision of liquidity support in the event of systemic runs provide free insurance benefits, banks have limited incentives to accumulate dollar liquidity on their own. Instead, competitive pressures will tend to penalize the more prudent banks.

A flexible approach, *one that requires banks to internalize risk but does not thwart sound risk management*, seems to be called for. In particular, additional capital requirements (in the form of specific reserves proportional to the risk associated with foreign currency loans to unhedged borrowers) may be needed. However, to ease the impact on the banking system of a large depreciation and limit the potential for a credit crunch, these reserves should not be part of the regular capital adequacy requirements. Instead, it would be preferable if transparent, preferably rules-based, arrangements could be set up to allow the reserves to be drawn down as warranted and gradually rebuilt once used.

As regards liquidity risk, the aim would seem to be to reduce the liquidity of banks' dollar liabilities and increase that of dollar assets. As local assets, such as short-term loans or treasury bills, can turn illiquid under a systemic crisis situation unless they can be freely used to obtain dollar liquidity from the central bank, a preferable option could be to generalize (and, when appropriate, increase) currency-specific liquidity requirements. The most liquid dollar liabilities should have the highest backing against liquid dollar assets held abroad or at the central bank, or against dollar public securities that can be rediscounted or repurchased against the central bank's dollar reserves abroad. Strong assurances of support from a bank's parent group or readily available contingent lines of credit from first line international banks might be acceptable, at least in part, as a substitute for holding liquid assets abroad.

However, to promote a viable, and more resilient, local currency based, path of financial development, measures to internalize the risks of intermediating in foreign currency would need to be reinforced by measures to enhance the attractiveness of the local currency and limit its riskiness. While the inherent difficulties in achieving sustained de-dollarization cannot be underestimated, comprehensive measures that promote the attractiveness of the local currency and simultaneously internalize the risks of dollarization, by being mutually reinforcing, seem to offer the best chances of gradual success towards de-dollarization. Countries should over time experience a 'virtuous cycle' in which dedollarization enhances the scope for monetary autonomy, leading in turn to a further decline of dollarization.

In particular, a strong and visible commitment to protect the long-term purchasing power of the currency should help enhance its credibility. Provided the necessary preconditions are in place (including in particular lack of fiscal dominance and sufficient central bank independence and technical expertise), the adoption of inflation targeting might help. Yet, to avoid destabilizing expectations and, in a worst case scenario, triggering a banking crisis induced by deposit outflows and a sharp exchange rate depreciation, a change in the monetary regime (including a shift in instruments, from the exchange rate to the interest rate) may need to be cautious and gradual, ensuring that proper conditions are in place.

The credibility of the currency does not only depend on being a stable store of value. It also depends on whether it constitutes a more useful buffer against large output shocks than the foreign currency, as this is likely to condition the extent of real dollarization. For this, a more active countercyclical monetary policy may be required (indeed, this would appear to be a case of using one's currency or losing it). The shift towards a more active monetary policy may not need to wait until the shift to full-fledged inflation targeting has been fully completed. Even when monetary policy continues to be conducted through the exchange rate, the rate of crawl could, in principle, be more actively managed through the business cycle.

What this would require, however, is that, through the build up of prudential buffers (as suggested earlier), the financial system be made less vulnerable to real exchange rate changes, particularly towards faster depreciations.

Measures to enhance the market acceptance of the local currency are also likely to be needed. In particular, this might require liberalizing financial intermediation in local currency (including in particular through the elimination or full remuneration of reserve requirements on local currency deposits), and an effort to gradually develop markets for local currency-denominated public securities. The introduction (or further promotion) of price-indexed instruments could complement these efforts and lower their cost. Price-indexed financial instruments seem to provide a prudentially superior alternative to dollar-denominated instruments for promoting financial deepening, particularly at the longer maturities. However, their introduction probably needs to be accompanied by a decisive effort to stabilize (to avoid indexation in the real sector) and should be properly presented and explained (so that it is not taken as a signal of the government's lack of resolve to fight inflation). A strengthening of monetary management in local currency, aimed at smoothing out the day-to-day volatility of interest rates, may also be required, consistent with a gradual freeing of exchange rates. Measures to enhance the quality of the payments system in local currency could also help give it a competitive edge over the dollar.

The nature of the policy response to dollarization is likely to depend on the degree of dollarization, its trend, and the monetary and exchange regime. Countries where inflation is low and monetary control is good, and the possibility of an abrupt regime switch is remote because the exchange rate is already mostly floating, and when dollarization is limited and stable, might not need to alter their prudential policies by much, if at all. The intermediate case of countries where dollarization is still limited but increasing, or could increase due to unstable (or potentially unstable) monetary conditions or a more open capital account, seems to call for a comprehensive, vigorous and prompt policy agenda aimed at addressing prudential issues raised by dollarization. On the other hand, the extreme case of heavily dollarized countries where lack of currency credibility is deeply rooted seems to call for a more careful and nuanced assessment of the nature, pace, and strategy of policy reform.

Conclusions

Central American countries are currently in the midst of major policy dilema as regards their exchange rate regime. Following the lead of Panamá and El Salvador, the remaining Central American countries could fully dollarize, or, following the example of the larger Latin American countries, including their northern neighbor, they could aim at asserting more fully their currency independence through a gradual move towards full-fledged inflation targeting. Or they might maintain an intermediate, dual-currency regime, closely tied to the dollar but not fully committed to it. Which of these options is preferable at this time is an obviously complex issue that has important strategic and even political ramifications and that goes much beyond the scope of this chapter.

This chapter limited itself to underscoring the potential pitfalls of the third option. In particular, it tends to generate a vicious cycle in which increasing dollarization and declining exchange rate flexibility feed back on each other. The vulnerability of financial sectors to large exchange rate fluctuations (together with their potential inflationary implications when the exchange rate is the main nominal anchor in the economy) discourage the monetary authorities from freeing the exchange rate. In turn, the closer the local currency is tied to the dollar, the more dollarized it becomes. Thus, while the option of adjusting the exchange rate in the case of a major shock remains available in principle, the resulting disruption, particularly to the financial system, is likely to be very large. Dual-currency regimes may thus have the same drawbacks as currency boards. They may temporarily help promote financial development but be exposed to financial crises. Relegating monetary policy to a 'spare tire' status, to be used only in the case of major accidents, could be highly inefficient and stressful.

The chapter argued that a possible way out of this dilemma is to adopt a two-pronged policy agenda that aims at restoring a more level playing field between the dollar and the local currency: (i) a tightening of prudential norms to internalize the risks associated with dollar intermediation and limit moral hazard; and (ii) the introduction of monetary and structural measures that enhance the attractiveness of the local currency as a medium of intermediation and reduce its risk. By being mutually reinforcing, such measures offer the best chances of limiting dollarization and encouraging a sounder and less brittle financial development. The main challenge on this path is to find a suitable policy mix that makes sufficient progress towards policy reform while taking into account the short-term constraints imposed by dollarization.

Notes

1. See Solnik (1974).
2. See Ize and Levy-Yeyati (1998 and 2003). Dollar assets may also be demanded as a hedge against real income fluctuations when returns on dollar assets covary negatively with output, that is, when countries have been repeatedly hit by shocks resulting simultaneously in output and exchange rate collapses.
3. Ize and Levy Yeyati (1998) show that this was the case for Bolivia and Perú. De Nicolo, Honohan, and Ize (2003) find some supporting preliminary evidence for a broad sample of countries. However, more empirical work appears to be needed before this hypothesis can be fully confirmed.
4. See Aghion, Bacchetta and Banerjee (2001) and Burnside, Eichenbaum, and Rebelo (2001).
5. Moral hazard is not the only factor leading to socially excessive levels of dollarization. Other factors discussed in the literature include market failures associated with debt defaults and inferior market equilibria derived from policy endogeneity. See Aghion, Bacchetta, and Banerjee (2001), Chamon and Hausmann (2002), Jeanne (2002), and Broda and Levy Yeyati (2003).
6. See Ize and Parrado (2002).
7. See Honohan and Shi (2002).
8. In Bolivia, for example, it now affects most utility prices, pensions, some elements of the tax system, accounting standards, and some supplier contracts. In Perú, a number of services, including residential and commercial leases, real estate, professional services and insurance premia, are priced in dollars.
9. Bosnia-Herzegovina, Lithuania and Slovenia, also experienced declines or halts in dollarization after having adopted strong stabilization policies, although these were not backed by formal inflation targeting.

References

Aghion, Bacchetta and Banerjee (2001) 'Currency Crises and Monetary Policy in an Economy with Credit Constraints', *European Economic Review*, Vol. 45, June: pp. 1121–50.

Broda, Christian and Eduardo Levy Yeyati (2003) 'Endogenous Deposit Dollarization', *Federal Reserve Bank of New York Staff Papers, No. 160.*

Burnside, Eichengreen and Rebelo (2001) 'Hedging and Financial Fragility in Fixed Exchange Rate Regimes', *European Economic Review*, Vol. 45, June: pp. 1151–93.

Chamon, Marcos and Ricardo Hausmann (2002) 'Why Do Countries Borrow the Way they Borrow?', prepared for *'The Currency and Maturity Matchmaking: Redeeming Debt from Original Sin'*, The Inter-American Development Bank, 21–22, November 2002.

De Nicolo, Gianni, Patrick Honohan, and Alain Ize (2003) 'Dollarization of the Banking System: Good or Bad?', *mimeo*, International Monetary Fund.

Honohan, Patrick and Anqing Shi (2002) 'Deposit Dollarization and the Financial Sector in Emerging Economies', *mimeo*, The World Bank.

Ize, Alain and Eduardo Levy-Yeyati (1998) 'Dollarization of Financial Intermediation: Causes and Policy Implications', *IMF Working Paper No. 28*.

Ize, Alain and Eduardo Levy Yeyati (2003) 'Financial Dollarization', *Journal of International Economics*, Vol. 59, No. 2, pp. 323–47.

Ize, Alain and Eric Parrado (2002) 'Dollarization, Monetary Policy, and the Pass Through', *IMF Working Paper No. 188*.

Jeanne, Olivier (2002) 'Why Emerging Economies Borrow in Foreign Currency', *mimeo*, International Monetary Fund.

Solnik, B. H. (1974) 'An Equilibrium Model of the International Capital Market', *Journal of Economic Theory*, Vol. 8, pp. 500–24.

Index